FALLEN ANGELS

ARCHIVES INTERNATIONALES D'HISTOIRE DES IDÉES

INTERNATIONAL ARCHIVES OF THE HISTORY OF IDEAS

165

FALLEN ANGELS

Balthasar Bekker, Spirit Belief, and Confessionalism in the Seventeenth Century Dutch Republic

by
ANDREW FIX

ANDREW FIX

Lafayette College,
Easton, PA, U.S.A.

FALLEN ANGELS

Balthasar Bekker,
Spirit Belief, and Confessionalism
in the Seventeenth Century Dutch Republic

KLUWER ACADEMIC PUBLISHERS

DORDRECHT / BOSTON / LONDON

A C.I.P. Catalogue record for this book is available from the Library of Congress.

ISBN 0-7923-5876-7

Published by Kluwer Academic Publishers,
P.O. Box 17, 3300 AA Dordrecht, The Netherlands.

Sold and distributed in North, Central and South America
by Kluwer Academic Publishers,
101 Philip Drive, Norwell, MA 02061, U.S.A.

In all other countries, sold and distributed
by Kluwer Academic Publishers,
P.O. Box 322, 3300 AH Dordrecht, The Netherlands.

Printed on acid-free paper

Printed in the Netherlands.

For Adam, the new man.

TABLE OF CONTENTS

All translations have been made by the author.

All biblical quotations have been taken from the King James Version of The Holy Bible (1611).

Acknowledgements

I would like to thank my home institution, Lafayette College, for its generous financial support of this project. Other major financial assistance was provided by the American Philosophical Society. I would like to thank my colleagues Wiep van Bunge of Erasmus University Rotterdam, Jacob van Sluis of Utrecht University, Jack Cell of Duke University, and H. C. Erik Middelfort of the University of Virginia for their reading and careful criticism of earlier versions of this manuscript. I would like to thank Simon Verheus and Rineke Nieuwestraten of Haarlem, The Netherlands, for their encouragement and support. I would also like to thank my editor and graphic designer Allison Coffin for her diligent and splendid work. Finally I would like to thank my family for their support and inspiration over the many years as this project became a book. It is to them that I owe my greatest debt.

PART ONE

Bekker and His Ideas

CHAPTER ONE

Balthasar Bekker and the Spirit Debate

Father Perreaud had been away from his home in Macon for five days, but because this was nothing unusual his maid continued her daily chores in expectation of his return. On the evening of September 14th, 1623, as the maid and another young lady were asleep in the same room, the young lady was awakened by a series of pulls on the curtain of her bed. Furniture in the room was suddenly thrown down, and when the lady tried to leave the room the door seemed to be held shut from the other side. When she later asked the maid why she had done these things to frighten her, the maid said that she had done nothing, but that perhaps the boy sleeping in the antechamber was responsible.

When Father Perreaud returned home and learned of these occurrences he too was baffled at first. Then he began to hear rattling all through the house that sounded like pieces of wood hitting on the oak screen in the kitchen. More furniture was thrown down, and copper pans were banged together. Father Perreaud concluded that such things could only be the work of an evil spirit. Occurrences of this sort continued for over a month. Then on November 25th, at nine o'clock in the evening, the spirit began to speak. He sang "two and twenty pennies, two and twenty pennies" in a hoarse voice and repeatedly called out "preacher, preacher" from a distance that seemed only three or four steps away from Father Perreaud. The good father was beside himself and said that only an evil spirit would know that a preacher lived in the house.

From November 25th through December 22nd the spirit's devilish activity continued. He mocked God by saying the Pater Noster and the Ten Commandments repeatedly and by singing Psalms. He brought Father Perreaud greetings from his elder brother in Vaux, who later said that at about the same time that the spirit did this he had been stopped on the road by a strange man riding a thin horse. Father Perraud's other brother was involved in a violent storm on Lake Geneva, which the spirit claimed to have caused. The spirit also claimed to have played pranks on a number of local people, and he told Father Perreaud gossip about many of his parishioners. He revealed the name of a man who had shot another parishioner with a musket, and the name of a woman who had murdered her husband. He told visitors to the house secrets that they said they had never revealed to anyone, and he continued to mock God by saying the Gloria Patri with "horrible words" and by claiming that he wanted to confess to the Pope. Finally the spirit began to prophesy the future, making predictions about the fate of the French Huguenots as well as about Father Perreaud's pregnant wife. Then on December 22nd several neighbors saw a big snake coming out of Father Perreaud's house, seized it, and paraded it around town saying "Look at the devil that came out of the preacher's house." [1]

[1]Balthasar Bekker, *De Betoverde Weereld, Zynde een Grondig Ondersoek Van 't gemeen gevoelen aangaande de Geesten, deselver Aart en Vermogen, Bewind en Bedrijf: als ook 't gene de Menschen door derselver kraght en gemeenschap doen* (Amsterdam, Daniel van Dalen, 1693), IV, 167-170.

Stories such as this one about the activity of evil spirits were, if not quite commonplace in the sixteenth and seventeenth centuries, at least not unusual. Such stories often met with a rather general acceptance since people considered it quite possible that a spirit could do such things. Yet when Dutch Reformed pastor Balthasar Bekker related the story of the so-called "devil of Macon" in 1693 in volume four of his work *The World Bewitched*, he rejected the argument made by Father Perreaud himself that an evil spirit had plagued his house. Bekker argued that the so-called spirit had not done anything that a person—or even a parrot—could not do. He suggested that a much more likely explanation for these events was that the father was the victim of pranks played by his spiteful maid or by the angry former inhabitant of his house who had been forced to move out to make room for the preacher. Bekker reached similar conclusions about other reports of activities carried out by evil spirits.

When Bekker addressed the issue of evil spirits the last fires to burn a witch in the Dutch Republic had been cold for nearly a century. The last execution for witchcraft had taken place in 1608, the last judicial complaint regarding witchcraft had been filed in 1643, after 1660 issues of witchcraft were no longer discussed at the synodal level of the Reformed church, and after 1670 accusations of witchcraft became ever more rare in the Republic.[2] Although capital punishment for witchcraft ended earlier in the Republic than elsewhere in Europe, by the 1690s the great "witch craze" that had convulsed Europe for over two hundred years had largely run its course. A remarkable, if horrific, chapter in European history was ending.[3] A great deal has been written in an effort to explain the causes of the sudden upsurge in judicial prosecutions of witchcraft and the parallel increase of belief in—and fear of—witches that began in the late fifteenth century and lasted through the late seventeenth. Less attention has been paid to the equally interesting question of why the witch craze suddenly came to an end with the dawning of the eighteenth century, vanishing almost as quickly as it had appeared.

One cause of this relative neglect is the common assumption that witch prosecutions, belief in witchcraft, and the closely allied belief in the existence, power, and temporal activity of evil spirits, ended for one obvious reason: the rise of the modern rational and scientific worldview after 1650 exposed and rejected such beliefs as ridiculous superstition. In the following pages this assumption will be tested by means of an investigation into the heated debate of the 1690s surrounding Balthasar Bekker's book *The World Bewitched*.

---

[2]Hans de Waardt, *Toverij en Sammenleven. Holland 1500-1800* (The Hague, 1991), 254-255; Jacob van Sluis, *Bekkeriana: Balthasar Bekker biografisch en bibliografisch* (Leeuwarden, 1994), 13.

[3]For a sampling of recent literature see Bengt Ankerloo and Gustav Henningsen, (eds) *Early Modern European Witchcraft: Centres and Peripheries* (Oxford,1990); Wolfgang Behringer, *Hexen und Hexenprozesse in Deutschland* (Munich, 1988); *Mit dem Feuer vom Leben zum Tod: Hexenverfolgung in Bayern* (Munich, 1988); Sydney Anglo (ed), *The Damned Art: Essays in the Literature of Witchcraft* (London, 1977); E. William Monter, *Witchcraft in France and Switzerland: The Borderlands during the Reformation* (Ithica, 1976); *Ritual, Myth and Magic in early Modern Europe* (Athens, Ohio, 1983); "The Historiography of European Witchcraft: Progress and Prospects," *Journal of Interdisciplinary History II* (1972), 435-451; "French and Italian Witchcraft," *History Today* (Nov. 1980), 31-35; Carlo Ginzburg, *Ecstasies: Deciphering the Witches' Sabbath* (New York, 1991); H.C.Erik Midelfort, *Witch Hunting in Southwest Germany 1562-1684: The Intellectual and Social Foundations* (Stanford, 1972); Gerhard Schorman, *Hexenprozesse in Nordwestdeutschland* (Hildesheim, 1977); Julio Caro Baroja, *The World of the Witches* (Chicago, 1961); Robert Mandrou, *Prophetes et Sorciers dans la Pays-Bas XVIe-XVIIIe Siecle* (Paris, 1978); Marijke Gijswijt-Hofstra and Willem Frijhoff (eds), *Witchcraft in The Netherlands from the Fourteenth to the Twentieth Century* (Rotterdam, 1991); H.R. Trevor-Roper, "The European Witch-Craze in the Sixteenth and Seventeenth Centuries,"

I

The dramatic increase in witchcraft trials and executions during the sixteenth and seventeenth centuries was accompanied by a lively and prolonged intellectual debate focussing on questions about the existence and activities of witches, sorcerers, angels, devils, and departed souls. This debate became most intense during a period from the late sixteenth century to the late seventeenth century, and it took place in all the major nations of western Europe. Although Bekker's book came at the very end of this debate, the lively and often heated controversy surrounding *The World Bewitched* demonstrated that Bekker's ideas touched a deeply sensitive nerve within the Reformed church and in society at large.[4] While Bekker's book is often credited with virtually ending spirit belief in the Dutch Republic and elsewhere, the intense controversy that surrounded it showed that many were far from convinced by Bekker's arguments.[5] Indeed, surprisingly few thinkers openly supported Bekker's position. Nevertheless, the Bekker controversy was the last great debate over spirits in the Dutch Republic. An analysis of the principal arguments put forward during this controversy can help illuminate some of the reasons behind the decline of belief in spirits, magic, and witchcraft in the Republic and elsewhere.

Despite continuing popular interest in the spirit world, the end of witchcraft trials in many countries in the late seventeenth century indicated in part a declining belief in the temporal power and activity of evil spirits. In Holland, as Hans de Waardt has shown, belief in witchcraft in the years after 1600 sharply declined among professions whose members were academically trained, such as physicians, jurists, and even some theologians.[6] This waning of belief was in its turn part of a more generalized but no less dramatic change in the intellectual climate of Europe: the replacement of the traditional, providential religious worldview with the secular and rational outlook of modern empirical science. Whereas the traditional worldview assumed the central importance of the spirit world and its constant interaction with the material realm, the intellectual system that replaced it grew increasingly skeptical about the possibility of such interaction and even about the very existence of the spirit world. For the greater part of

---

in *Religion, the Reformation and Social Change* (London, 1967); Robert Muchembled, *La sorcière au village, XVe-XVIIIe,* 2nd ed., (Paris, 1991);"The Witches of Cambresis: Acculturation of the Rural World in the Sixteenth and Seventeenth Centuries," in James Obelkevich (ed), *Religion and People 800-1700* (Chapel Hill, 1979); Gustav Henningsen, *The Witches' Advocate: Basque Witchcraft and the Spanish Inquisition 1609-1614* (Reno, 1980); Alan Macfarlane, *Witchcraft in Tudor and Stuart England* (London, 1970); Keith Thomas, *Religion and the Decline of Magic* (London, 1981); Norman Cohn, *Europe's Inner Demons*(London, 1975); Kieckhefer, Richard, *European Witch Trials, 1300-1500: Their Foundations in Popular and Learned Culture* (London, 1976); Klaniczay, Gabor, *The Use of Supernatural Power* (Princeton, 1991); Labouvie, Eva, *Zauberei ind Hexenwahn: Landlicher Hexenglaube in der fr,hen Neuzeit* (Frankfurt, 1991); Larner, Christina, *Enemies of God: The Witchhunt in Scotland* (Baltimore, 1981); Levack, Brian, *The Witch-Hunt in Early Modern Europe* (New York, 1987); Soman, Alfred, "The Parlement of Paris and the Great Witch-Hunt," *The Sixteenth Century Journal* 9 (1978), 31-45.

[4]Marijke Gijswijt-Hofstra, "Mennonite Views on Magic and Witchcraft," in J. Lambo (ed.), *Oecumennisme: Essays for Henk B. Kossen on the Occasion of His Retirement as Church Teacher* (Amsterdam, 1989), 69-70.

[5]Robin Attfield, "Balthasar Bekker and the Decline of the Witch Craze: The Old Demonology and the New Philosophy," *Annals of Science* 42 (1985), 383-395; G.J. Stronks, "The Significance of Balthasar Bekker's The Enchanted World," in Marijke Gijswijt-Hofstra and Willem Frijhoff (eds.), *Witchcraft in the Netherlands from the Fourteenth to the Twentieth Century* (Rotterdam, 1991), 149-156.

[6]de Waardt, 282-283.

the nineteenth and the early twentieth centuries, scholars influenced by Enlightenment positivism assumed a direct causal relationship between the coming of modern science and the end of the traditional European religious worldview. The victory of science could only come, they believed, with the defeat of the superstition and obscurantism of traditional religion.[7]

The experiences of the two world wars of the twentieth century bred a great deal of scepticism concerning the supposed inherently adversarial relationship between science and religion. Beginning with the 1920s, scholars like Alfred North Whitehead and Robin G. Collingwood argued for the constructive influence of religious ideas in the formation of many of the key concepts of modern science, while Robert K. Merton stressed the contributions of Puritanism to the growth of modern science. A large group of younger scholars has examined various aspects of the positive interaction of religion and science in the early modern period, and as a result a new picture has begun to emerge of the complex evolution of the modern scientific worldview against the background of traditional religious culture, an evolution resulting from a creative interaction between key concepts of both worldviews.[8]

Despite changing views about the general relationship between early modern science and religion, ideas concerning the end of belief in witchcraft and spirits have not changed much. Jeffrey Burton Russell, for example, has argued that the declining belief in the devil after 1700 was caused in part by the rise of modern science and a longing for a "calm and rational" view of the cosmos. With the advent of empirical science and the mechanical philosophy, Cartesian dualism destroyed any real connection between the material world and the spiritual world, Russell held, and "the latent

---

[7]See W.E.H. Lecky, *History of the Rise and Influence of the Spirit of Rationalism in Europe*, two vols. (New York, 1865); John W. Draper, *A History of the Conflict between Religion and Science* (New York, 1875); Andrew White, *A History of the Warfare of Science with Theology in Christendom*, two vols. (New York, 1896); Basil Wiley, *The Seventeenth Century Background* (London, 1934); E.A.Burtt, *The Metaphysical Foundations of Modern Science* (London, 1925); R.F. Jones, *Ancients and Moderns* (St. Louis, 1961); Paul Hazard, *The European Mind 1680-1715* (Cleveland, 1964).

[8]Alfred North Whitehead, *Science and the Modern World* (New York, 1925); R.G.Collingwood, *The Idea of Nature* (Oxford, 1945); Charles E. Raven, *John Ray, Naturalist: His Life and Works* (Cambridge, 1950); *Natural Religion and Christian Theology* (Cambridge, 1953); Michael Foster, "The Christian of Creation and the Rise of Modern Natural Science," *Mind* 43 (1934), 446-468; "Christian Theology and the Modern Science of Nature," *Mind* 44 (1935), 439-466; George Rosen, "Left-Wing Puritanism and Science," *Bulletin of the History of Medicine* 15 (1944), 375-380; Robert K. Merton, "Science, Technology and Society in Seventeenth-Century England," *Osiris* 4 (1938), 360-632; Richard S. Westfall, *Science and Religion in Seventeenth-Century England* (New Haven, 1958); Eugene Klaaren, *The Religious Origins of Modern Science* (Grand Rapids, Mich., 1972); Reijer Hooykaas, *Religion and the Rise of Modern Science* (Grand Rapids, Mich., 1972); T. Aston (ed.), *The Intellectual Revolution of the Seventeenth Century* (London, 1974); D. Stimson, "Puritanism and the New Philosophy in Seventeenth-Century England," *Bulletin of the Institute for the History of Medicine* 3 (1935), 321-334; J.R. Jacob and M.C. Jacob, "Scientists and Society: The Saints Preserved," *Journal of European Studies* 1 (1971), 87-92; "The Anglican Origins of Modern Science," *Isis* 71 (1980), 251-267; Douglas Kemsley, "Religious Influences on the Rise of Modern Science," *Annals of Science* 24 (1968), 199-216; Barbara Shapiro, "Debate, Science, Politics, and Religion," *Past and Present* 66 (1975), 133-138; *John Wilkins, 1614-1672: An Intellectual Biography* (Berkeley, 1969); *Probability and Certainty in Seventeenth Century England* (Princeton, 1983); T.K. Rabb, "Puritanism and the Rise of Experimental Science in England," *Journal of World History* 7 (1962); R.L. Greaves, "Puritanism and Science: The Anatomy of a Controversy," *Journal of the History of Ideas* 30 (1969), 346-360; John Morgan, "Puritanism and Science: A Reinterpretation," *Historical Journal* 22 (1979), 535-560; P.H. Kocher, *Science and Religion in Elizabethan England* (San Marino, 1953); J.E. McGuire, "Boyle's Conception of Nature," *Journal of the History of Ideas* 33 (1972), 523-542; Francis Oakley, "Christian Theology and

skepticism about the devil that only a few hardy souls dared to express in 1600 had by 1700 become part of that treasury of unspoken commonplace assumptions which any society holds." [9]

Writers who have focussed more specifically on the decline of witchcraft have reached similar conclusions. Hugh Trevor-Roper argued that the end of the witch craze should not be attributed to the arguments of writers like Johannes Weyer and Reginald Scot, who urged an end to witchcraft trials, but rather to a gradual erosion of the worldview that supported belief in witchcraft. This erosion resulted from the ideas of thinkers such as Bacon, Grotius, and Descartes, who seldom specifically mentioned witchcraft. Likewise, Keith Thomas has argued that the assumption of a regular and ordered universe unlikely to be upset by supernatural intervention, along with an increasing belief that science would find answers to all unexplained phenomena, were key factors in the decline of belief in witchcraft. Thomas pointed out that witchcraft prosecutions in England subsided when the educated class refused to administer the witchcraft laws. In similar fashion, both Hans de Waardt and Jacob van Sluis have pointed out that in the Dutch Republic in the second half of the seventeenth century judges came to see witchcraft accusations as unprovable (largely because of the impact of two critical judicial decisions in 1593 and 1594), physicians rarely considered witchcraft as a cause of illness, and church councils attached little practical weight to accusations of sorcery. [10]

A few writers have questioned the assumption that the advent of modern science and philosophy brought an end to belief in spirits and witchcraft. In his 1980 book *Witch-hunting, Magic and the New Philosophy: An Introduction to Debates of the Scientific Revolution 1450-1750,* Brian Easlea argued that the mechanical philosophy was not as powerful a force against witchcraft as Thomas and others held. The spread and influence of Cartesianism did not necessitate a rejection of belief in spirits, Satanic magic, or witchcraft. As evidence he pointed to thinkers like Joseph Glanville, who supported Cartesianism but also believed in the power of demons. In addition, Cartesianism had many problems of its own and was far from being the all-conquering force that many positivists and Enlightenment historians have supposed. [11]

The present study of the controversy surrounding *The World Bewitched* will argue that the assumption that the end of spirit belief in the Dutch Republic was caused in large part by the rise of empirical science and Cartesian philosophy is questionable. Bekker did make use of Cartesian arguments to criticize traditional beliefs about spirits, but his attack on spirit belief did not arise from Cartesian foundations, nor did his

Newtonian Science: The Rise of the Concept of the Laws of Nature," D. O'Connor and F. Oakley (eds.), *Creation: The Impact of an Idea* (New York, 1969); Margaret J. Osler, "Descartes and Charleton on Nature and God," *Journal of the History of Ideas* 40 (1979), 445-456; "Providence and Divine Will: The Theological Background to Gassendi's Views on Scientific Knowledge," *Journal of the History of Ideas* 44 (1983), 549-560; Edward B. Davis, "Creation, Contingency, and Early Modern Science: The Impact of Voluntaristic Theology on Seventeenth-Century Natural Philosophy,"(doctoral dissertation, Indiana University-Bloomington, 1984).

[9]Jeffrey Burton Russell, *Mephistopheles: The Devil in the Modern World* (Ithica, 1986), 77, 83, 128. See also Robert West, Milton and the Angels (Athens, Ga., 1955).

[10]Attfield, 383-384; de Waardt, 279, 10; van Sluis, 13.

[11]Brian Easlea, *Witch-hunting, Magic and the New Philosophy: An Introduction to Debates of the Scientific Revolution 1450-1750* (Sussex, 1980), 196-210.

critique rest primarily on Cartesian principles. The more important issues at stake between Bekker and his opponents, and the issues upon which the controversy ultimately turned, were questions of biblical exegesis and Calvinist confessionalism—issues buried deep within the traditional religious worldview.

II

On the surface the controversy that arose around *The World Bewitched* seems to lend support to the views of those who have seen spirit belief succumbing to the power of the new mechanical worldview. Closer investigation of the Bekker controversy suggests, however, that in Holland it was not the triumph of rationalistic philosophy that destroyed belief in spirits and witchcraft. Cartesian arguments were in fact used by both Bekker and his opponents to argue for, as well as against, traditional spirit belief. Cartesianism was just as easily employed as a prop for traditional spirit belief as it was used as a weapon against such belief. In addition, Cartesianism in Holland was weakened by serious internal philosophical problems, and, as a result, the controversy over spirits became intertwined with a debate within Cartesian philosophy over causal and epistemological difficulties resulting from Descartes' dualism of spirit and matter.

The fundamental issues in dispute between Bekker and his opponents indeed had little to do with the impact of Cartesian philosophy on spirit belief. The main questions underlying this debate were far more traditional in nature: how was the Bible to be interpreted, and what were the roles of ecclesiastical discipline and doctrinal orthodoxy within the Reformed church? Bekker's position on spirits should be seen as part of a broader intellectual and religious position that he adopted concerning the nature of the Dutch Reformed church and the meaning of Scripture.

Spirit belief in the Dutch Republic in large part fell victim to changes taking place within the traditional religious worldview itself. These changes issued from a long-running conflict within the Reformed church between a conservative, confessionally-oriented party of biblical literalists and a more liberal party of thinkers who interpreted the Bible in a broader context. Opposition to Dutch Reformed confessionalism was a central feature of the spirit controversy. This opposition, with its rejection of biblical literalism, in turn opened the way for a broader acceptance of the new science and philosophy among the educated classes of the Dutch Republic. The new philosophy, however, did not itself play a causal role either in the opposition to Calvinist confessionalism or in the critique of traditional spirit belief.

Many historians who have discussed Bekker's arguments against the temporal activity of evil spirits have focussed on Cartesianism as his principal and most effective weapon against spirit belief. The debate around *The World Bewitched* has thus often been interpreted as a contest between Cartesians and their opponents, with the victory going to the Cartesians, a result that made spirit belief intellectually untenable. Many of Bekker's critics during the controversy itself took aim primarily at his Cartesian philosophical arguments, although these composed only a small part of one volume of the four-volume work. The reason for this focus on a small part of Bekker's overall argument becomes clear when it is seen within the larger context of Dutch intellectual and religious life during the late seventeenth century. Conservative clerics in Bekker's day were driven by a profound fear of what they believed to be the dangers posed by Cartesianism for traditional religious belief. These conservatives felt that Cartesian dualism would cut people off from the spirit world and lead inevitably to materialism and atheism. Although this fear of dualism was somewhat exaggerated, writers like Henricus Brinck and Melchior Leydekker attacked Bekker as a Cartesian who gave too much power to human reason in matters of religion. Similarly, Johannes Verrijn and Jacobus Koelman maintained that Bekker's entire critique of spirit belief flowed from Cartesian sources.[12]

Later historians of the Bekker controversy have tended to follow these contemporary assessments. R.B. Evenhuis saw *The World Bewitched* as a Cartesian work in which reason was made the primary guide to truth.[13] In his book on Pieter Rabus, Johannes de Vet described the controversy around Bekker as primarily a dispute between Cartesians and their conservative Calvinist opponents.[14] Likewise, Robin Attfield has recently argued that "Bekker's original contribution lay in his application of Cartesian reason and of Cartesian premises to theology and demonology....[H]is cohesive and original system and his evocative propaganda represent the most explicit example of the deployment of the mechanical philosophy to contest the old demonology."[15] Similarly, Hans de Waardt has written that Bekker's greatest contribution was to provide a Cartesian theoretical foundation for the largely pragmatic scepticism about spirit activities expressed by earlier Dutch Mennonite writers such as Abraham Palingh and Antonie van Dale.[16]

These assessments of the Bekker controversy from Bekker's own time and after rest upon the assumption that Cartesianism was by its very nature opposed to traditional spirit belief. Richard Popkin has suggested, however, that it was not Cartesian ideas themselves that threatened traditional religion. Rather, it was the application of Cartesian methodology and standards of scientific truth to religious issues that revealed a basic conflict between the knowledge claims of science and those of religion, thus promoting religious scepticism.[17]

Descartes considered himself a religious thinker and attempted to use his philosophy to provide a framework for defending the faith, Popkin has pointed out, noting that Descartes offered proofs for God's existence and for the immortality of the soul that were compatible with a mechanistic picture of the world. Many Catholic and some Protestant theologians adopted and defended major portions of Descartes' philosophy, and other theologians saw no essential conflict between Cartesianism and Christianity as long as Cartesianism was restricted to the investigation of nature. It was when

---

[12]See Johannes Verrijn, *Aenmerckingen op de Betoverde Werelt van Dr. Balthasar Bekker...*(Amsterdam, 1692); Jacobus Koelman, *Schriftmatige Leere der Geesten...*(Utrecht, 1695) and *Het Vergift van de Cartesiaansche Philosophie...*(Amsterdam, 1692); Henricus Brinck, *De Godslasteringen van de Amsterdamsche Predikant Dr. Bekker...*(Utrecht, 1691); Melchior Leydekker, *De Godlikheid der H. Schriften* (Utrecht, 1692).

[13]R.B. Evenhuis, *Ook Dat Was Amsterdam: De Kerk der Hervorming in de Tweede Helft van de Zeventiende Eeuw* (Amsterdam, 1971), III, 285-294.

[14]Johannes de Vet, *Pieter Rabus: Een Wegbereider van de Noordnederlandse Verlichting* (Amsterdam, 1980), 285.

[15]Attfield, 391.

[16]de Waardt, 255.

[17]Richard Popkin, "Cartesianism and Biblical Interpretation," in Thomas M. Lennon, John M. Nicholas, and John W. Davis (eds.), *Problems in Cartesianism* (Montreal, 1982), 62-63; Etienne Gilson, *Etudes sur la role de la pensee medievale dans la formation du systeme Cartesian* (Paris, 1930); Henri Gouhier, *La Pensee religieuse de Descartes* (Paris, 1924); Alexandre Koyre, *Essai sur l'idee de Dieu et les preuves de son existence chez Descartes* (Paris, 1922).

Cartesian ideas became intermingled with the historical-critical approach to biblical interpretation—developed from humanistic, Reformation, and Counter-Reformation impulses—that the result was disastrous for traditional religion. Such was the case with Benedict Spinoza, whose *Tractatus Theologico-Politicus* (1670) put forward a method of biblical interpretation little different from the rational investigation of nature sponsored by Descartes, and in the process Spinoza found that Scripture had little cognitive content. Many important religious doctrines could not stand up to the Cartesian criterion of truth.[18]

If Popkin is correct in arguing that it was not Cartesian metaphysics itself but rather the application of the Cartesian criterion of scientific truth to biblical exegesis that was the real threat to traditional religion, then it can be argued that Bekker's Cartesian critique of the foundations of spirit belief was not nearly as dangerous to traditional religion as his exegetical methods were. Indeed, Klaus Scholder has remarked that Bekker "raised the question of the biblical world of spirits and submitted it to a comprehensive critical examination in connection with the new philosophy." Scholder further attested that *The World Bewitched* "belongs in the first rank of those works with which modern biblical criticism begins."[19]

Bekker employed several techniques of biblical interpretation found in Spinoza's work, including the doctrine of accommodation.[20] This method, which had been employed by none other than Calvin himself and which was also popular with Cartesians and other opponents of biblical literalism, assumed that Scripture was the result of an effort by God to accommodate his divine message to the limited understanding of humankind. Many passages in the Bible thus could not be understood literally because in them God had used the language and the concepts of ignorant people to express much more sophisticated truths in ways that those people would be able to understand. Such accommodation accounted for numerous apparent contradictions in Scripture.

Accommodationist exegetics did not pose a direct threat to traditional religion itself. Indeed, this approach was often used to reconcile traditional religion with apparently divergent modes of thought. Proponents of the new science and philosophy used accommodation to argue that the mechanical worldview did not contradict Scripture, and Descartes himself made use of this doctrine in his reply to the second objection to the *Meditations*. The doctrine of accommodation did, however, directly threaten the literal interpretation of the Bible that was the cornerstone of Dutch Reformed confessionalism. By using accommodation and thus threatening this cornerstone Bekker embroiled himself in a heated controversy within the Reformed church between the proponents and opponents of confessionalism. It was to the outcome of this dispute, and not to the fate of Cartesianism in Holland, that Bekker's arguments against spirits were ultimately tied.

[18]Popkin, 66-70.

[19]Klaus Scholder, *The Birth of Modern Critical Theology: Origins and Problems of Biblical Criticism in the Seventeenth Century*, trans. by John Bowden (London and Philadelphia, 1990), 128-129.

[20]Wiep van Bunge, "Balthasar Bekker's Cartesian Hermeneutics and the Challenge of Spinozism," *British Journal of the History of Philosophy* 1:1 (Spring 1993), 55-80.

III

In his recent biographical sketch of Bekker, Jacob van Sluis pointed to the paradoxical fact that the great controversy over *The World Bewitched* took place at a time in which belief in sorcery and diabolic activities was already in rapid decline in the Dutch Republic. Why did so many writers defend ideas about spirits that were less and less accepted in learned society at that time? While van Sluis attributed a great part of the Bekker controversy to Bekker himself and his often difficult personality,[21] there is another way to explain this paradox. The principal issue in dispute between Bekker and his critics was not spirit belief but biblical exegesis.

The controversy surrounding Bekker's use of Cartesian dualism to criticize traditional spirit belief also took place at a time in which the great controversy that initially had surrounded the introduction of Cartesian metaphysics into the academic and intellectual life of the Dutch Republic had largely played itself out. By 1680 most serious opposition to Cartesianism in the Dutch intellectual world had collapsed. For this reason it is difficult to attribute the great upwelling of criticism of Bekker's ideas primarily to opposition to the Cartesian philosophy itself. The underlying issues of exegesis and confessionalism were what attracted such great attention to Bekker's book.

Many historians have seen Bekker as a key figure in the early Enlightenment in the Dutch Republic, one of the first important centers for the emergence of the modern rational and secular worldview. Many years ago Paul Hazard saw Bekker as a key figure in the "triumphant rationalism" of the early Enlightenment, while more recently Jonathan Israel has described Bekker as "steeped in Cartesian thought" and *The World Bewitched* as "one of the key books of the early Enlightenment in Europe."[22] Margaret Jacob has seen Bekker as a typical Dutch example of that "crisis of the European mind" that Hazard located in the last twenty years of the seventeenth century and the first fifteen years of the eighteenth century. In this crisis, brought about by the intellectual tensions and uncertainties resulting from the breakdown of the traditional European religious worldview and the growing acceptance of a secular culture, Bekker combined liberal Christianity with the new science and philosophy in a creative tension that formed a moderate response to the intellectual upheaval of the day.[23]

The present study suggests a revised view of Bekker and his role in the early Enlightenment. Bekker's intellectual outlook did indeed combine a liberal, non-confessional Calvinism with Cartesian rationalism, but his Cartesianism was more a weapon to be used against religious authority than a deeply felt conviction. If, because of the reaction to and influence of *The World Bewitched*, Bekker can be seen as a hero of the Enlightenment who advanced the cause of secularism in the Republic, such was in no way his intention. Religious issues were always Bekker's primary concern, in particular the struggle against the spread of Calvinist confessionalism within the Dutch

[21]van Sluis, 13-15, 41-44.

[22]Paul Hazard, *The European Mind 1680-1715* (Cleveland and New York, 1964), 168-172; Jonathan Israel, *The Dutch Republic: Its Rise, Greatness, and Fall 1477-1806* (Oxford, 1995), 925-931.

[23]Margaret Jacob, "The Crisis of the European Mind: Hazard Revisited," in Jacob and Phyllis Mack (eds), *Politics and Culture in Early Modern Europe* (Cambridge, 1987), 251-267. See also Wijnand Mijnhardt, "The Dutch Enlightenment: Humanism, Nationalism, and Decline," in Mijnhardt and Margaret Jacob (eds), *The Dutch Republic in the Eighteenth Century: Decline, Enlightenment, and Revolution* (Cornell, 1992), 198-212.

Reformed church. Bekker's combination of Calvinism and Cartesianism, old and new, produced in him no crisis of conscience, but merely reaffirmed his religious views.

This reinterpretation of Bekker's role in the spirit controversy of the 1690s in Holland suggests a reinterpretation of that controversy itself and its place in the history of the early Enlightenment. It suggests as well a re-evaluation of the role of Cartesianism in the end of spirit belief in the Dutch Republic. Rather than being one of the opening shots fired in the battle between Enlightenment rationalism and traditional religious belief, the controversy around Bekker's book can better be seen as one of the last conflicts between confessionalists and anti-confessionalists within the Dutch Reformed church. It was a struggle that took place largely on the terrain of the traditional religious worldview.

If fallout from this struggle promoted the advance of a secular worldview, the fading of the traditional religious outlook had much less to do with the coming of the new science and philosophy than it did with internal divisions within the old worldview itself. By introducing Cartesianism into the struggle against Reformed confessionalism, Bekker and fellow liberal Calvinists helped to spread the influence of the new philosophy within the Republic. Bekker's critique of spirit belief, however, was born not of his love for philosophical rationalism but rather from his hatred of Calvinist literalism and confessionalism, which he saw as disastrous distortions of the true religion.

This is not a book just about one exceptional individual, Balthasar Bekker. It is a book about the intellectual and spiritual world in which he lived; it is a book about spirit belief and its critics, Cartesian philosophy and its Dutch academic variant, and Dutch Reformed confessionalism and its opponents. It is a book about the interactions among these belief systems, the men who shaped them and were shaped by them, and at the center of this intellectual whirlpool: Balthasar Bekker.

CHAPTER TWO

Bekker, the Sabbath, and Dutch Reformed Confessionalism

Balthasar Bekker's participation in the spirit controversy was the culmination of a life of intellectual and spiritual development that led him away from traditional norms in philosophy and theology and ultimately set him in opposition to the confessional hierarchy of the Dutch Reformed church. The two intellectual pillars upon which *The World Bewitched* would be built, Cartesianism and anti-confessional theology, were set in place early in Bekker's career. His interest in Cartesian philosophy started to develop after his first exposure to this philosophy when he entered the University of Groningen. The theological position that placed Bekker in opposition to Calvinist confessionalism and thus involved him in a religious controversy that would envelop his entire adult life also began to develop during his university days in Groningen and Franeker. His early theological views were nourished by an enduring friendship with Jacobus Alting, his Groningen professor of Hebrew, and were first highlighted in an unfortunate clash with the church hierarchy occasioned by the death of his first wife.

The beginnings of Bekker's anti-confessional theology were evident in his doctoral disputation, but these ideas were first fully expressed in his adult catechism, entitled *De Vaste Spyze der Volmaakten* (The Sound Food of Adults). The publication of the catechism involved Bekker in one of the defining religious controversies of the seventeenth century within the Dutch Reformed church: a dispute over the origin and nature of the Christian sabbath. Because the sabbath controversy was a key conflict in a long-running battle between the confessional and anti-confessional wings of the Dutch church, Bekker's involvement in this debate solidified his opposition to Reformed confessionalism, made him powerful enemies within the church, and set the theological stage upon which the spirit controversy would later be played out.

I

Balthasar Bekker was born on the twentieth of March, 1634, in the tiny Friesian village of Metslawier, the son of the village pastor. His father educated him in the Bible at home from an early age. In 1646 the family moved to Warfhuizen in the province of Groningen, and in 1650, at the age of sixteen, Bekker entered the University of Groningen.

At this early age Bekker became acquainted with the ideas of Descartes through his association with Tobias Andreae, teacher of Greek literature and history at the university and a Cartesian. Bekker observed numerous controversies within the university between Andreae and a group of conservative clerics who campaigned against the new philosophy. He witnessed disagreements of a different kind between two other professors, Jacobus Alting (1618-1679), a teacher of eastern languages, and Samuel Maresius (1599-1673), a theologian. Maresius was a proponent of the strict confessional Calvinism ascendant in the Reformed church since the Synod of Dordrecht in 1619, while Alting was critical of confessional theology. Through his association with Alting, Bekker began to develop the latitudinarian religious position that would become the driving force behind much of his life's work. He took Alting's courses in eastern languages at Groningen and the two became friends and correspondents in later life. Bekker acknowledged a great debt to Alting in the preface to *The World Bewitched*. Despite his relationship with Alting, however, Bekker was also impressed with the theological ideas of Maresius.[1]

In 1654, after four years of study in Groningen, Bekker moved to the Friesian university in Franeker, where his studies focussed on theology. In Franeker he took philosophy and Hebrew with Bernardus Fullenius and theology with Christianus Schotanus Sterrenga, Nicolaus Arnoldus, and Johannes Valckenier. After completing his studies, Bekker was examined by the Reformed church classis of Franeker and made a Proponent, a candidate minister, in April 1655. Because he did not immediately receive a call to be pastor of a Reformed congregation, Bekker took a position as head of the Franeker latin school. Then, in April of 1657 he received a call from the congregation of Oosterlittens, a village two miles from Franeker, and he left the university town to take up his first pastoral office. In this post he worked with great zeal, preaching and holding catechism classes for children.[2]

While in Oosterlittens Bekker married Elske Walkens, daughter of a Franeker preacher. All three children the couple had died in infancy, and Elske followed them in April 1664. This unfortunate series of events led to the beginning of Bekker's troubles with the hierarchy of the Reformed church. At his wife's funeral Bekker asked a colleague to give an oration, in keeping with Friesian custom. But this practice went against the rules of the Reformed church, and complaints were made to the Synod of Bolsward. As a result, friction developed between Bekker and church leaders.

After the funeral incident Bekker became increasingly aware that some conservative clerics disliked his religious views. This knowledge played a role in Bekker's decision to pursue a doctorate in theology at Franeker, and in the years that followed his ideas evolved in the direction of a liberal, non-confessional Calvinism, spiced with a fondness for Cartesian philosophy. Bekker invited the entire synod of the Friesian Reformed church to attend his final doctoral disputation in theology at Franeker in May of 1665. In the disputation he successfully defended one hundred propositions in twenty chapters covering the full range of Reformed belief, but the disputation also made it clear that the funeral incident had launched Bekker in a theological direction opposed to Calvinist confessionalism. One of the propositions that Bekker defended stated that funeral orations were permitted by the Bible, which was superior in authority to all church resolutions. This was a direct attack on the confessional conception of the church, which placed great emphasis on obedience to church law and the church's

---

[1]W.P.C. Knuttel, *Balthasar Bekker: De Bestrijder van het Bijgeloof* (Groningen, 1979, reprint of Den Haag, 1906 edition), 11-16.
[2]Ibid., 16-19.

confessional documents in addition to the Bible. By taking such a controversial public stand before the members of the synod so early in his career, Bekker indicated the central role that an anti-confessional, biblically-based religious position would play in his overall intellectual outlook. The fact that Bekker's early anti-confessional stance stemmed from this defense of Friesian custom in the funeral oration incident suggests that it was not his interest in Cartesianism that was the organizing principle of Bekker's worldview. Perhaps in response to Bekker's actions, the Synod of Dokkum in 1666 passed a resolution saying that academic disputations could not deal with synodal law.

After receiving his doctorate in theology Bekker was no longer obliged to seek church approval for his writings, a situation that he no doubt found pleasing. Bekker's position on the authority of church resolutions led some in the church to suspect that he lacked respect for church authority, and even a simple rhymed catechism that he wrote for the use of children in his catechetical classes (the *Gerymede Kinder-Leer* or Rhymed Child Instruction) aroused grumblings about his orthodoxy in conservative circles.[3] As a result of his reading of Descartes and other sources, Bekker began to develop positions that further angered his conservative critics and seemed to confirm their earlier suspicions about him. Among other things, Bekker came to believe that heliocentricism was not contrary to Scripture even though he had defended the contrary in his doctoral disputation. This position immediately raised questions about his methods of biblical interpretation.

In January of 1666 Bekker moved to Franeker as pastor, replacing his late father-in-law Ds.Walkens. Shortly before or just after he moved to Franeker Bekker married for a second time, his new wife being Froukje Fullenius, daughter of the man who had taught Bekker Hebrew during his student years in Franeker. During his stay in Franeker Bekker maintained close contacts with the university there, and it was during this period in his career that his Cartesian ideas began to take definite shape.

In Franeker, Bekker wrote a catechism for older children entitled *Gesneden Broodt* (Cut Bread) and one for adults, *De Vaste Spyze der Volmaakten* (The Sound Food for Adults). Difficulties with the adult catechism soon arose as it became a target for Bekker's growing army of critics. In the *Vaste Spyze* Bekker took a liberal position in a long-running dispute within the Reformed church concerning the origin and nature of the Christian sabbath. This position in turn further embroiled him in the battle against Reformed confessionalism as well as in volatile exegetical debates surrounding Johannes Coccejus, a controversial professor of theology at Leiden University (about whom more in due course). Bekker's role in the sabbath controversy has been underestimated by historians examining his ideas, but in fact it was an event of first importance for his career. It not only made Bekker's religious position widely known within the church, but also it cemented the enmity of the confessional party for Bekker's ideas and set the stage within the Reformed church for the central drama of Bekker's career that was to take place twenty years later. Bekker's role in the sabbath controversy foreshadowed the later upheaval surrounding *The World Bewitched*.

---

[3]Ibid., 19-23.

II

The sabbath debate that took place within the Dutch Reformed church during the seventeenth century was a central part of a broader controversy concerning the nature of the Reformed church and the proper method for interpreting Scripture. In this struggle a party of confessional Calvinists battled more moderate elements within the Reformed community for control of the Dutch church, and ultimately society as well. The roots of this battle were entwined with the very beginnings of the Reformed church in The Netherlands.

Calvinism first arrived in the Low Countries from France in the years around 1560 and came to play a crucial role in the Dutch revolt against Spain. Calvinism's early influence was greatest in the highly urbanized and commercially prosperous southern Netherlands. Here, Calvinists encountered religious persecution by Hapsburg government authorities that reached a level of intensity unequalled elsewhere in Europe: between 1523 and 1566 some 1,300 inhabitants of The Netherlands were put to death for their religious beliefs.[4] As a result of this persecution, a militant, confessionalist, and highly doctrinaire form of Calvinism developed in the southern Netherlands.

In the province of Holland, the history of Reformed Protestantism was somewhat different from that in the southern Netherlands. Holland had a smaller Calvinist community that had to compete with a large Anabaptist movement for the loyalties of those disillusioned with the Catholic church. Habsburg persecution was considerably less intense in Holland than in the south because of the smaller Calvinist community there, its distance from the center of government power in Brussels, and the effective resistance of local authorities. Partly as a result of these circumstances, and partly as a result of contact with other Protestant groups, Calvinism in Holland was for the most part more moderate and less doctrinaire than that in the southern Netherlands.

When the Reformed church began to publicly organize itself in Holland after the Spanish were expelled in 1572, it built on the foundations of local Calvinism. Following Spanish military victories in the south in the 1580s, however, a wave of Calvinist refugees arrived in Holland, bringing with them their own more strict views about how the Reformed church should be organized and run.[5] In addition, during the last quarter of the sixteenth century the influence of English Puritanism entered the Dutch Reformed church through congregations in Zeeland and reinforced the strict views of the southern refugees, helping to make these views a powerful force within the Dutch church.

A conflict thus developed within the Reformed church from its earliest days over the organization, doctrine, and indeed the very nature of the church. One group of believers, often called the *preciezen* (the precise), advocated strict adherence to a defined set of church doctrines (especially the doctrine of predestination) and rules of conduct, along with rigorous ecclesiastical discipline that would define the Reformed church as the community of the elect. These believers upheld a literal interpretation of the Bible and stressed the importance of confessions of faith, catechisms, and other confessional formulas in defining and guaranteeing the doctrinal purity of the church. In their view part of the task of church discipline was to enforce conformity with these

---

[4]Andrew Pettegree, *Emden and the Dutch revolt: Exile and the Development of Reformed Protestantism* (Oxford, 1991),
[5]Ibid., 188-225.

confessional statements. This party within the Dutch Reformed church found itself in harmony with the great wave of confessionalism that swept the Protestant churches of Europe during the immediate post-Reformation era.

Another group of Reformed believers favored a more inclusive church. They argued that the Dutch revolt against Spain was not only a national struggle but also a struggle against religious intolerance and persecution, and thus religious freedom should find a place in the church that was a partner in that struggle. These believers de-emphasized ecclesiastical discipline and doctrinal orthodoxy as defining character-istics of the Reformed religious community. They questioned the authority of Reformed confessional documents and even some specific theological doctrines, and they did not adhere to strict biblical literalism. This moderate party saw its influence within the Reformed church wane during the last decades of the sixteenth century as the influ-ence of the confessional party was on the rise. The conflict that developed between these two groups and their differing views of the church centered around two profes-sors of theology at Leiden University: Jacobus Arminius and Franciscus Gomarus.

Arminius (1560-1609) was a spokesman for the moderate wing of the Reformed church in Holland. He was deeply troubled by the deterministic doctrine of election and damnation contained in the doctrine of predestination as it was held by Theodore Beza in Geneva and by the Dutch *preciezen*. This doctrine seemed to him to make God the author of sin. Arminius held that God predestined sinners as a group to be damned, but that each individual who sinned did so through free will. Arminius also believed that God predestined all who had faith to be saved, but in this case human free will did not play a role: God's grace made it possible for the individual to choose faith.[6]

In 1603 Arminius was appointed one of three professors of theology at Leiden University, where he immediately came into conflict with his colleague Franciscus Gomarus (1563-1641), a leader of the confessional wing of the church. In a public disputation held in 1604, Arminius maintained that original sin had been contingent upon free will, not predetermined as the *preciezen* believed. In response Gomarus condemned Arminius's views, and by 1606 a major controversy over predestination raged in Leiden. Arminius and Gomarus also disagreed over the authority of confes-sional documents within the church. The *preciezen* considered the Dutch Confession of Faith and the Heidelberg Catechism to have doctrinal authority equal to that of the Bible itself, and they further believed that adherence to the theological doctrines con-tained in those writings was a necessary test of Christian orthodoxy. Arminius and his followers, on the other hand, believed that the confessional basis of the church should be founded only on the Bible, which alone was divinely inspired. All other forms of biblical interpretation and theological doctrine were, in their view, human products that were provisional and fallible.

The dispute between Arminius and Gomarus reached a climax in 1608 when Arminius made a public declaration of his beliefs before the States of Holland.[7] When Arminius died in 1609, he left behind a party of supporters who carried on his struggle. In 1610, the Arminians filed a remonstrance with the States of Holland asking for toleration of their views. From this plea for toleration and anti-confessionalism the party came to be

[6]Carl Bangs, *Arminius and the Dutch Reformation* (Nashville, 1971), 52-147, 195-216. See also Cornelis Graafland, *Van Calvijn tot Barth: Oorsprongen en Ontwikkeling van de Leer der Verkiezing in het Gereformeerd Protestantism* (The Hague, 1987) for an overview of Dutch views on predestination.
[7]Bangs, 308-315.

known as the Remonstrants, while their opponents were often called Contra-Remonstrants. The States of Holland reacted to the remonstrance by issuing a general admonishment to religious peace, but agitation between the two sides continued. In 1611 the States of Holland organized a peace conference between the parties in The Hague, but little was accomplished. The Contra-Remonstrants called for the convening of a national synod of the Reformed church to settle the dispute, but the States of Holland, whose deputies represented a regent class generally sympathetic to the Remonstrants, blocked the meeting from fear that it would be dominated by Contra-Remonstrant clergy, who were in a majority outside the province of Holland.

The actions of the States of Holland showed that the religious controversy had become entangled with a political struggle that was taking place in the Dutch Republic between the province of Holland and the party of the Stadholder, commander of the Republic's military forces and one-time governor of the northern Netherlands for the king of Spain. During the Twelve-Year Truce (1609-1621) in the war with Spain, political tensions in the Republic reached a climax over the question of where sovereignty was to be located in the new state. Count Maurice of Nassau (1567-1625), Stadholder of Holland, Zeeland, Utrecht, Gelderland, and Overijssel, joined with the States General of the Republic in an effort to mold a powerful central government under the leadership of his House of Orange. Maurice was supported in his efforts by the Dutch nobility, long-time backers of the House of Orange; by the rural provinces of Utrecht, Groningen, Gelderland, and Overijssel, which resented the dominant position within the Republic of the maritime province of Holland; and by the Contra-Remonstrants, who favored a strong central government to resume the war against Catholic Spain.

The Stadholder's party was opposed by the province of Holland, led by its chief minister Johan van Oldenbarnevelt (1547-1619). Oldenbarnevelt favored a loose federal government for the Republic that could easily be dominated by Holland, by far the wealthiest province. His policy was backed by the urban regent class that governed the prosperous towns of Holland, whose commercial interests would suffer from the renewed war with Spain favored by the Stadholder, and by the Remonstrants, who sought Oldenbarnevelt's protection because of his Erastian views. While many in the ruling regent class favored the Remonstrants, a large segment of the general population favored the party of Nassau and viewed the Remonstrants as dangerous troublemakers.

This mixture of religious, political, and social conflict created an explosive brew that became more and more unstable as tensions mounted with the nearing end of the truce with Spain. In Amsterdam, hostile mobs broke up Remonstrant meetings and ransacked the homes of leading Remonstrant citizens. During the summer of 1617, the States General voted to call a national synod of the Reformed church for the following year to settle the religious dispute. In August, Oldenbarnevelt convinced the States of Holland to empower municipalities, many of which were controlled by Remonstrant sympathizers, to raise special citizen militias to protect public order. These militias were outside the authority of Count Maurice and amounted to an attempt by the regent party to arm itself against Nassau's forces. These steps led the Stadholder to take drastic action. In January 1618 he used his special governmental powers to replace Remonstrant governments in the city of Nijmegen and the province of Overijssel. He did the same in the city of Utrecht in the summer. In July the States General disbanded the city militias, and in August Maurice arrested Oldenbarnevelt and several key supporters. He then replaced the municipal governments of Holland with his own supporters and had Oldenbarnevelt executed.

When the national synod of the Reformed church met in Dordrecht in November 1618 it was dominated by the victorious Contra-Remonstrants, and thus the outcome was hardly in doubt. The synod condemned Remonstrant ideas and deposed all Remonstrant preachers, who were given the choice of signing a pledge never to preach again or of leaving the country. Most chose exile, ironically enough in the Spanish southern Netherlands. The synod adopted the Heidelberg Catechism and a revised version of the Dutch Confession of Faith as obligatory rules of belief for the Reformed church. The victory of the confessional party appeared complete.

In the first two decades after Dordrecht, the confessional party within the church was without serious opposition, and thus the vigor of the party and the church it dominated began to wane. But the vitality of the confessional party was soon restored by the appearance of a dynamic new element in Reformed religious life. A group of Reformed clergy influenced by English Puritanism attempted to lead a revival of discipline, belief, and commitment within the church beginning in the early 1620s.

As early as the closing decades of the sixteenth century, Puritan beliefs and practices had begun to play an important role in the Dutch Reformed church. The Puritan "doctrine of precision," which taught strict adherence to divine law in the form of the Bible and theological doctrines drawn from it, influenced many of the followers of Gomarus, lending them the name of *preciezen*. After the Synod of Dordrecht, a group of Reformed clergy influenced by Puritanism began to assume a leadership role within the church by advocating renewed moral and doctrinal rigor. Led by such men as Willem Teellinck, Jacobus Koelman, William Ames, and Gisbertus Voetius, this movement called for a spiritual regeneration of the church and a purification of Reformed religious life using fiery penitential preaching as its main weapon. This new movement came to be called the *Nadere Reformatie* or "Further Reformation" because its advocates called for a second Reformation to follow upon and complete the work of the first by making the Reformed church a body of ethically upright, spiritually pure, and personally regenerate believers whose faith was individually experienced and active in everyday life.[8]

Voetius, Teellinck, and their followers met together in conventicles to practice their piety. They were bound together by a series of beliefs many of which were held by earlier *preciezen* as well. They held that the literal truth of Scripture was clear, explicit, and evident through itself; they held that this truth could be formulated into doctrinal rules, obedience to which was the mark of faith; they believed that all knowledge

[8]R.B. Evenhuis, *Ook dat was Amsterdam; De Kerk der Hervorming in de Tweede Helft van de Zeventiende Eeuw: nabloei en inzinking* (Amsterdam, 1971), III, 207-208; T. Brienen, et.al., *De Nadere Reformatie: Beschrijving van haar voornaamste vertegenwoordigers* (The Hague, 1986). Leszek Kolakowski in *Chretiens sans eglise: la conscience religieuse et le lien confessionel au XVIIe siecle* (Paris, 1969) calls this movement the Calvinist Counter-reformation because it was in part a reaction against Arminianism within the Dutch church, and Thomas A. McGahagan, *Cartesianism in The Netherlands 1639-1676; The New Science and the Calvinist Counter-Reformation* (dissertation, University of Pennsylvania, 1976) follows this terminology. The nature and role of the *Nadere Reformatie* within the Reformed church have not been without controversy. See F.A. Lieburg, *De Nadere Reformatie in Utrecht ten tijde van Voetius. Sporen in de gereformeerde kerkeraadsacta* (Rotterdam, 1989); T. Brienen, et.al., *De Nadere Reformatie en het Gereformeerd pietisme* (The Hague, 1989) and *Theologische aspecten van de Nadere Reformatie* (Zoetermeer, 1993); Cornelis Graafland, *De zekerheid van het geloof. Een onderzoek naar de geloofsbeschouwing van enige vertegenwoordigers van Reformatie and Nadere Reformatie* (Wageningen, 1961) and "De verhouding reformatie en nadere reformatie, een voortdurend onderzoek," *Documentieblad Nadere Reformatie* XVII:2 (1993), 94-111.

served faith; and they maintained that an important role of the church was to make binding dogmatic decisions for its members. Like earlier *preciezen*, the followers of the *Nadere Reformatie* tended to see any move away from biblical literalism as subjecting faith to reason, leading inevitably to subjectivism, scepticism, and atheism.[9]

In the decades after Dordrecht, the confessional party within the Reformed church, renewed and reinforced by the adherents of the *Nadere Reformatie*, worked to enforce doctrinal orthodoxy based on the church's three "Formulas of Unity:" the Heidelberg Catechism, the Dutch Confession of Faith, and the Post-Acta (decrees) of the Synod of Dordrecht. These documents were considered concise formulations of the fundamental articles of Christian belief found in the Bible, obedience to which was necessary for church membership. The confessional documents drew their authority directly from the Bible in the form of scriptural citations that accompanied major doctrinal points. This use of biblical "proof texts" to lend scriptural authority to the church's confessional documents—and by extension to the entire confessional structure of the church—depended in turn on the primacy of a literal interpretation of Scripture. Thus biblical literalism provided the scriptural foundation and religious authority for Reformed confessionalism.

The process of confessionalization that took place in the Dutch Reformed church after Dordrecht was accompanied by the development of an increasingly systematic Reformed theology. Scripture increasingly came to serve as an arsenal of passages mustered to support various points of Reformed theology. As the systematic confessional statements of the church became the focus of religious belief and practice, the Bible became a servant of theology. The Reformed church was developing its own form of scholasticism.[10]

The conception of religious belief that came to dominate the church in the years after Dordrecht was the one long held by the *preciezen*: belief was seen as a kind of knowledge based on intellectual assent to the elements of Reformed doctrine. To believe was to understand and accept. Voetius and his followers championed this conception of faith, in part no doubt because faith based on consent to doctrine made it relatively easy to identify individual orthodoxy, thus making the strict discipline favored by the confessionalists easier to enforce.[11] The intellectual structure of Dutch Reformed confessionalism and Bekker's principled opposition to it will be examined more closely in the concluding chapter of this study.

III

Within this structure of an increasingly confessionalized Dutch Reformed church, the theology of Johannes Coccejus (1603-1669) exploded like a bombshell. With an approach to the Old Testament that virtually ruled out literal interpretation, Coccejus reignited the controversy over the nature of the Dutch church. If literalism could no

[9]McGahagan 87, Theo Verbeek, *Descartes and the Dutch: Early Reactions to Cartesian Philosophy 1637-1650* (Carbondale, Ill, 1992), 89.
[10]Evenhuis, 115-116. See also J. Platt, *Reformed Thought and Scholasticism. The Arguments for the Existence of God in Dutch Theology, 1575-1650* (Leiden, 1982).
[11]Evenhuis, 115-116.

longer be accepted as the sole means for interpreting Scripture, then the meaning and importance of the proof texts were called into question, and with them the scriptural authority of the church's confessional documents. Thus the entire intellectual structure of Dutch Reformed confessionalism threatened to collapse.

Johannes Coccejus was born in Bremen in 1603 and taught there and at Franeker before being appointed in Leiden in 1650 with the recommendation of Abraham Heidanus. A talented linguist, Coccejus specialized in biblical exegesis that closely analyzed the language of sacred text. He was primarily a biblical theologian who saw his task as explaining Scripture to the faithful. Because Coccejus stressed biblical over systematic theology, his thought was fundamentally anti-confessional: he was little interested in theology and dogmatics. Coccejus's exegesis focussed primarily on the New Testament. He viewed the Old Testament as a preparation for, or a prefiguring of, the New. He interpreted Old Testament passages chiefly as foreshadowings of Christ, his work, and the events of the New Testament. Coccejus thus did not consider the Old Testament to be as important as Voetius and other confessionalists did.

Coccejus's view of biblical interpretation was fundamentally opposed to that of the confessionalists. Coccejus believed that the meaning of Scripture was not to be found in individual words or expressions but in the whole of Scripture: the words had meaning not in isolation but only when they were considered within the context of the entire system of Scripture. Coccejus's denial of the historicity of the Old Testament further angered literalists, as did the fact that the church's confessional writings had little influence on his exegetics.

In 1648, while a professor at Franeker, Coccejus published a study of God's covenants with mankind that was to give his distinctive theology its name. In the work he wanted to show how God's revelation to man had gradually unfolded throughout history. In paradise, Coccejus maintained, God concluded a covenant of works with man. After the fall, God proclaimed a covenant of grace with humanity, a covenant that concluded with the Israelites in the wilderness. Then with the coming of Christ a new covenant was proclaimed. In this historical process each successive covenant replaced the foregoing one. The Ten Commandments belonged to the ceremonial laws of the covenant of grace, Coccejus held, and thus they were no longer valid after the coming of Christ. This idea was to assume great significance in the sabbath controversy. In working out his covenant theology Coccejus divided Christian history into seven periods, beginning with the ascension and including the time of Constantine and the Christianizing of Europe, the period of Catholic supremacy, the Reformation, and his own time. Coccejus saw the Bible as a history of God's revelation to man and he stressed the preaching of the Gospel as the proclaiming of God's kingdom.[12]

Among confessional theologians, Gisbertus Voetius led opposition to Coccejus's ideas. He was sharply critical of Coccejus's conception of the relationship between the New and Old Testaments, arguing that both Testaments were of equal importance. The followers of Coccejus and Voetius also differed fundamentally in their methods of Scriptural exegesis and preaching. While Coccejus and his followers favored figurative interpretation of many places in the Bible, a method made necessary by their conception of the Old Testament as a prefiguring of the New, Voetius and his party

[12]Otto de Jong, *Nederlandse Kerk Geschiedenis* (Nijkerk, 1978), 233-234, Evenhuis, 117; J.C. Trimp, *Jodocus Lodensteyn: Predikant en Dichter* (Kampen, 1987), 29; F. Ernest Stoeffler, *The Rise of Evangelical Pietism* (Leiden, 1965), 113-114.

insisted on literal interpretation. The Voetians tended to give each Bible passage equal weight based on its literal meaning, while Coccejus stressed examination of Scriptural language within the overall context of the Bible to decide which passages were more important than others. Coccejus did not deny that biblical texts had literal meaning, but to this he added a second level that he called spiritual meaning. Coccejans also used typology, seeing in Old Testament persons and events types or representations of what would later happen. Using these methods they reinterpreted passages that they felt were otherwise unintelligible, offensive, or confusing.[13]

The exegetical disagreements between Coccejans and confessionalists were brought into sharp focus by the sabbath controversy, which burned with its greatest fury during the middle years of the seventeenth century. Although the dispute over the nature and meaning of the Christian sabbath had raged in the Republic for well over half a century before Coccejus and his followers got involved, the intervention of the Coccejans opened a new and intense phase in the controversy, a phase that would involve Bekker as well. The sabbath debate became a defining dispute in the long-running battle between confessional Calvinists and their opponents in the Reformed church. It brought the confessional/anticonfessional split in the church to the attention of a broad public for the first time since the days of Arminius and Gomarus, and it showed that confessionalism had by no means entirely won the day. Because it focussed on the question of how to interpret one of the most important of the Ten Commandments, the sabbath controversy became part of the exegetical debate between literalists and proponents of figurative interpretation. The Decalogue was a part of the Bible considered to be of paramount importance by the confessional party, and thus a debate about how to interpret one of the Ten Commandments became a debate about the biblical foundations of Reformed confessionalism. It was into this complex network of controversy that Bekker stepped with his *Vaste Spyze*, and his involvement in this intense controversy became by far the most important event in his early career as a Reformed pastor.

IV

The central issues at stake in the sabbath controversy were the meaning of the Fourth Commandment and the relationship between the Old and New Testaments. Was the commandment's injunction to remember the sabbath day by resting from work to be interpreted literally and obeyed by Christians in the New Testament just as it had been by the Jews of the Old Testament? Or was it to be interpreted figuratively, historically, and contextually as one of the ceremonial commands given specifically to Israel and no longer binding on Christians? A number of other issues revolved around this central question. What was the relationship between the Fourth Commandment and the rest of the Decalogue? What was the relationship between the Old Testament Sabbath of the seventh day and the Christian observance of Sunday as the Lord's Day? Was the Lord's Day instituted by Christ, by the apostles, or by the later church? Should there still be a special day set aside for religious service? If so, how should this day be

---

[13]De Jong, 234; Evenhuis, 126-127. Willem J. van Asselt, *Amicitia Dei: Een Onderzoek naar de structuur van de theologie van Johannes Coccejus* (1603-1669) (dissertation, University of Utrecht, 1988).

observed and to what extent did the Fourth Commandment injunction to rest apply to it?[14] Lurking beneath most of these questions was the crucial issue of biblical exegesis.

These questions had been debated throughout the entire history of the Christian church, with discussion reaching an especially sophisticated level by the late Middle Ages. Thomas Aquinas recognized both a literal and a spiritual meaning in the Fourth Commandment. Literally taken, the sabbath commandment was partly moral and partly ceremonial. It was moral, and thus of enduring importance, that a person set aside a certain part of his or her life for divine things, but the appointment of a specific day to do this was ceremonial, and thus changeable. The commandment's spiritual meaning was both allegorical and anagogic: allegorically the sabbath was a foreshadowing of Christ's future rest in the grave after completing the work of reconciliation, and anagogically the sabbath foreshadowed mankind's future rest from sin in Christ.

Aquinas maintained that the Christian observance of the Lord's Day was instituted by the church in memory of Christ's resurrection, not as a result of a specific command of the Decalogue. Activities that diverted people from the religious purpose of this day were forbidden, including servile labor and anything disturbing the peace. But manual work that was necessary or especially beneficial to oneself or others was permitted on Sunday, Aquinas held.

During the Protestant Reformation it was especially the Calvinists, with the Old Testament orientation of much of their ecclesiology, who decried sabbath profanation that they believed had arisen because of Catholic laxity with regard to the Fourth Commandment. For English Puritans during the later sixteenth century, strict observation of the sabbath based on a literal interpretation of the Fourth Commandment was central to their conception of divine law and true piety. Puritan religious idealism was built to a large extent upon a legalistic adherence to the commands of the Decalogue, and this idealism and legalism exercised great influence on the confessional party within the Dutch Reformed church. Proponents of the *Nadere Reformatie* built upon earlier Reformed complaints about sabbath profanation by introducing into the Dutch church a much stricter idea of sabbath observation than had prevailed before the Synod of Dordrecht. It was this idea and the reaction to it that gave rise to the sabbath controversy within the Dutch Reformed church.

The Fourth Commandment and the sabbath held a prominent place in Puritan religious life. Puritans saw divine law as the disclosure of God's plan for mankind, and thus they believed obedience to this law to be man's highest moral obligation. This deep commitment to divine law and its application to every aspect of individual life led to the kind of piety often called "precision." A list of precepts drawn from the Bible and formulated with the help of human reason provided a standard of conduct to be followed by the Elect in thankfulness for their election, transforming the practice of piety into a habit of life. In this list of precepts the Ten Commandments took first place.

The most important Puritan work on the sabbath was Nicholas Bound's *The Doctrine of the Sabbath, Plainly Laid Forth and Soundly Proved* (1545), in which Bound declared the Fourth Commandment "an immortal commandment of almighty God" valid for all people in all times, a basic feature of the divine law to be observed forever by Christians as well as by Jews. The fourth was the foundation for the

---

[14]Hugo Visser, *De Geschiedenis van den Sabbatsstrijd onder de Gereformeerden in de Zeventiende Eeuw* (Proefschrift, Vrije Universiteit te Amsterdam, 1939), 1.

other commandments and was obeyed by the church from the very beginning of the world, long before its formal proclamation at Sinai. While the Jews celebrated the sabbath of the seventh day, the Holy Spirit caused the apostles to change this day to the first day of the week, or the Lord's Day, in memory of the resurrection. On this day all daily work, recreation, and pleasures were banned.[15]

Dutch Reformed theologians prior to the Synod of Dordrecht generally adopted a more moderate position on the nature of the sabbath and its observance. Lambert Danaeu (1530?-1595), for example, professor of theology at Leiden in 1581-1582, discussed the sabbath in his *Ethices Christianae* (1588). In his view, the sabbath was a solemn holy day for the Jews and a sign of the covenant God had made with them, but not a divine command eternally binding on all mankind. Since the coming of Christ, the ceremonial part of the sabbath was no longer necessary and the strict rest observed by the Jews was no longer demanded of Christians. But because God chose one day of the week for his service, Christians had to devote one day a week to God, and on that day they had to stop their daily work in order to attend religious services.[16]

It was in the maritime province of Zeeland that the influence of English Puritan ideas on the sabbath gave rise to increasing controversy within the Dutch Reformed church during the last years of the sixteenth century and the first decade of the seventeenth century. Gottfried Udemans (1580?-1649?), preacher at Zierikzee from 1604-1649, was influenced by Puritan ideas and introduced the form of legalistic piety known as precision into the Dutch church. In Udeman's view, the practice of piety consisted mainly in obeying God's law revealed in Scripture, and thus he urged his followers to adhere closely to the Apostles' Creed, the Lord's Prayer, and the Ten Commandments. Faith was dead without works, he believed.

In his *Practijcke, dat is werckelijcke Oeffeninge vande Christelicke hooft-deuchden, geloove, hope en liefde* (Practice or Real Exercise of the Chief Christian Virtues of Belief, Hope, and Love, 1612) Udemans treated the issue of the sabbath. For Udemans there was no ceremonial element in the Fourth Commandment: it was entirely moral, eternal, and applicable to all people in all times and places. For Christians, Christ had changed the day of observance to the first day of the week. This day was to be devoted to God's service in body and soul, public and private, Udemans declared. Everything that could profane Sunday or prevent people from observing it was forbidden: drinking, dancing, fighting, idleness, buying, traveling, harvesting, holding meetings, field work, riding, skating, and other recreations of spirit or body. Rest, pious conversation, and holy walks after the religious service were permitted, along with works of charity and necessary work that could not be done another day.

Another Zeeland advocate of strict sabbath observance was Willem Teellinck (1579-1629), preacher at Middelburg from 1613. A founder of the *Nadere Reformatie*, Teellinck believed that, along with a reform of doctrine and polity, a reform of church life was badly needed. Daily life had to be governed by the ethic of the Bible, and he favored rigid obedience to divine law as a means to the higher end of both temporal and eternal happiness. He favored scrupulous observance of Sunday and worked hard toward this end. His efforts in Middelburg involved him in a controversy over the sabbath with one Gillis Burs, a figure about whom little is known beyond the fact that he was among the few figures who in this early period in Zeeland raised a voice against Puritan ideas

[15]Ibid., 35-42.
[16]Ibid., 42-50.

on the sabbath. Teellinck's pastoral colleague in Middelburg, the famous theologian and leader of orthodoxy Franciscus Gomarus, also adopted a position on the sabbath that was less strict than that of Teellinck, indicating that Puritan ideas on the sabbath had taken the Reformed church establishment somewhat by surprise. The dispute over the sabbath that developed in Middelburg, although mild by comparison with later developments, caused enough disruption within the church that the issue was brought before the Synod of Dordrecht in 1619.[17] After long debate the synod largely upheld the moderate position of Reformed theologians like Danaeu.[18]

Despite the work of the synod, however, the issue of the sabbath remained alive after 1619 and the church continued to spend considerable time on the issue. In Zeeland the debate over the sabbath continued due to the efforts of Teellinck, who became the most vocal proponent of stricter observance. In 1622, he wrote *De Rusttijdt ofte Tractaet van d' onderhoudinge des Christelyken Rustdachs, diemen ghemeynlyck des Sondach noemt* (The Rest Time or Tract about maintaining the Christian Rest Day, which is commonly called Sunday), in which he declared that Sunday observance was directly ordered by God. But many did not share Teellinck's strict views. In 1627 Jakob Burs, preacher in Tholen and son of Teelinck's earlier opponent, wrote *Threnos ofte Weeclaghe aanwijzend de Oorzaken des Jammerlyken Stands van 't Land* (Threnos or Complaint Showing the Causes of the sorry State of the Country), accusing advocates of strict sabbath observance of Judaism and deviation from the ideas of the reformers. Burs defended the moderate position of the Synod of Dordrecht and rejected a complete ban on all labor on the sabbath.

Burs' work annoyed those in Teellinck's camp enough that Udemans wrote to Leiden theology professor Antonius Walaeus, formerly a preacher in Middelburg and colleague of Teellinck, asking him to compose a refutation of Burs' ideas. When the refutation came, however, it was not the work of Walaeus but of Gisbertus Voetius, at that time pastor in nearby Heusden in the Generality Lands. Voetius accused Burs of pretending to advocate the opinion of the majority in the church when in fact many favored a much stricter observation of the sabbath.[19]

In the early years of the debate, practical considerations about the nature of sabbath observance and the problems of sabbath profanation dominated the discussion, but that began to change in the 1630s with the growing involvement in the controversy of Leiden theology professors. This academic turn in the controversy inevitably introduced larger issues of scriptural exegesis that produced dramatic results when the controversy heated up again in 1655 at Leiden University. It was there that Johannes Coccejus dropped the exegetical bombshell that ignited the most intense phase in the sabbath controversy and tied it directly to the raging battles surrounding Calvinist confessionalism.

It was not Coccejus himself but his Leiden theology colleague Johannes Hoornbeek (1617-1660) who opened the Leiden phase of the sabbath controversy. A disciple of Voetius who was greatly pained by sabbath profanation, Hoornbeek published V*an des Heeren Dags-heyliginge* (Concerning the Veneration of the Lord's Day) in 1655. In this work he argued that the Lord's Day was based on God's word, making it clear that his views closely followed those of Voetius and other advocates of a strict view of the sabbath. The Coccejans did not long delay their reply.

---

[17]Stoeffler, 127-131; Visser, 58-59.
[18]Visser, 60-71.
[19]Ibid., 72-114.

Leiden theologian and Cartesian Abraham Heidanus (1597-1678), who had been instrumental in bringing Coccejus to Leiden, first put forward Coccejus's views on the sabbath in two disputations held in 1658. In the first disputation, Heidanus held that Sunday observance was not an essential part of belief but merely part of church order and policy. In the New Testament, all distinction of days, like all distinction of places, foods, and the like, had come to an end with the coming of Christ and the end of the Jewish ceremonial laws. Strict observation of the seventh day in rest from all work without the appropriate inward rest of the soul was not the real sabbath, Heidanus argued. The real sabbath was a sabbath of inward spiritual fulfillment that did not simply consist of stopping otherwise permitted work on Sunday. The real sabbath consisted of stopping all bad work all of the time through the grace of Christ. Thus Sunday need not be observed with the strict rest that some advocated.[20]

Coccejus himself stepped into the fray in 1659 with his *Indagatio naturae Sabbati et quietis Novi Testamenti*, immediately translated as *Ondersoeck van den Aert ende Natuyre des Sabbaths* (Investigation of the Nature and Character of the Sabbath), one of the most influential works in the sabbath dispute and one that more than any other was responsible for launching the debate into its climactic phase.[21] True to the basis of his Covenant Theology, Coccejus approached discussion of the sabbath from the point of view of the relationship between the Old and New Testaments. God proclaimed the Ten Commandments from Sinai with great fear and trembling, intending them to be a part of the covenant of grace, Coccejus argued. With the Ten Commandments, God demanded belief in his promise to save mankind from sin, a promise of freedom and salvation in the future new covenant of Christ. The Ten Commandments thus were signs that God was ready to sanctify his people: they were signs of a future salvation. But the Jews misunderstood the commandments as part of a law of works simple obedience to which would earn salvation. The Israelites showed that they had not understood God's demand for belief in future salvation when they erected the idol of the golden calf. In response God declared them unclean and placed upon them many burdensome laws and commands of purification, such as offerings for sin and guilt, dietary laws, and other distinctions between pure and impure things.

But the coming of Christ removed these burdens from God's people and brought them rest in the pouring out of the blood of the New Testament, Coccejus continued. It was this rest from the burden of sin that was properly called the Christian sabbath. It was a great mistake to place upon a people sanctified by the blood of the New Testament the burdensome old laws and distinctions of the Jews that did not belong to the new rest brought by Christ.[22]

Just as the Ten Commandments in general were signs of a future salvation belief in which God demanded from his people as a proof of their conversion, so too the Fourth Commandment was a sign of the expected salvation. The rest ordered by the commandment was therefore a foreshadowing of the future rest from sin to be brought by Christ in the New Testament, Coccejus declared. To rest from work that was otherwise permitted and useful on that day was no service to God.

In a perfect example of figurative interpretation Coccejus added that the words of the Fourth Commandment—"Remember the sabbath day and keep it holy"—really

---

[20]Ibid., 115-121.

[21]Ibid., 121-127.

[22]Johannes Coccejus, *Ondersoeck van den Aert ende Natuyre des Sabbaths, En der Ruste des Nieuwen Testaments...Waer by Komen Getuygenissen van Oude en Nieuwe Leerars* (Leiden, 1659), 6-18, 134-138.

referred to the day on which God's work of satisfaction would be finished and ordered that that day should be observed as a day of rest to thank and glorify God. Thus "in the Old Testament foreshadowing of the New Testament, the sabbath did not mean a day of emptiness and rest from permitted works," Coccejus argued. Rather, the rest of the sabbath day foreshadowed the entire time of the New Testament, which was a rest from sin but not from all useful works. The sabbath was a sign of God's covenant with his people and his intention to sanctify them. Such sanctification would not come to those who merely rested from work on the sabbath, but only to those who had faith in God's promise. Thus the Fourth Commandment bound Christians to keep holy the time of rest that was the New Testament: the true spiritual sabbath of the Lord.[23]

After the appearance of Coccejus's work, the sabbath debate intensified dramatically. In Leiden, Hoornbeek and Heidanus continued to cross swords, and the dispute soon spread to other Dutch universities. The Synod of Leiden in 1658 tried to end the debate by ordering all parties to adhere to the articles of the Synod of Dordrecht, but to no avail. Church authorities pleaded with Coccejus, Heidanus, Hoornbeek, and their followers to reach a compromise. Finally, on 18 December, 1659, the States of Holland forbade the professors from writing further on the subject. This ban, however, had only limited effect.[24]

Meanwhile the sabbath debate flared up in both church and university in Utrecht. Voetius, by now leader of the Utrecht church and professor of theology at the university, had been involved in the debate since his early days in Heusden. In 1658, he published all of his disputations on the sabbath together in one volume strongly opposing the views of Coccejus. The issue of the sabbath by this time had come to be a key dividing line between the confessional and anti-confessional parties, and, while Voetius's ideas on the topic were well known, he left the polemics largely to his students and colleagues. Among Voetius's most vocal supporters was his Utrecht pastoral colleague Jodocus Lodensteyn (1620-1677).

Preacher at Sluis and Zoetermeer before coming to Utrecht in 1653, Lodensteyn studied both with Voetius in Utrecht and with Coccejus when he was in Franeker. From Voetius, Lodensteyn learned a legalistic and ascetic piety, and in his earlier posts he had already shown himself an advocate of Puritan ideas on the sabbath. In 1668 he could remain silent in the debate no longer. He felt that Coccejus's position on the sabbath threatened a key part of the practical piety that lay at the heart of the *Nadere Reformatie*: adherence to divine law, especially the Decalogue.[25]

In his *Kort en Zedig Onderzoek van 't Bericht nopende den Sabbath* (Short and Moral Investigation of the Report about the Sabbath) Lodensteyn rejected the position that the sabbath was only a foreshadowing of the rest to be brought by Christ, as well as the claim that the Lord's Day was not divinely instituted. Lodensteyn held that the Fourth Commandment had both moral and ceremonial aspects, and that while the ceremonial parts were abolished with the coming of Christ, the moral obligation to observe the sabbath remained.

According to Coccejus, the Ten Commandments were part of the covenant of grace and not the covenant of works, but in Lodensteyn's view the commandments were a renewal of the covenant of works meant to provide God's people with a moral law that

[23]Ibid., 18-19, 21-22, 63-72, 89-97.
[24]Visser, 130-149.
[25]Trimp, 21-50, 111-113.

was distinct from ceremonial or political laws. God distinguished this moral law from other laws by special signs: he gave it to his people amidst fire, thunder, and lightening, and he wrote it into stone with his own fingers so that it would be an eternal law (in reply to this argument Bekker would later say that the commandments written in stone would last only as long as the stone tablets lasted!). Lodensteyn declared that this law was a moral rule "for all of God's people for all times and ages." Christ and the apostles taught people this law, which they would not have done were it simply ceremonial and abolished with Christ's coming into the world. Obedience to all Ten Commandments was necessary for salvation, Lodensteyn stressed.

The Lord made Ten Commandments, Lodensteyn continued, not nine or three or seven. And all Ten Commandments were of the same nature, given as such to Israel without any exception being mentioned. No man could except one of the commandments without damaging the entire moral law. The Fourth Commandment was part of the moral law and binding on all people for all time because the command of the rest day had an eternal goal. "The rest day commanded in the Fourth Commandment is a certain time, defined by God in His Word, to rest and to sanctify or to spend in holy works," Lodensteyn declared.[26] Lodensteyn ended his argument in the spirit of confessionalism by pointing out at some length that his position and not that of his opponents was in agreement with the Heidelberg Catechism and the decrees of the Synod of Dordrecht.[27]

V

From Utrecht the sabbath debate spread to Groningen, where the two main contestants were professors Alting and Maresius. It was at this stage of the controversy that Bekker got involved, with decisive results for the rest of his career in the Reformed church. As both a student and a friend of Alting, Bekker inclined to Alting's position on the sabbath, a position in its turn influenced and defended by Coccejus, who was Alting's friend.

Bekker's interest in the sabbath question began in 1665, the year of his doctoral disputation at the university of Franeker. His defense of theses 79 and 95 showed that his conception of the sabbath was indeed influenced by Alting and Coccejus. In article 79 he held that while the Fourth Commandment spoke specifically of the weekly sabbath, it also referred to yearly and monthly religious feasts and to all outer religion of that time. In article 95 he said that holding public religious service was necessary and commanded in the New Testament, but that the definition of the first day of the week or Lord's Day for this service came not from divine ordination but from church tradition. The second of these propositions was clearly Coccejan, and the first raised questions as well. It was in this same disputation that Bekker took a clearly anti-confessional stand on the issue of funeral orations.[28]

[26]Jodocus Lodensteyn, *Kort en Zedig Onderzoek van 't Bericht nopende den sabbath, Ende de Korte Aanmerkingen over het gene dies aangaande zederd enigen tydt tot Utreght geleert zoude zyn. Benevens de Laatste Gedagten over de Zedelykheit des Vierden Gebodts, Ofte Verdediging van het Kort en Zedig Onderzoek* (Groningen, 1740), 3-5, 82-97.

[27]Ibid., 5-6.

[28]Visser, 203.

Even more disturbing for the confessionalists was the stand on the sabbath taken by Bekker in his adult catechism, the *Vaste Spyse*, published in 1670. The catechism was, after all, not a university disputation but a document intended for the general public. Bekker had been working on the catechism since his arrival in Franeker as a preacher in 1668, and during the writing of the work he maintained close contacts with Alting in Groningen. In the preface to the *Vaste Spyse*, Bekker criticized several of Voetius's opinions about Sunday. In chapter 27 he held that the Ten Commandments were God's conditions for his covenant with Israel, and as such they were not just part of the moral law but also part of the ecclesiastical and civil law. Bekker argued that it was clear that the commandments were not just moral and eternal because "the words as they are speak mainly of outward obedience," while the moral law focussed on inward obedience. Furthermore, while the Commandments' "words and style are suited to the conditions of the Jewish people in particular," the moral law applied to all nations. Just because the commandments were proclaimed by God with such majesty, written by him with his own finger into the stone tablets, and preserved in the ark of the covenant did not mean that they were exclusively moral and everlasting in nature, Bekker argued. The fact that they were written in stone only meant that they would last as long as the tablets, but no longer. "Now the tablets are lost and the law is abolished," he declared. The law of morals was never written in stone, but in the flesh tables of the heart.[29]

Bekker stressed that the Ten Commandments did have to be upheld by Christians as a rule of life and prescription for belief. Nevertheless, Christians could only realize the importance of the Decalogue by keeping in mind the difference between the Old Testament and the New Testament. "All of the Ten Commandments still bind us, but with these differences: 1) some apply to us just as their words express," while 2) "All of the special circumstances expressed in the Ten Commandments applied only to the Israelites. But the thing itself therein expressed also applies to us Christians. This is principally the case with the Fourth Commandment," Bekker argued.[30] In effect, Bekker held that some of the Ten Commandments were to be interpreted literally, while others could not be. The Fourth Commandment fell in this latter category. It applied to Christians only in a very general way. Such ideas on the Decalogue were far from those of the Puritan-influenced party that saw adherence to the divine law as a fundament of piety.

On other points, Bekker's ideas were even more Coccejan. In chapter 29, he argued that the laws given by God to Israel created distinctions among persons, foods, places, and times, but that Christians were free of these distinctions. In the New Testament true belief had replaced such disciplinary regulations, Bekker argued, and thus God had set Christians free. "Places are now all alike—one can serve God equally well in all places." There could be no distinction of foods because God gave all foods to everyone. Likewise there could be no distinction of times in the New Testament because "God has given the times as well as the cause of times—the sun, moon, and stars—to all people under the whole heavens. So long as God himself makes no distinction, it is all the same for us," Bekker argued.[31] The basis of the Fourth Commandment was that there were certain times to serve God, Bekker continued, but since the

---

[29]Balthasar Bekker, *De Vaste Spyze der Volmaakten, Bestaande in een grondige en Schrifmatige Verklaringe van de Leere die begrepen is in den Heidelbergse Catechismus gebruikelik by de Gereformeerden kerken der Vereende Nederlanden* (Leeuwarden, 1674), 500-501.

[30]Ibid., 501-502; Visser 202-204.

[31]Bekker, 562-563.

distinction of times had been abolished, Christians were no longer bound by it to observe the weekly sabbath. The sabbath had been a sign between God and Israel meant to remind the people that God was their Lord who had created the world in six days and then rested on the seventh. By themselves resting from their work on the seventh day the people of Israel showed their trust in God. And the sabbath rest was "a prefiguring of a bigger and better rest," Bekker argued. Thus Bekker, like Coccejus, held that the Jewish sabbath had been a sign and foreshadowing of the spiritual sabbath of Christ in the New Testament. In response to Question 116: "How ought a Christian Sabbath to be?" Bekker replied: "One day seems to me too little. The Christian church must go beyond the Jews in rational religion." He went on to say that the Christian sabbath should be "constant, day by day," and "spiritual, as God himself demanded," very much as Coccejus had argued.[32]

"So it appears that the sabbath was only instituted for one people—the Jews," Bekker argued. And it was first instituted in the wilderness, when God took Israel as his special people and gave them the manna. There was no evidence that the sabbath had been instituted before the fall or that it dated from the creation of the world, Bekker added, "Because we do not read about it earlier. And they did not know about it earlier."[33]

In the New Testament, the Jewish sabbath was replaced by the Lord's Day. "Because thinking of and praising God's works can take place just as well on any other day as the seventh, during the time of the Messiah and for reasons suited to that time God abolished the Law of the Seventh Day and left the congregation free to choose other days," Bekker argued. On the question of the divine authority of the Lord's Day, Bekker claimed that Sunday observance was an old and general practice of the church, but not one instituted by either Christ or the apostles. "Christians solemnly observe Sunday since this day has been observed by the church since the days of the apostles. It is an old and common use in the Christian church," that was made official during the time of Constantine, Bekker added. But this day was not instituted by Christ or the apostles themselves: "Christ and the apostles gathered with believers on the first day of the week, but also on other days," Bekker noted.[34] "It is not a human institution that people gather in the congregation at certain times dedicated to religious service. That was instituted by God himself. But which day, that was the choice of the church," Bekker argued.[35]

Bekker finished with a bold attack on the Synod of Dordrecht, an attack all the more astounding because it came in a public catechism. Question 115 asked: "How do you understand the actions of the Synod of Dordrecht regarding the sabbath?" Bekker replied that the synod had not expressed the feelings of the entire Reformed church but only of the Netherlands' clergy, and not even all of them, but only those few in attendance. Those preachers in attendance were not allowed to refer the matter back to their congregations for the opinions of members, a practice that "was naturally necessary for a church law," Bekker added. And the synod had not intended to bind the entire church to its decisions some 50 years later and thus "to take away our freedom to investigate the thing further." The synod's decision was only meant to be valid until a future body took up the issue of the sabbath, Bekker concluded.[36]

[32]Ibid., 566-567, 575.
[33]Ibid., 564-565.
[34]Ibid., 568-569.
[35]Ibid., 569.
[36]Ibid., 574.

By taking this Coccejan-influenced position in the sabbath debate Bekker clearly aligned himself in opposition to the powerful confessional wing of the Reformed church. An intense controversy immediately developed around the *Vaste Spyze*, and the enmity of the confessional party that Bekker earned in this episode would follow him for the rest of his life.

Even before Bekker published his catechism, confessionalists such as Franeker philosophy Professor Abraham Steindam and history professor Michael Busch began to spread the rumor that the *Vaste Spyze* contained "heresies."[37] Bekker took Steindam and Busch to the Court of Friesland, but the States of Friesland prohibited the court from considering the matter, saying that it was a church issue. The States, as overseer of both the church and university of Franeker, took up the issue itself and sought advice about *De Vaste Spyze* from the Franeker theology faculty, in the meantime forbidding further circulation of the book. In its *Advies* (Advice) to the States the faculty, led by Professor Arnoldus, condemned Bekker's claim that the Ten Commandments were part of civil and ecclesiastical law as well as the moral law, and his statement that the Ten Commandments often spoke only of outward obedience. The faculty said that these opinions demeaned the commandments by contrasting them unfavorably with the Gospels and by suggesting that the commandments were no longer relevant for Christians. The faculty also condemned Bekker's ideas on the Fourth Commandment as "Socinian."[38]

Arnoldus and his colleagues further declared that the book contained no fewer than 37 offensive ideas and unsound doctrines, as well as novelties and other strange ideas. The faculty thus recommended that the catechism not be used in the church because it would give rise to misunderstandings. After receiving this advice, the States sent the professors' comments to the six Reformed church classes of Friesland, requesting that they consider what should be done about the catechism in light of the professors' opinions. The classes were asked to send their judgements to the upcoming synod of the Reformed church of Friesland. The States then forbade the printing of *De Vaste Spyze*.[39]

Bekker reacted to these events by publishing several letters of approval that he had received from prominent scholars concerning his catechism and by calling on the States to rescind their edict against its printing. The States, however, bought up the remaining 80 unsold copies of the first printing and sent them to the classes for their inspection. In order to defend himself, Bekker composed a refutation of the faculty's report on his work. Entitled the *Nodige Antwoord* (Necessary Answer), the work took up the theologians' objections point for point. In defense of his conception of divine law, Bekker referred to the ideas of Alting and Heidanus, and he repeated his claim that the Ten Commandments were not solely moral. In Matthew 5:17, Christ spoke of the Ten Commandments as not being separate from the other laws of Moses, and from this it was clear that they were no more spiritual than the other laws, Bekker argued. But Christ did not contrast the commandments with the Gospel as if the two were contradictory, and neither did he, Bekker insisted. On the issue of the Fourth Commandment, nobody denied that it was at least partly other than moral, Bekker said, and he went on to claim that his ideas about the rest day had been distorted. He conceded that the Fourth

---

[37]Jacob van Sluis, *Bekkeriana: Balthasar Bekker biografisch en bibliografisch* (Leeuwarden, 1994), 20-21.

[38]Visser, 206.

[39]Knuttel, 50-70.

Commandment did divinely institute the seventh day sabbath, but he denied that this applied to Christians. The Lord's Day was a human institution, but it was observed according to God's Word.[40] Bekker sent the *Nodige Antwoord* to the Friesian classes, at the same time offering to come before them in person to explain his ideas.

Meanwhile, Alting's old enemy Maresius entered the fray against Bekker with his work *Catechesis Publica*. Maresius argued that the Fourth Commandment dated from the creation of the world, was observed by the patriarchs but neglected in Egypt, then was restored with the falling of the manna in the wilderness. Thus the sabbath command was partly ceremonial and specific to Israel, as Bekker held, but it was moral and applicable to all Christians when it ordered a set day for rest and religious exercise. The apostles had, on divine authority, changed the seventh day sabbath to the first or Lord's Day, Maresius insisted.

Maresius and others in the confessional party feared Bekker as an innovator in theology who not only harbored Coccejan sympathies but who was also critical of the authority of the confessions and dogmatic writings of the Reformed church. It was therefore not surprising when the Friesian Synod of Bolsward in 1671, acting on the advice of the classes, forbade the printing and sale of Bekker's catechism until it could be purged of "offensive" passages. At this point Bekker volunteered to collect and reply to all objections to his work, but the States were not satisfied and once again condemned the *Vaste Spyze*, forbidding anyone from writing either for or against it.[41]

Conditions in Franeker grew steadily worse for Bekker. Arnoldus and Sterrenga, who had played key roles in the Franeker faculty's condemnation of the *Vaste Spyze*, refused to go to communion with Bekker, and only after great effort could the church council make peace among the three men. The classis of Franeker was unrelentingly hostile, criticizing Bekker for delivering sermons in which he expressed ideas taken from the *Vaste Spyze*. The classis demanded that Bekker promise not to teach anything from the catechism that it found objectionable, either in writing or orally, but Bekker refused. On top of all of this, some professors objected to the fact that Bekker taught theology to students in his Franeker home. They complained to the States that these teaching sessions broke university rules and were un-biblical in content. Despite Bekker's protestations the States forbade his private teaching.

As a result of all of these problems in Franeker, Bekker began to look around for another position. On Alting's suggestion he looked in Holland. Groningen was another possibility, even though the Synod of Groningen condemned the *Vaste Spyze* in 1672, largely due to the efforts of Maresius. Bekker made changes in the *Vaste Spyze* after reading the reports on it made by the classes of Friesland, and he put the revised work before the Synod of Friesland in Franeker in 1672 for its approval. The synod took no action, however, because of the traumatic invasion of The Netherlands by the French armies of Louis XIV that threw the entire country into a panic and brought down the government of Grand Pensionary Jan de Witt. During the crisis, Bekker chaired a gathering of Friesian preachers who met in Leeuwarden and gave advice to the States. His role in the war crisis was later to be of great help to Bekker in Friesland because of the contacts that he made in court and government. Bekker was also chosen by his colleagues in the Friesian church to be their observer at the Synod of Overijssel in 1672, which was never held because of the war. Bekker's position in the church

[40]Visser, 206.
[41]Ibid., 70-80; van Sluis, 20-21; see also D. Nauta, *Samuel Maresius* (dissertation, Vrije Universiteit Amsterdam, 1939).

during the war crisis showed that he had the respect of many of his colleagues despite the attacks made by others on his orthodoxy.[42]

After the war crisis had passed, a committee appointed by the Franeker synod of 1672 investigated the changes that Bekker had made in the *Vaste Spyze* and approved the work for printing and use within the church. Bekker then began preparing the new edition for the press, and it seemed as if good fortune had come at last. But in 1673 Maresius published his *Tractatus brevis de afflicto statu studii Theologici in foederato Belgio et commoda illius restituendi ratione,* in which he attacked the theological innovations of Cartesianism and Coccejanism, criticized Coccejus's ideas on divine law, and labeled the opponents of confessionalism a "Cartees-Loevesteyns-Remonstrantsche" faction (Cartesian-Lovesteyn-Remonstrant faction. Castle Lovesteyn was where Arminian sympathizers were imprisoned after the coup that toppled Oldenbarnevelt, and later it played host to jailed opponents of William II). Maresius specifically targeted Bekker with his criticism, and he called for the upholding of the authority of Reformed church confessions and formulas.

Bekker replied in his *Defensio justa et necessaria* in 1673, a long open letter in which he reprinted earlier correspondence with Maresius and defended his own ideas.[43] Bekker not only replied to Maresius but also referred insultingly to Maresius's ally, the Leiden theologian Fridericus Spanheim. Spanheim complained to the States of Friesland, which passed the complaint on to the Friesian synod meeting in Harlingen. The States reproached Bekker for his conduct and the synod made him write a letter of apology to Spanheim. The synod also forbade Bekker from publishing anything further without prior inspection by the States, and it began a new investigation into the revised *Vaste Spyze,* forbidding its sale in the meantime.

Due to lack of paper caused by the war, the catechism had not yet been completely printed, so the synod assigned inspection of the work to a new set of deputies different from those who had read the revised work in 1672. These investigators made new objections to the work but agreed to allow Bekker to publish it if he would address several issues that concerned them in an appendix. Bekker wrote the appendix and presented it to the review committee at the synod of Dokkum in 1674, but the committee was not satisfied. Additional revisions also proved insufficient, and Bekker was further humiliated by the fact that he had prematurely asked and received permission to dedicate the book to the States, which fined him when the book was not approved for publication. It was in the midst of this demoralizing affair that Bekker left his post in Franeker and accepted a call to Loenen, a village between Amsterdam and Utrecht. The appendix was finally approved by the Synod of Leeuwarden in 1675, and the revised *Vaste Spyze* was published at last. After Bekker had departed Friesland, the States forbade him from being nominated for a position at the university of Franeker in July 1676, a parting shot that no doubt hurt him deeply.[44]

The long and drawn out struggle by Bekker to publish his adult catechism was a complex affair fought on several levels. Bekker's liberal position on the sabbath placed him clearly on one side of an ideological divide within the Dutch Reformed church separating two distinct visions of the nature of the church and the interpretation of Scripture. The highly charged nature of Bekker's stand on the sabbath question, given

---

[42]Knuttel, 79-96.
[43]Visser, 207-209; Knuttel, 98-112.
[44]Knuttel, 96-112; van Sluis, 20-21.

the long and intense debate on that issue within the church, accounted for much of the heat generated by opponents of the *Vaste Spyze* as they defended their confessional vision of the church against Bekker's ideas. In this sense, the debate around the *Vaste Spyze* provided both sides with a full dress rehearsal for the later drama surrounding *The World Bewitched.*

Long before the spirit controversy broke out, therefore, the battle lines had been drawn and Bekker's enemies had marshalled their forces. Having lost their struggle to prevent the publication of the *Vaste Spyze,* they had nevertheless succeeded in bringing Bekker's views under synodal scrutiny. All that was left was to await the opportunity for a final and decisive battle. As it turned out, they would have to wait nearly 20 years.

CHAPTER THREE

Cartesianism and the Spirit Controversy

Balthasar Bekker's interest in Cartesian philosophy developed alongside his anti-confessional religious position during his early years in Groningen and Franeker. Cartesianism had been highly controversial in the Republic since it began to gain a foothold there in the 1640s, drawing intense opposition from the confessional wing of the Reformed church, which saw philosophical rationalism as a threat to religious belief. Bekker's interest in Cartesianism therefore further embittered his confessionalist opponents and involved him in another complex web of intellectual controversy, this time between Dutch Cartesians and their clerical opponents.

Cartesianism provided Bekker with a powerful weapon against traditional spirit belief, and his use of Cartesian arguments in *The World Bewitched* became one of the most controversial aspects of the work. While the fundamental issues at stake in the spirit controversy were those of biblical exegesis and the confessional nature of the Reformed church, Bekker's use of Cartesian dualism to assault traditional spirit belief made the ideas of Descartes and their relationship to religious belief another focus of the debate.

I

The influence of Cartesian philosophy upon Dutch intellectual and religious life in the period between 1640 and 1700 was substantial. The Netherlands was the first country outside France in which Descartes' ideas gained a significant following, both inside and outside the universities. The influence of his philosophy within the academic world gave rise to a native Dutch Cartesianism with its own distinctive characteristics that reached a peak of influence and creativity during the 1660s. A central concern of Dutch academic Cartesianism was its relationship to religious orthodoxy as defined by the Reformed Church, but despite repeated efforts by Cartesians to demonstrate their religious orthodoxy, conservative members of the church viewed the new philosophy with alarm.

Rene Descartes lived and worked in The Netherlands at various locations during the years 1623-1648. His *Meditations on First Philosophy* was first published in Leiden in 1637, and, in 1644, Elsevier published his *Principles of Philosophy* and *Discourse on Method*. Editions of his *Opera philosophica* were published by Elsevier in Amsterdam in 1650, 1656, 1662, 1672, and 1677. Unlike their conservative counterparts elsewhere in Europe, Dutch universities initially proved quite open to Cartesian ideas, ideas that caused much debate both within and among the faculties.

Cartesianism had its earliest influence at the University of Utrecht, where Henry Regius (1598-1679), professor of medicine, was Descartes' closest associate in the Dutch academic world. Soon Leiden university became the leading center of academic Cartesianism, in part because of the influence there of Johannes De Raey (1622-1702), a pupil of Regius who gave private lessons in Cartesianism, and Abraham Heidanus (1579-1678), professor of theology and one of Descartes' earliest supporters. From these two centers Cartesianism spread to the other Dutch universities. Cartesian ideas were defended at Groningen as early as 1645, and at the Friesian university in Franeker, scholars sought to reconcile the new philosophy with the older Aristotelian tradition. At Harderwijk, questions about the religious impact of Cartesianism did not stop the new philosophy from being widely discussed.[1]

The influence of Cartesian ideas led to heated debates over the method of doubt, dualism, and Descartes' idea of God, and, eventually, to considerable rancor among university scholars. As a result, university administrators repeatedly forbade the teaching of Cartesian metaphysics in order to avoid conflict. Nevertheless, Cartesians continued to be appointed to university posts, and their ideas continued to spread, becoming well established in Leiden and Utrecht by 1650. Aristotelians objected to Cartesian metaphysics much more than to Cartesian physics, while confessionalist clerics in the Reformed church objected to the religious implications of Descartes' method of doubt as well as to his evil demon argument.[2] The new philosophy became involved in numerous theological disputes from the mid-seventeenth century onward, and it was largely these controversies that carried the influence of Cartesianism beyond the academies.

Dutch university Cartesians were not single-minded followers of Descartes, nor was Dutch Cartesianism a monolithic movement. In fact, many Dutch Cartesians had only a very imperfect grasp of the new philosophy, and as a result they often misrepresented Descartes' ideas. Many of Descartes' Dutch students saw his philosophy in the traditional university manner—as a series of theses, each to be upheld separately—rather than as a revolutionary new method of thought.[3] University Cartesians were especially interested in making Cartesianism into an academic discipline and in neutralizing theological and religious objections to the new philosophy, two points of little concern to Descartes himself.[4]

Dutch academic Cartesians were for the most part orthodox Calvinists who favored innovation in philosophy but not in theology, and Bekker's own Cartesianism was at first very much in this mold, although he was not an academic Cartesian. To defend themselves against charges of religious heterodoxy, university Cartesians insisted on a much more strict separation between philosophy and theology than Descartes himself allowed. They held reason to be the primary criterion for truth in philosophy, but they retained faith as the criterion for religious truth. The goal of philosophy was knowledge,

---

[1]C. Louise Thijssen-Schoute, *Nederlands Cartesianisme* (Amsterdam, 1954), 554-555.

[2]Theo Verbeek, *Descartes and the Dutch: Early Reactions to Cartesian Philosophy 1637-1650* (Carbondale, 1992), 82-88.

[3]Thomas A. MaGahagan, *Cartesianism in the Netherlands 1639-1676: The New Science and the Calvinist Counter-Reformation* (dissertation, University of Pennsylvania, 1976), 106.

[4]Verbeek, 76.

while the goal of theology was salvation, and therefore the two disciplines could not be in conflict. Moderate Dutch Cartesians made great efforts to show the harmony of Cartesianism with Reformed theology, and they emphatically rejected thinkers (like Lodewijk Meyer and Benedict Spinoza) who seemed to make philosophy the judge of religion. The few truly radical Dutch Cartesians were found outside the university system, were a small minority, and attracted strong criticism from all sides, including from academic Cartesians.[5] Bekker's early Cartesianism followed in the moderate academic tradition and thus drew little opposition from conservative clerics, but when his ideas became more radical in *The World Bewitched,* uproar resulted.

Very few university Cartesians endorsed the whole of Descartes' metaphysics—in part because of philosophical problems presented by dualism, in part because dualism seemed to pose a serious threat to traditional religious doctrines, and in part because Cartesian metaphysics was the initial focus of attacks by Reformed opponents of the new philosophy. Academic Cartesians were generally more interested in Descartes' physics than his metaphysics, and for this reason Cartesianism more easily spread and won acceptance within the universities. As Cartesianism became an academic discipline within the arts faculties it encountered problems in its relationships with the higher faculties. Cartesian philosophers tried to avoid conflict with theology faculties by maintaining the strict separation between philosophy and theology that was also their first line of defense against Reformed critics.[6]

In Utrecht there was Regius, a physician who Theo Verbeek suggests was probably the only professional Dutch academician to grasp the full significance of Descartes' *Discourse on Method.*[7] As professor of theoretical medicine and botany, Regius developed his own physical system based on Cartesian ideas. In a series of disputations in 1641 he put forward Cartesian ideas about the soul and its relationship to the body, but he did not incorporate dualism into his conceptual system. He was unsympathetic as well to other points of Cartesian metaphysics. His epistemology was empiricist, and he rejected innate ideas. Regius accused the Aristotelians of atheism for holding that substantial forms—among them, the soul—were produced from matter, a position that gained him little favor with the university administration. He was also openly critical of Utrecht pastor and professor Voetius, and he was personally advised by Descartes when he composed a reply to Voetius's attack on Cartesianism.

Like other Dutch Cartesians, Regius separated the realms of philosophy and theology in order to protect both his own religious orthodoxy and the autonomy of reason. He believed that faith and reason could not be in conflict because they rested on separate principles: faith depended on revelation, while reason was founded on sense experience. And they had different ends—the end of faith was salvation, while that of reason was utility. Descartes did not accept such an absolute separation of faith from reason, and this, along with other issues, led to a break between Descartes and Regius in 1647.[8]

The leader of the Leiden Cartesians was Abraham Heidanus, professor of theology. Heidanus believed that philosophy was not to be used in theology, where Scripture

---

[5]McGahagan, 3.

[6]Verbeek, 88-90; McGahagan, 109.

[7]Verbeek, 13.

[8]See Theo Verbeek (ed), *Descartes et Regius: Autour de l'Explication de l'esprit humain* (Amsterdam and Atlanta, 1993).

ruled supreme, nor could Scripture and theology be used to understand natural science. This latter position earned him the scorn of Voetius and his followers, who saw Scripture as a source for all truth.

Another prominent Leiden Cartesian was Adriaan Heereboord (1614-1661), who tried to combine Cartesianism, Aristotelianism, Baconianism, and Gassendism in his thought. Born in Leiden, Heereboord graduated from the university in 1637 and went to Amsterdam as a private tutor. In 1640 he became a professor at Leiden. Even before he came under the influence of Cartesianism, he was already at work revising Aristotelian philosophy. A popular teacher, Heereboord led a stormy family life influenced by alcoholism and made numerous personal enemies, some of whom carried their dislike for the man into attacks on his philosophical positions. Like Heidanus, Heereboord saw philosophy as having no real role in theology beyond definition of terms and defense of orthodoxy. Revealed truth in Scripture could not be interpreted with reason, he felt, and he also insisted that theology had no role in philosophy.[9]

Perhaps the most important of all the Leiden Cartesians was Johannes De Raey, who taught at the university beginning in 1651 before becoming ordinary professor of philosophy in 1661. He had studied with both Regius and Heereboord. Like Heereboord, De Raey tried to reconcile Cartesianism with the Aristotelian tradition, seeking to "purify" Scholastic philosophy using a new method based partly on Descartes. De Raey believed that there was a greater difference between Aristotle and the Scholastics than between Aristotle and Descartes, and he saw Cartesian philosophy as the key to restoring the true Aristotle. De Raey held Cartesian disputations in 1651-1652 and adopted most of Descartes' physical theory, but he did not subscribe to much of Cartesian metaphysics, the method of doubt, the *cogito* argument, or the proofs of God's existence.

De Raey maintained that Cartesian methods could not be used to solve problems of theology, politics, or medicine, and he also held that reason could not be used to criticize the Bible. He developed a radical separation of philosophy not only from theology but from all other knowledge as well. For De Raey, philosophical knowledge had a unique character that distinguished it from all other forms of knowledge. Truth in philosophy was of a different nature than truth in theology, medicine, or law (the higher university faculties) because philosophy developed clear and distinct ideas, while the other sciences dealt in interpretation. Even philosophical language was fundamentally different from ordinary language, the two being independently functioning semantic systems that were not interchangeable. With this radical separation, De Raey defended academic Cartesianism both from conservative theologians and from radical philosophers like Spinoza, who saw in Cartesianism implications for religion and politics. De Raey resigned from Leiden in 1669 to accept the post of philosophy teacher at the Atheneum in Amsterdam, and he later worked on the Amsterdam edition of Descartes' works published by Elsevier.[10]

In Amsterdam, Cartesianism exercised considerable influence, especially at the Atheneum and the Remonstrant Seminary. The Atheneum did not witness the bitter disputes over Cartesianism that took place in Leiden and Utrecht. In part this was

---

[9] Verbeek, *Descartes and the Dutch*, 70-71, 228-229; Thijssen-Schoute 96-99, 125.

[10] Theo Verbeek, "De Vrijheid van de Philosophie: Reflecties over een Cartesiaans Thema," *Quaestiones Infinitae: Publications of the Department of Philosophy, Utrecht University*, IV: 1994, 4-7; Verbeek, *Descartes and the Dutch*, 72-73; Thijssen-Schoute 126-140.

because De Raey taught a moderate Cartesianism there that he hoped would be reconcilable with Aristotelianism, while Arnoldus Senguerd's Cartesian teaching at the Atheneum was confined to physics. When Etienne de Courcelles became a teacher at the Remonstrant Seminary in 1643, Cartesianism entered that liberal theological institution. Courcelles knew Descartes personally and translated his *Discourse on Method* into Latin, but there was little Cartesian influence in his own works of exegesis and theology.

It was outside the academic setting that the most radical Cartesians were to be found in Amsterdam. These men ignored the separation of religion from philosophy favored by most university Cartesians, and, in so doing, they showed the serious consequences that could result when Cartesian epistemological methods and criteria for truth were applied to biblical interpretation. As a non-academic Cartesian, Bekker, in his later works, began to drift into this world where Cartesian ideas were applied to theology and exegetics, but he was always far more cautious in this area than were the real radicals. Among the most important of these radicals was Lodewijk Meyer (1630-1681), physician and center of a group of Cartesian professionals in Amsterdam. He was also for a time director of the city theater. While still a young man, he busied himself writing poetry and drama, after which he entered Leiden University at the age of 25 to study medicine. Meyer was influenced by Spinoza and became a friend and correspondent of the great philosopher. In 1663, he wrote a preface for Spinoza's *The Principles of Descartes' Philosophy* and edited the work's Latin style. He helped to prepare Spinoza's later works for publication after the author's death in 1677.

In his *Philosophia Sacrae Scripturae Interpres* (1666), Meyer held that philosophy was an infallible key for interpreting Scripture because reason could determine which sense of Scripture best agreed with the intentions of the writers. According to Meyer, whose exegesis contrasted starkly with the biblical literalism of Reformed conservatives, the Bible could not explain itself nor was its true sense readily apparent in the text itself. The Holy Spirit was not essential for interpreting Scripture, according to Meyer. Reason alone could establish the divine nature of the Bible. The *Philosophia Sacrae Scripturae Interpres* was quickly condemned by the theology faculty of Leiden University, but in 1673 it was published together in one edition with Spinoza's *Tractatus Theologico-Politicus*, an edition that was condemned by the States of Holland. Despite Meyer's close relations with Spinoza, the great philosopher himself did not agree with the arguments made in Meyer's book, which he believed inverted his own method.[11]

The extreme ideas that Meyer produced by linking philosophical rationalism directly to theology and exegesis frightened moderate Cartesians, but his ideas did find a few followers. Lambert van Velthuysen (1622-1685) was an Utrecht physician who took a degree in philosophy in 1644 and became an advocate of Cartesianism, agreeing with some of the radical ideas of Meyer. He also wrote on natural law, defended the ideas of Hobbes, and speculated on methods of biblical exegesis. Like Spinoza, with whom he corresponded, van Velthuysen argued that any explanation of Scripture had to take account of the circumstances under which the Bible was written. In 1655 he published a work arguing that heliocentricism did not contradict Scripture.[12]

---

[11]Thijssen-Schoute, 356-362, 380-381, 395-404.

[12]Wiep van Bunge, "Van Velthuysen, Batelier and Bredenburg on Spinoza's Interpretation of the Scriptures," in Paolo Cristofolini (ed), *The Spinozistic Heresy: The Debate on the Tractatus Theologico Politicus 1670-1677 and the Immediate Reception of Spinozism* (APA Holland University Press, 1995), 1-4.

University Cartesians tended to be more moderate than their non-academic counterparts, like Meyer and van Velthuysen, in part because of the need to guard their religious orthodoxy in order to insure their university positions. The civil authorities responsible for university appointments were generally not reluctant to appoint Cartesians to faculty positions despite the repeated objections of the Reformed clergy, but neither did these authorities relish the often violent controversies that resulted when Cartesian professors provoked their more conservative colleagues with radical claims, especially on topics of religious importance. More than once, university and civil authorities intervened in such disputes in Leiden and Utrecht and, in the interests of public and academic peace, forbade the discussion of controversial Cartesian ideas. Cartesian professors did not always comply with the pacific wishes of the authorities, but there were risks involved: as will be seen below, Heidanus lost his position at Leiden in 1676 for refusing to comply with official instructions not to teach certain controversial propositions of Cartesian metaphysics.

The spread of Cartesianism in The Netherlands was not slowed by either the controversies surrounding it or the often bitter opposition of some of the Reformed clergy. Many pastors of the Reformed church were not concerned about Cartesianism, while others, like Bekker, looked favorably on the new philosophy. But some conservative clergy, often with formal philosophical training, saw the new philosophy as a serious threat to religious belief. In particular, the confessional wing of the Reformed church led by the Utrecht's Gisbertus Voetius took it upon themselves to oppose Cartesianism at every possible opportunity. This opposition, unrelenting throughout most of the seventeenth century, helped to define the nature of Dutch Cartesianism as it evolved under fire from the confessional party. As a Reformed minister, Bekker found defending Cartesianism among his own colleagues to be one of his most difficult tasks.

II

Voetius placed himself in the forefront of the struggle against Cartesianism, on several occasions personally clashing with Descartes and Regius and writing many works against their ideas. Philosophically Voetius was an Aristotelian Neoscholastic who believed that science was only useful when it furthered piety. For Voetius, to defend the autonomy of science as many Cartesians did was to defend license and libertinism. He saw reason as a servant of faith, not a judge of faith, and while he did not object to philosophy or rational theology as such, he did object to their autonomy from the demands of faith. The authority of God in Scripture was the only infallible standard of religious truth.

Just as Voetius and the confessionalists disagreed with Cartesians over reason's relationship to faith, so too the two sides fundamentally disagreed over reason's role in scriptural exegesis. On this point, the division of confessionalists from Cartesians was much like the earlier one between *preciezen* and Arminians. While Voetius did not believe that the truths of faith were based on reason, like earlier *preciezen* he saw reason as one important tool among others to be used to interpret Holy Writ. An important job for reason in this context was to extract the truths of faith from Scripture and cast them in rational-propositional form in order to create Reformed theology and the confessional formulas of the church. Voetius held faith to be an act of explicit intellectual consent, the object of which had to be cast in rational form. While reason's role in religion was to grasp the evident truth of Scripture and cast it as doctrine, Voetius believed that no real interpretation was involved in this process. Biblical truth was clear through itself and reason added nothing to it in the process of understanding.[13] Scripture had one clear sense for Voetius—its literal sense—and he rejected all figurative, parabolic, or allegorical readings; indeed, he rejected the need for any external authority whatsoever in interpreting the Bible. In Voetius's view, scriptural interpretation was unproblematic: it was simple perception of truth, a kind of intellectual seeing.

Somewhat ironically, most academic Cartesians, like the Arminians before them, had a more limited view of the role of reason in religion. Reason could not extract truth from Scripture and formulate it as authoritative doctrine because the vital points of belief were largely beyond the powers of reason to grasp. When reason was used to understand the Bible, human interpretation was involved, Cartesians believed. Interpretations varied and carried no divine authority because each individual interpreter read the Bible in the light of his own reason. Voetius, on the other hand, rejected the possibility of multiple interpretations of Scripture, charging that this would lead to subjectivism and scepticism. Cartesians thus tended to see faith as implicit, as an act of the will, not an explicit act of intellectual consent.[14] This is why academic Cartesians avoided using reason to interpret Scripture, and this is why many of them were critical of claims to divine authority made for Reformed confessional documents. Cartesian theologians followed in the line of earlier Arminians who had stressed that the Bible alone carried divine authority, that there were many parts of it that could not be interpreted by reason, and that confessional and theological formulas were fallible because they were produced by human reason.

This exegetical position tied Cartesians to earlier Arminian theologians and cast both groups in the role of opposition to the rising tide of Dutch Reformed confessionalism. It is not at all surprising, therefore, that Voetius and his party understood the threat of Cartesianism in categories stemming from the earlier Arminian controversy.[15] They saw their clash with the new philosophy as an extension of the earlier conflict, and they interpreted the threat of Cartesianism to what they perceived as religious orthodoxy to be much the same as that posed by earlier Arminianism.[16] This view was, in its broad outlines, accurate. While the danger of Cartesian metaphysics was exaggerated by Reformed opponents, Cartesian exegetics was a serious threat to the confessional conception of the church that defined faith in terms of intellectual consent to a set of theological doctrines that were supposed to carry divine authority.[17]

Beyond Cartesianism's threat to the confessional conception of the church, Voetius saw in Descartes' method of doubt a danger to all of traditional religious belief. Voetius did not approve of questioning the basic truths of the Bible, and anyone who did so he branded an incipient atheist. Descartes had in fact doubted the existence of God in the

---

[13]McGahagan, 54-63.

[14]Ibid., 64, 139, 362.

[15]McGahagan points out the conception of reason's role in scriptural interpretation held by Arminians and Cartesians, while both he and Verbeek, *Descartes and the Dutch*, highlight the link made by Voetians between the Arminian controversy and the threat of Cartesianism.

[16]McGahagan, 3, 363-370; Verbeek, *Descartes and the Dutch*, 5-6.

[17]McGahagan, 363.

Meditations. Furthermore, Voetius believed that Cartesianism was built upon a principle of subjectivism (the *cogito*) that was incompatible with the authority of Scripture. Thus the Cartesian attack on authority, central not only to the method of doubt but to the entire Cartesian philosophical revolution, was seen by Voetius as seminal atheism.[18]

The strident opposition to Cartesianism offered by Voetius and the confessional wing of the church resulted in a series of conflicts between Cartesians and their opponents at Leiden and Utrecht beginning in the 1640s. These conflicts themselves helped to shape the tradition of Dutch Cartesianism that Bekker would inherit. By the time Bekker used Cartesian arguments in *The World Bewitched* these ideas had a long history of debate and confrontation surrounding them.

Tensions first began to build in Utrecht, the earliest home of Cartesianism in the Republic. In several disputations held in late 1641, Regius rejected the Aristotelian conception of substantial forms and came very close to maintaining Cartesian dualism. When he held that the union of body and soul in man was merely accidental, not substantial, an uproar resulted. Opponents declared that if the body were not essential to man then the doctrine of the resurrection of the body was thrown into doubt. Voetius declared that the suggestion that man was an accidental being was atheistic because of the many truths of faith that it contradicted. The ideas of Descartes were new and unproved, Voetius insisted, and thus it was a serious mistake to favor them over the proven Aristotelian philosophy.

Regius composed a reply to Voetius's criticisms that was read and revised by Descartes himself. In this reply, Regius accused the Aristotelians of atheism for maintaining that substantial forms—including the soul—were produced from matter. University officials were not at all pleased with such charges against the philosophy long sanctioned by university teaching, and the academic senate condemned Regius's reply. The senate proceeded to condemn Cartesianism in general as incompatible with ancient philosophy, prejudicial to the higher faculties, and as having an adverse affect on student efforts to learn the technical terms used by the great philosophers. Utrecht thus became not only the first university to welcome the influence of Cartesianism, but also the first to forbid its teaching.[19]

The second edition of Descartes' *Meditations* appeared in Amsterdam in the spring of 1642, and to it was appended a letter by Descartes attacking Voetius and the actions of the Utrecht University senate. Descartes also made a veiled appeal to the city magistrates of Utrecht to depose Voetius from his university position. Infuriated, Voetius complained vigorously to the university senate and secretly engaged his student Martin Schoock, a Groningen Aristotelian philosopher, to compose a vicious and personal attack on Descartes. The *Admiranda methodus* (1643) accused Descartes of scepticism and atheism, among other things. In an open reply to Voetius, Descartes attacked the pastor and asked the magistrates of Utrecht for protection against Voetius's slander. The burgomasters, however, sided with Voetius (who, as pastor and professor, was a municipal employee), accused Descartes of libel, and demanded that he publicly answer the charge. The city instituted a lawsuit for libel against Descartes, which was only cancelled when Descartes got the French ambassador to intercede on his behalf with the Stadholder. Nevertheless, despite its spirited defense of Voetius the Utrecht city government took no real steps to suppress Cartesianism in accord with the decree

---

[18]Ibid., 11-81, 158-182, 290-293.
[19]Verbeek, *Descartes and the Dutch*, 16-19; Thijssen-Schoute 96-99.

of the university senate. Indeed, another Cartesian, Johannes de Bruyn, was appointed to the Utrecht philosophy faculty in 1652.[20]

In Leiden, Jacobus Revius (1586-1658), theologian, poet, former pastor in Deventer, and regent of the States College, together with theologian Jacobus Trigland (1583-1654), led the opposition to Cartesianism. Revius objected to the method of doubt, the suggestion that God could be a deceiver, and other points of Cartesianism. In a disputation over which he presided Revius accused Descartes of Pelagianism for attributing too much freedom of the will to man. Much like Voetius, Revius called the method of doubt an insult and provocation of God and a step toward scepticism and atheism.

In a letter of May 4, 1647, Descartes complained to the curators of Leiden University about these attacks, and on May 20th the curators ordered the regents and professors to stop mentioning the name and ideas of Descartes in their disputations. The curators also specifically ordered Professor Heereboord to stick to Aristotelian philosophy in his lectures and disputations. They informed Descartes of this order and asked for his silence as well, but he was predictably infuriated. Nor did Heereboord or his primary rival, the Aristotelian professor Adam Stuart, obey, and noisy disputes took place on several occasions. Stuart attacked Descartes in a disputation that caused an uproar among the spectators, and, in 1648, both Heereboord and Stuart were censored by university officials and forbidden to teach metaphysics. The seizure of various writings of Revius, Stuart, and Heereboord was also ordered in the interests of academic peace. Nevertheless, Revius continued to attack Descartes, claiming that his doubt of the existence of material bodies meant that he doubted the incarnation of Christ. He also attacked Descartes' evil demon argument as well as his proofs of God's existence. Heereboord defended Descartes, but the curators reprimanded him along with Stuart and Revius for continuing to discuss Cartesian ideas. Again the curators forbade such discussions and again the professors ignored them. Despite these repeated decrees against teaching Cartesian ideas, nothing was really done to prevent the spread of Cartesianism in Leiden, and a large circle of Cartesians formed there.[21]

In 1647-48, the controversy around Cartesianism took a new turn when Regius himself came into conflict with Descartes. Regius held that reason could not prove the immortality of the soul, and he warned that Cartesian dualism made the interaction of body and soul hard to explain. He approached a position on the soul similar to that of Aristotle and the Scholastics, suggesting that the soul could be a modification of body, an idea he had earlier condemned. But he added that it could also be the case that mind and body were two distinct substances. Since man's reason was insufficient to make this distinction, it was fortunate that God had revealed to man that mind and body were indeed two separate substances. To soften this dualism, he maintained that while spirit and matter were indeed different, that difference did not make them contradictory or mutually exclusive.

Descartes was critical of Regius's ideas in the preface to his *Principles of Philosophy* (1647), and Regius responded in a disputation in which he held that he could not clearly and distinctly conceive of mind as a substance distinct from body. In a disputation in 1648, Regius rejected innate ideas and said that the mind was not always and essentially thinking. In addition he rejected the Cartesian proof of God from innate ideas, saying that only the authority of Scripture provided certainty of God's existence.

---

[20]Verbeek, *Descartes and the Dutch*, 20-33.
[21]Ibid., 44-50, 59-70; Thijssen-Schoute 101-104.

Regius rejected Cartesian dualism and other key points of Descartes' metaphysics primarily for religious reasons, and the oldest of Descartes' Dutch alliances crumbled.[22]

Conflict between Descartes and his opponents flared again in 1656 when Voetius wrote several pamphlets charging that Cartesianism was damaging to religious orthodoxy. Heidanus replied in defense of Descartes, and various pamphlets followed warning of the dangers of Cartesianism and Coccejanism and stressing the links between the two systems. Shortly thereafter, the university senate in Leiden instructed philosophy professors not to discuss matters of Scripture or Cartesian philosophy. The States of Holland also issued a decree designed to keep the academic peace, requiring professors to stress divine authority over human judgement in their teaching. The decree also forbade the teaching of offensive Cartesian ideas. But these measures did not stop the spread of Cartesianism at Leiden, which reached its peak influence in the period 1660-1668.[23]

In the years after 1660, Cartesianism increasingly became a part of normal philosophical discussions at Leiden and elsewhere. Grumbling within the Reformed church, however, did not subside despite the lack of success that the clergy experienced in stemming the tide of Cartesianism. By 1676, mounting anti-Cartesian sentiment within the Reformed church synods of north and south Holland prompted the curators of Leiden University to renewed action, largely from fear that inaction would lead to the intervention of the synods or even the Prince of Orange in university affairs. The curators drew up a list of 20 propositions that could not be taught in the university because they endangered orthodoxy. On the list were many central propositions of Cartesian metaphysics as well as some Coccejan ideas. Specific warnings were included against the ideas of Meyer, Christopher Wittich (1625-1687), a Cartesian theologian at Leiden who opposed biblical literalism, and Coccejus. It was Heidanus, however, who chose to write a reply to the decree. The curators were none too happy with this challenge to their authority and demonstrated that they were indeed serious about the prohibition by dismissing Heidanus from his university post. After this debacle, Wittich and others were for a time more cautious.[24]

As the years went by, Cartesianism became more and more a part of academic routine in the Dutch Republic, and the new philosophy was gradually transformed into an academic discipline. By the time of the spirit controversy in the 1690s, Cartesianism had for some years occupied a secure place in the Dutch universities and there was no longer any realistic prospect that its advance in wider intellectual circles in the Republic would be stopped or even significantly slowed. Not all voices of opposition within the Reformed church had been silenced, but years of frustrated efforts to hold back the new philosophy had taken their toll. The great outburst of hostility against Bekker's Cartesian arguments about spirit belief, coming as it did at a time when the real battle against Cartesianism had largely been lost, was just as much a venting of frustration and exasperation by confessionalist clerics as it was an attempt to make a last stand against the new philosophy.

---

[22]Verbeek, *Descartes and the Dutch*, 52-54; Thijssen-Schoute 4-13.
[23]McGahagan, 303-310, Thijssen-Schoute 20-41, 104.
[24]McGahagan, 344-346; Thijssen-Schoute 48-59.

III

Bekker's interest in Cartesianism went back to his student days in the 1650s, a period during which the controversy over Descartes' ideas was most intense. He was not himself swept into this widening web of conflict until the mid-1660s, when he became embroiled in the beginnings of a Cartesian controversy in Franeker. As with the earlier funeral oration episode, a personal incident was again involved in drawing Bekker into an intellectual dispute. Johannes Wubbena, a Cartesian, had been named professor of philosophy at Franeker in 1666. Wubbena was a person whose morals were generally known to be weak, and as a pastor in Franeker it fell to Bekker to exercise church discipline against him, excluding him from communion. But Wubbena had important friends in government circles as high up as the States of Friesland, and he became a troublesome enemy for Bekker.[25]

By 1667, Professor Arnoldus was complaining to the academic senate about Wubbena's teaching, and the Franeker church council became alarmed over the teaching of Cartesianism in the university. Soon the classis of Leeuwarden began to press for synodal and governmental action against the Cartesian threat. In particular, the classis asked the States of Friesland to forbid any mention of Cartesianism in the academy. The classis also declared that all preachers who were called to posts in Friesland would in the future be required to expressedly reject twelve Cartesian theses.

Although no friend of Wubbena, Bekker was disturbed by the actions of the Reformed classis and worried that a relatively small number of anti-Cartesian pastors would be able to manipulate the majority of Friesian clerics who were not trained in philosophy and therefore could not reach any independent judgement on the dangers of Cartesianism to religion. For this reason, Bekker decided to write a defense of the ideas of Descartes in which he argued that the new philosophy posed no threat to Reformed belief. *De Philosophia Cartesiana admonitio candida et sincera*, published in 1668, maintained in typical Dutch Cartesian fashion that philosophy and theology had their own separate terrains of investigation, philosophy dealing with reason while theology dealt with revelation. Scripture revealed things that reason could not understand, Bekker argued, and thus it was an error to submit theology and God's Holy Word to the judgement of reason. But philosophy itself was not contrary to Christian theology. If it sometimes appeared to be, this was only because man erroneously applied philosophy to questions beyond its competence. Philosophy and theology each had its own proper limits. Philosophy needed compelling proof and was understood, while theology depended on the authority of Scripture and had to be believed. One could not learn the truths of salvation from nature and natural reason, nor could one learn about natural things, like the motion of the earth and the position of the sun, from Scripture. God was the author of both reason and revelation, and for this reason philosophy and theology, could not contradict each other.[26]

Klaus Scholder has pointed out that the two Cartesian rules of the separation of philosophy from theology and the non-contradiction of the two realms of knowledge necessarily clashed with each other because the latter principle called for accord

---

[25]Jacob van Sluis, *Bekkeriana: Balthasar Bekker biografisch en bibliografisch* (Leeuwarden, 1994), 4.
[26]W.P.C. Knuttel, *Balthasar Bekker, Bestrijder van het Bijgeloof* (Groningen and Castricum, 1979) 31-45.

between two realms that the former principle held to be completely separate from one another. Scholder has also pointed out the dangerous consequences of the non-contradiction principle: "What manifestly contradicts philosophy cannot be believed in theology, nor can one know in philosophy something that Scripture disputes."[27]

In the *Admonitio*, Bekker divided Cartesians into three groups: those who merely followed Descartes and tried to explain his ideas, those who followed Descartes on some points but disagreed with him on others, and those who went further than Descartes by using Cartesianism to defend propositions reaching beyond philosophy into the realm of theology. He could not discuss or defend all of Descartes' philosophy because he himself was not a philosopher, Bekker declared, but he did judge Descartes to be correct in the broad outlines of his thought. Certainly Descartes could have made mistakes since philosophy was a human endeavor. But Descartes did not teach things contrary to Reformed belief, Bekker asserted. For this reason, one could find many Reformed theologians who followed Descartes. Some claimed that Descartes' thought was damaging to religion because it began with doubt, Bekker continued, but Descartes only used scepticism as a tool with which to find certainty. Bekker then went on to discuss a number of specific points of Descartes' thought that had been attacked by conservative thinkers, such as his claim that God was self-caused instead of uncaused, his assertion that people could not imagine limits to the world (which some took as a claim of the eternity of the world), and his claim that God could not have created a world other than the one he did create. Bekker concluded the *Admonitio* by declaring that it was absurd to call Descartes an atheist when he had offered such powerful proofs for the existence of God.[28]

Some Reformed theologians attacked Bekker over the *Admonitio*, but the synod of Friesland was convinced enough by Bekker's arguments to reject the anti-Cartesian complaints of the classis of Leeuwarden. The *Admonitio* had the further effect of making Bekker's Cartesian sympathies well known in Reformed circles and thus the enmity toward him on the part of confessionalists continued to increase. But no great debate arose around the *Admonitio*, and Bekker's introduction into the controversies surrounding Dutch Cartesianism was a relatively gentle one.

The next several years of Bekker's life were consumed by his struggle with the confessional party over the *Vaste Spyze*. After leaving Friesland, partly as a result of the bitterness of this controversy, Bekker took up his new pastoral office in Loenen. He had always been earnestly dedicated to his normal pastoral responsibilities as well as to his studies, showing himself a conscientious shepherd of his flock wherever he served.[29] He took up his duties in Loenen with great energy and helped the community deal with the lingering shock of the French war. During this busy time, as during the struggle over the *Vaste Spyze*, Bekker gave little attention to Cartesianism and the continuing controversies surrounding it in the Republic. After only 21 months in Loenen, Bekker moved again, this time to a post in Weesp, a larger town closer to Amsterdam. In 1678, Bekker became a preacher in the army, serving in a hospital and later with cavalry in the field.[30] During the years in which Bekker was quietly serving in these positions, his confessionalist enemies continued to work against him behind the scenes.

[27]Klaus Scholder, *The Birth of Modern Critical Theology: Origins and Problems of Biblical Criticism in the Seventeenth Century* (London and Philadelphia, 1990), 123.

[28]Knuttel, 45-49.

[29]Wiebe Bergsma, "Balthasar Bekker als Predikant: diener en doctor," in *It Beaken: Tydskrift fan de Fryske Akademy*, 58, 2-3, (1996), 73-91.

[30]Ibid., 112-122.

In 1679, a pastoral vacancy developed in Amsterdam, and Bekker was nominated to fill it. His nomination immediately gave rise to conflict between confessionalists and their opponents within the Amsterdam church. Five years earlier, when Bekker had been called to Loenen, conservative Amsterdam pastor Laurentius Homma had raised objections to the calling to a nearby pulpit of such a controversial minister. Homma, of course, opposed the calling of Bekker to Amsterdam in 1679, but others supported it. Bekker invited Homma to a conference with him before six Amsterdam pastors—three liberals and three confessionalists—in order that the differences between them could be worked out. At the conference Homma presented several pamphlets from the *Vaste Spyze* controversy in Friesland that accused Bekker of unorthodoxy, and he also raised 13 specific objections to Bekker's ideas, most of which had been made by earlier opponents. Bekker replied to each point individually and tried to show that his views were orthodox. But Homma was not convinced, and Bekker volunteered to provide a written explanation of the points objected to by his opponent. At a follow-up meeting an agreement was finally reached: Bekker signed a document explaining his views on each disputed point and promised not to publish further theological works without the prior approval of the classis. Homma also signed the document to indicate that he was satisfied with Bekker's explanations. With this agreement Bekker's call to Amsterdam went forward and he was installed in his new post on December 31, 1679.[31] Homma's resistance, however, was a sign of things to come.

After taking up his post in Amsterdam, Bekker was, at first, little inclined to write anything. He was very busy with his pastoral duties and tired from earlier controversies, and he knew that anything that he wrote would be closely scrutinized by the confessional wing of the church. Nevertheless, he quickly found a circle of intellectual friends with whom he could discuss ideas, and he did not moderate his convictions despite the unpopularity of some of them among his Reformed colleagues.

Bekker's first years in Amsterdam were far from uneventful. During the winter of 1680, and again in 1681, comets appeared in the sky to the fright of much of the population. Comets were widely believed, even by some educated opinion of the time, to be portents of impending disaster. Many pamphlets appeared in Amsterdam to explain what disasters the comets of 1680 and 1681 foretold, but Bekker warned his congregation from the pulpit not to become upset by such ideas about comets, which he found absurd in the extreme. A number of people were angered by his position on comets, but others were thankful for his efforts to calm people and urged him to publish his sermon discussing the issue. Bekker responded to these suggestions by doing further reading on comets in order to prepare a more elaborate treatment of the topic. He soon came forward with a book on comet beliefs that was published by his friend Hero Nauta in Leeuwarden in 1683, Bekker's first publication since the *Vaste Spyze* controversy.[32]

Bekker opened the book by discussing the ideas of Descartes, Hevelius, and Bernoullie regarding comets, concluding from this that it was not known with certainty what comets were. Given this fact, Bekker argued, no one could say with any certainty what comets meant. Predictions could not be made from comets, he argued, because they varied so much in form, movement, and direction. Some said that the country over which a comet appeared was headed for disaster, but how

[31]Ibid., 145-148.
[32]Ibid., 149-150.

could this be when comets moved over so many countries? And comets were so rare and hard to see that God would not use them as signs. Bekker then went on to discuss some of the comets that had appeared during the previous 80 years in order to strengthen his argument.[33]

A great deal was made of the comet of 1618 because it was seen for 30 days and afterwards war broke out in Germany for 30 years, Bekker related. It was said that the number of days the comet was seen foretold the length of the war. Did this mean that all the other disasters supposedly predicted by comets had to last the same number of days that the comet was seen? Bekker asked. In any event, it was not even true that the comet was seen for 30 days. In fact, several different comets were seen in 1618. Nor was it true that the war lasted for 30 years. The Bohemian crisis was already underway before the comets appeared, and Christendom had already been involved in various religious and civil wars for 30 years prior to the comets' appearance. Indeed, just as many bad things happened before the comets of 1618 appeared as after they were observed, and many good things occurred after the comets as well as before them, Bekker argued.[34]

The comet of 1607 supposedly predicted the domestic disturbances in the United Provinces surrounding the Arminian controversy and the fall of Oldenbarneveldt, Bekker noted, but he added that the Twelve Year Truce with Spain also followed this comet. The comet of 1652 was said to predict the disaster of the first Dutch war with England, but four bloody battles in that conflict had already been fought before the comet appeared. The comet of 1664 appeared just prior to the outbreak of the second Anglo-Dutch war and was believed by some to have foretold that struggle, but bad feelings had been building up between the two nations for years previous. And no comet at all announced the terrible disasters brought by the French invasion of 1672. In fact, comets did not appear before every disaster, nor did disasters follow every comet, Bekker concluded.[35]

After having rationally analyzed comet belief, Bekker next turned to what Scripture had to say about comets, a pattern of argument he was later to repeat in *The World Bewitched*. The Bible did not support popular beliefs about comets, he argued. Some scriptural places that had been interpreted as speaking of comets and their supposed predictions—for instance Jeremiah 1:11-13 and Micha 6—did not really do so when understood correctly. In fact, the Bible condemned belief in any predictions or signs other than God's Word, especially astrology. To believe that comets were predictions of the future was a sin, Bekker proclaimed. Those who believed comets to be signs of the future even though God never appointed them as such robbed God of his supreme power because only he could know the future, Bekker argued.[36] This same basic argument would later be the core of Bekker's attack on spirit belief: it was wrong, he believed, to detract from God's absolute power by assigning to other agents powers that belonged to God alone. This emphatic belief in God Almighty was at the center of Bekker's religious thought.

Even though Bekker's comet book rejected a widely held belief, showed Bekker's inclination to Cartesianism, and gave a preview of the kind of argument and the

[33]Balthasar Bekker, *Ondersoek van de Betekening der Kometen, By gelegenheid van de gene die in de Jaaren 1680, 1681, en 1682 geschenen hebben* (Amsterdam, 1692), 11-18, 26-30.
[34]Ibid., 34.
[35]Ibid., 34-35.
[36]Ibid., 39, 59-74.

controversial exegetical methods that would re-appear later in *The World Bewitched*, the work gave rise to no real controversy. Comets were of little importance in the Bible and, unlike spirits, played no real role in contemporary religious discussion. For these reasons Bekker's exegetical methods in dealing with scriptural accounts of comets, went largely un-noticed. The success of the comet book encouraged Bekker to start writing again.

In 1685, Bekker finished a work on ecclesiastical history in which he commented on the ideas of Spinoza, whom he had met several years earlier in The Hague. Bekker was highly critical of Spinoza's metaphysical position and also of his exegetics. The latter critique is surprising given the similarities of Bekker's own exegesis to that of Spinoza, similarities apparent in the comet book and even more so in *The World Bewitched*. In the *Kort Begryp der Algemeine Kerkelyke Historien Zedert het Jaar 1664 daar Hornius eindigt tot den Jare 1684* (Short Resumé of General Church History from the Year 1664 Where Hornius Ended to the Year 1684), Bekker called both the *Tractatus Theologico-Politicus*, published anonymously in 1670, and the *Ethics*, left by Spinoza upon his death in 1677 and published posthumously, "absurd and full of errors." Bekker listed six of these errors, including Spinoza's contention in the *Ethics* that there was no independent substance outside of God, as well as his claim that creatures were modes of God. Bekker clearly felt more comfortable with Cartesian dualism than with Spinoza's monism. He also rejected Spinoza's suggestion that along with the two essential characteristics of substance, thought and extension, there might be an infinity of other characteristics that men did not know about. Bekker was no more ready to accept Spinoza's determinism, and thus he rejected Spinoza's contention that there was an infinite number of causes in the world following upon each other in an infinite order.

The final two objections that Bekker made focussed on Spinoza's view of Scripture presented in the *Tractatus*. He rejected Spinoza's claims that the Bible was not divinely inspired in its entirety and that its authors had made mistakes in writing it. He also rejected Spinoza's contention that miracles were produced by natural causes. While Bekker's criticism of Spinoza's metaphysical position is not surprising coming from a Cartesian whose commitment to dualism came out clearly in the spirit controversy, his comments on Spinoza's exegetics are more difficult to interpret. As a Reformed pastor, Bekker had to distance himself from Spinoza's radical views on the Bible, but, as will be seen below, Bekker's own exegetical methods in *The World Bewitched* at points closely resembled those of Spinoza. Bekker firmly held to the divinely inspired nature of Scripture, but he made use of the doctrine of accommodation in much the same way that Spinoza did. These similarities to Spinoza's position led some of Bekker's later critics to brand him a Spinozist, and indeed Bekker's exegetical methods were perhaps the most radical element of his thought. His critique of Spinoza on these points, therefore, has a strange ring.

But on other points Bekker was no Spinozist. He accused Spinoza of violating the Dutch Cartesian principle of the separation of religion from philosophy by making philosophy the master of things of belief. Indeed, perhaps the most revolutionary contribution of Spinoza's *Tractatus* was to bring the Bible and all of religion before the bar of philosophical reason in this way. Bekker himself, however, was to considerably narrow the gap between philosophy and theology in his later discussion of spirits. Bekker ended his comments on Spinoza by lamenting the fact that the philosopher's ideas were so widespread and that they had poisoned some of the best minds of the time while tempting pious people to unbelief.[37]

Soon after completing his ecclesiastical history Bekker was at work on a commentary on the *Book of Daniel*, a work in which he was critical of some of the exegetical theories of Coccejus, especially Coccejus's prophetic speculations. Bekker also tarred with a broad brush all millennarian interpretations of Daniel's prophecy, saying that the *Book of Daniel* was written by Jews and for Jews in Old Testament times and had absolutely nothing to do with Christian history. Like his comet book, Bekker's commentary on Daniel was generally well received.[38] In 1689, Bekker published a work on child baptism at the request of a friend who wanted to understand the Mennonites' objections to the practice.[39] Again his ideas met little opposition, perhaps giving Bekker a false sense of security and leading him to greater boldness in the public expression of his opinions. As the year 1690 dawned, Bekker had little reason to suspect that he was about to become involved in the greatest struggle of his life.

IV

Bekker's interest in spirit belief arose in part from the practical demands of his job. As a minister active in pastoral care, Bekker had experience dealing with a wide variety of popular beliefs often at variance with educated opinion. At Oosterlittens, Franeker, and Amsterdam, Bekker repeatedly came into contact with people who claimed to be possessed by the devil or evil spirits, and he began to develop an interest in such cases. After his study of popular beliefs regarding comets, Bekker began to examine both popular and learned views of spirits and their temporal activities. Despite the fact that it had been nearly a century since the last execution for witchcraft in the Dutch Republic, popular belief in sorcery, witchcraft, and spirit activity remained alive. In addition to popular belief, the existence and activities of spirits continued to be the subject of a lively debate in learned circles for most of the seventeenth century. Bekker's interest in spirit belief was heightened by the fact that he came to see fear of the devil as an offense against the power of God in the same way that belief in comets as portents was.

As a result of these reflections, Bekker wrote a short work entitled *Ondersoeck over 't Stuk van Tovery en Spokery* (Investigation into the Matter of Sorcery and Spooks), which he intended to publish with his friend Hero Nauta in Leeuwarden as an appendix to a reprint of his comet book. Then Bekker read, translated, and published an account of the so-called Beckington witch in England, adding to the work his own argument against believing such reports. His study of the Beckington case caused

---

[37]Balthasar Bekker, *Kort Begryp der Algemeine Kerkelyke Historien, Zedert het Jaar 1664 daar Hoornius Eindigt, tot den Jare 1684* (Amsterdam, 1739), 38-39; Knuttel, 171-173. See also Wiep van Bunge, "Balthasar Bekker's Cartesian Hermeneutics and the Challenge of Spinozism," *British Journal for the History of Philosophy* I (1993), 55-79.; Andrew Fix, "Bekker and Spinoza," in *Disguised and Overt Spinozism Around 1700*, ed. by Wim Klever and Wiep van Bunge (Leiden, 1996); and Theo Verbeek, "De Vrijheid van de Philosophie: Reflecties over een Cartesiaans Thema."

[38]Knuttel, 173-180; Wiep van Bunge, "Balthasar Bekker over Daniel: Een Zeventiende Eeuwse Kritiek op Millenarisme," *It Beaken: Tydskrift van de Fryske Akademy* 58 2-3, (1993), 138-145.

[39]Knuttel, 180-186.

Bekker to revise the *Ondersoeck* and delay its publication. The work began to grow rapidly in size and scope as Bekker broadened his investigation. Even at this early point in his research some of his friends began to warn Bekker of the trouble that could result if he published a major work on the devil and his power. Nevertheless, in early 1691, after much work, Bekker sent Nauta the first two volumes of a planned multi-volume work, now re-named *De Betoverde Wereld* (The World Bewitched).

In a preface to the work, Bekker wrote that the purpose of his book was to protect God, religion, and the Bible from atheism by showing that common beliefs about the devil's power were exaggerated. In Bekker's view, people who feared the devil excessively really believed in two Gods—one good and one bad—much as the ancient Manichees had. He thus proclaimed his own rejection of the devil's power true monotheism.

Volume One of *The World Bewitched* provided an historical account of belief in God, good and evil spirits, the immortality of the soul, fortune-telling, sorcery, and related practices among the Greeks, Romans, Jews, Moslems, Catholics, Protestants, and heathensa. Bekker intended to show that there were prejudices essentially pagan in nature that had been handed down over the ages from pagans to Jews to Christians, and that these prejudices caused Christians to find a world of spirits in the Bible. Bekker himself wanted to examine Scripture free from these prejudices, and to explain Scripture "as though no one had ever explained it."[40]

The Moslems believed in good and bad angels as well as in the devil, Bekker argued.[41] The Jews believed in one God and did not originally believe in spirits or demigods, but they later took over these beliefs from the heathens, along with belief in sorcery and ghosts. Early Christians adopted many beliefs from the heathens as well as from the Jews, Bekker argued, and he traced belief in evil spirits and sorcery back to the Manichees.[42] He blamed Catholics for perpetuating belief in two Gods in the guise of fear of the devil, and he argued that Catholic belief in the devil and

---

[40]Scholder, 129.

[41]Balthasar Bekker, *De Betoverde Weereld, Zynde een Grondig Ondersoek van t' gemeen gevoelen aangaande de geesten, deselver Aart en Vermogen, Bewind en Bedrijf: als ook t' gene de Menschen door deselver kraght en gemeenschap doen* (Amsterdam, Daniel van Dalen, 1691), I, 52-72. This is probably the third printing of the work from 1691, the second by van Dalen in Amsterdam, and the first edition of the work to contain thirty-six chapters in book two, rather than the thirty-five of earlier editions. The added chapter, chapter seven, is a reply to occasionalist objections made by Bekker's opponents. It was added probably during the late summer or early fall of 1691. The edition of the work used here is in private ownership, but essentially the same as the one held by the Royal Library in The Hague and classified as 141 B1. The printing history of *De Betoverde Weereld* has been shown by J. van Sluis to have been extremely complex. Perhaps five to six thousand copies of the work were sold in 1691, which necessitated continuous printing of the work by van Dalen beginning in the early summer and running through the end of the year. During this printing process Bekker was continually making revisions, some minor rearrangements of sentences or paragraphs, along with a few more important changes such as the addition of chapter seven to book two. The most changes were made by Bekker between the first 1691 edition, published in octavo in the spring by Hero Nauta in Leeuwarden, and the first Amsterdam edition of June, in quarto. Bekker carefully noted all of these changes at the end of book two of the first Amsterdam edition. Additions, deletions, and rearrangements were made. After this edition, the addition of chapter seven of book two in the third printing was the most important change to the text. Because of the continuous printing process, however, many different variations of the work appeared, all dated 1691, with differing arrangements of preface material, different type sizes, and differing text paginations. It is difficult, therefore, to speak of distinct editions during 1691. The version employed here was perhaps the earliest complete one.

[42]Ibid., 73-94.

spirits had produced the ideas of purgatory and the saints.[43] The Protestant Reformation had done a great deal to end many superstitious Catholic beliefs, but unfortunately belief in the devil and evil spirits was still prevalent even in the Reformed church.

Bekker went on to discuss the temporal influence of the devil, supposed intercourse with the devil, witches, and the tests used to uncover them. He concluded that belief in the power of the devil and evil spirits was a pagan idea rooted in ignorance, prejudice, and fear. It had crept into the Christian church in antiquity and been perpetuated over the centuries. Belief in the devil's power was not based on either reason or Scripture despite the large number of biblical passages usually cited to support it, Bekker declared, adding that such passages had not been correctly understood.[44]

Volume Two of Bekker's work contained his controversial Cartesian arguments against the power and temporal activity of evil spirits, the core of this discussion taking place in the first 11 chapters. Bekker's goal in this section was to show that there was no rational basis for belief in the temporal power of the devil and evil spirits. He made it clear from the beginning of his argument that in investigating the problem of spirits he would rely on both Scripture and reason. Somewhat modifying his established separation of religion from philosophy, Bekker explained that both sources were needed because neither was in itself sufficient to treat the subject. Reason could not teach people about the mysteries of the Christian religion—only Scripture could provide that kind of knowledge. But on other issues Scripture was silent, and thus reason was needed. Scripture was never intended to explain nature or to instruct men in things beyond the bounds of religion, Bekker argued. Christians should not reject reason in favor of belief because reason could act to strengthen faith with its investigations of things outside of Scripture.

Even Scripture itself could in some cases be better interpreted by using reason, Bekker suggested, and the gap between philosophy and theology began to narrow as his argument progressed. Much that the Bible taught could be investigated with the help of reason by comparing different parts of Scripture with each other to see how best to interpret them, Bekker held.[45] As Bekker allowed interpretive reason to cross the boundary into exegetics, his confessionalist opponents saw danger to biblical literalism, which lay at the foundation of the confessional conception of the church.

Bekker showed how reason could be used in exegesis, and at the same time opened his assault on biblical literalism, when he began to discuss the ways in which spirits were referred to in Scripture. The Bible was intended to show God's works in a way that ordinary people could understand, he argued, and for this reason the language of the Bible was tailored for the common man. The Bible often called God a spirit, but in fact God was so far superior to mankind that there was no adequate word to describe him. Thus in order to speak of God, man had to borrow words for things that God had created, and among created things the most perfect was a spirit. So God was called a spirit in order to indicate the perfection of his being, but he was not actually a spirit at all.[46] By thus appealing to the principle of accommodation, employed by Calvin himself but increasingly popular in the seventeenth century among thinkers uncomfortable with the strict literalism of Reformed confessional theology, Bekker staked out his own position in the exegetical controversy. He also indicated in advance that his

[43]Ibid., 95-111.
[44]Ibid., 111-128.
[45]Bekker, II, 1-3.
[46]Ibid., 8-9.

Cartesian arguments about spirits could not be applied to God, as some of his critics would later try to do in order to accuse him of deism or even atheism.

When the Bible used the words "angel" and "devil" for particular spirits, it was not describing their essence or nature, but rather their actions, Bekker continued. In the original Hebrew text of the Old Testament the word later translated into Dutch as "angel" (engel) was "Malach," which meant "messenger." This was a name often given to people who acted as messengers, and therefore it was necessary to determine from the context of each Scriptural passage whether the word was used to refer to a man or a spirit. The same was true for the Hebrew word later translated as "devil" (duivel), which originally meant "slanderer," and the word "Satan," which originally meant "opponent." These words too were originally used to refer to both men and spirits. Unfortunately, later translators of the Bible had made no distinction between these different uses, Bekker argued.

Bekker left no doubt, however, about what he meant by the term spirit. "By spirit I mean a being that is immaterial and has not the least thing in common with a body," he explained in good Cartesian fashion.[47] A spirit had no community of nature or essence with a body and was thus entirely distinct from body, he continued. Spirit and body were independently existing substances created by God, each having its own essential characteristic without which it could neither exist nor be conceived of. The essential characteristic of spirit was thinking, while that of body was extension—length, breadth, and depth. Through these essential characteristics, each substance was active according to its nature. Spirits acted through thinking, while bodies acted through movement.[48]

All that was neither God nor body had to be spirit, Bekker declared. Man alone consisted of two distinct natures—both spirit and body—miraculously united by God, and for that reason man was often called "a small world." Angels, on the other hand, were spirits that were neither limited by, nor united to, body. They were purely thinking substances. Bekker then went on to point out what was no doubt already obvious to most readers: in his definition of spirit he followed Descartes "as far as that serves my purpose."[49]

What reason could prove about spirits was limited, Bekker argued. Reason could establish the possibility of the existence of spirits, and it could define what their nature would be if they existed, but reason could make no final judgement as to whether or not there actually were spirits aside from the human soul. The Bible, on the other hand, clearly showed that there were spirits other than human souls, and it called them angels and devils. Only Scripture made the distinction between good and bad spirits, or angels and devils. Reason taught nothing about the origins of spirits, while Scripture had a bit more to say on this point. By contrast, reason clearly taught that spirit and body were of such distinct natures that they had nothing in common, whereas Scripture alluded only vaguely to this distinction.[50]

Bekker emphasized that the spirits mentioned in the Bible were not demigods, *daemones*, or divine intermediaries that shared with God the government of the world, as some ancients had believed. There was only one God and governor of the world and he needed no intermediate beings like the intelligences of Aristotle, Plato's Ideas, or any of the other subordinate gods that the ancients had worshipped. The ancient Persians and

[47]Ibid., 4-6.
[48]Ibid.
[49]Ibid., 6-8.
[50]Ibid., 2-3.

Indians actually had three gods: one doled out the souls, one took care of the needs of life, and the third ruled over death. Other ancients believed in gods of trees, draughts, vegetables, and even garbage, Bekker continued. But while the ancient pagans simply appointed whatever gods they desired, Christians believed in one God who was master of nature. No creature, spirit or otherwise, could have such power. This for Bekker was the essence of monotheism: both spirits and bodies were created by God, were dependent on God, and were in their nature and power limited by God.[51]

In order to better understand the nature and actions of spirits, Bekker began by examining the only spirit that man had first-hand experience of: the human soul. The soul was united to the body by God, Bekker noted, but it did not depend on the body for its existence. As long as the union of body and soul lasted the soul acted on the body and the body acted on the soul, although man could not understand how this happened. The soul carried on some actions in cooperation with the body, such as speaking, hearing, seeing, reading, and writing, but the soul carried on other actions independently from the body, such as thinking and willing. Because the soul could act without the body, it followed that the soul could also exist without the body. The soul was not made from material that could be divided or destroyed, and thus it could not be diminished or destroyed by things that diminished or destroyed the body. It was thus not within the power of a body to destroy a soul or spirit. While some people believed that souls reappeared after the death of their bodies, either in their own body or in some other body, Scripture said nothing about this. Why would the soul, having lost its own body at death, reappear later in that same body? Bekker asked. And what if the soul reappeared so long after the death of the body that the body was already rotted?[52]

It would be reasonable to assume, Bekker continued, that if there were other spirits aside from the human soul they would share many of the soul's characteristics—the major exception being union with a body. Even though reason alone could not prove that such spirits existed, Christians followed the Bible in believing that God had created other spirits. A number of Christian philosophers had maintained that the existence of angels could be proved from sources other than the Bible, but Bekker rejected this claim. Aquinas argued that the perfection of the universe demanded that there be creatures comparable to God in intelligence and will, but Bekker objected that no creature, spirit or body, could resemble the creator God. The nature of angels contained no necessity of their existence as God's nature did according to Descartes, Bekker pointed out. And he added that no necessity of existence flowed forth from God's nature to that of lower creatures as proposed in "the absurd idea" of Spinoza. "I can have no thought of God that does not include his necessary existence, but I can think of creatures without thinking that they necessarily exist," Bekker explained. He concluded that when the existence of angels was investigated with reason alone "...we cannot find any reason why there must be such spirits as we call angels. If we can know anything about them from nature it would be only *a posteriori*: from their actions."[53]

Bekker's claim that reason could not prove or disprove the existence of angels and devils was a direct attack on rationalistic and scholastic theology, both Catholic and Protestant. His attempt to make the Bible the primary foundation for spirit belief paralleled the efforts of Coccejus to replace the confessional and dogmatic theology of

[51]Ibid., 18-21.
[52]Ibid., 21-25.
[53]Ibid., 32-35.

the Reformed church with a more biblically based belief. Bekker's argument led some to conclude that he was claiming that belief in angels was irrational or that reason held that angels did not exist, but Bekker did not suggest either of these things. Reason could not prove that angels did not exist, he argued, even if their activities were never observed. God might well have made things that people never observed. An infinite number of creatures were unknown to man, so it did not follow that if there were spirits man would know what they were and how they acted.

Because angels could not be rationally proved to exist, Bekker believed that their actions observed by people and recorded in Scripture provided the best way to know of their existence. This made the veracity of biblical accounts of angels crucial. This was also why Bekker's investigation of spirits focussed on their actions. These actions were key for man's belief in the very existence of angels, so Bekker was concerned with the question of whether or not the nature of angels—which could be established by reason independent of their existence—would permit them to do what the Bible said they did.

It was at this crucial point that Bekker applied the test of reason, in the form of Cartesian dualism, to Scripture. If angels' nature did not permit them to do what the literal text of Scripture reported, then the text had to be interpreted in some other way so as to preserve an account of angelic activities as evidence for their existence. The logical alternative was unacceptable to Bekker (although not to Spinoza): that the Bible was in error and that angels did not exist. It was thus Bekker's application of Cartesian principles to Scriptural texts about angels, along with his faith that angels did exist and that the Bible was not in error, that necessitated his rejection of biblical literalism. By allowing philosophy to cross over into the realm of exegesis, Bekker gave his opponents the chance that they had been waiting for.[54]

In examining the actions of spirits Bekker accepted Cartesian dualism of spirit and matter as his essential operating premise. He rejected the view of some ancients that there were creatures whose essences were half spirit and half body, such as the Greek *daimones*. Such middle creatures were impossible, Bekker argued, because of the mutually exclusive nature of body and spirit. Just as a spirit could not be moved nor a thought measured, so no one nature could include both substances. Even though man appeared to be an example of such a middle creature, in fact God made man from two entirely distinct natures that he miraculously united in one being. Man's nature was

---

[54]The idea that angels' actions were key evidence for their existence emerged once again in Bekker's discussion of the vexed question of whether spirits could be in a place. Bodies as extended substances occupied space and were said to be in a place, Bekker argued, but spirits lacking extension could only be located by their actions. One did not ask where a spirit was, but rather where it acted. A spirit had no place except insofar as it acted on a body that was in a place, in which case the spirit could be said to be in the same place as the body. For example, the common place of the human soul was the human body, which it acted on and through. Bekker then continued by making a strange argument that would give his opponents much ammunition for ridicule later. If the soul thought about things or persons in another place, he maintained, then that could be said to be the soul's place. If the soul thought about the largeness of a city, then the soul could be said to be the same size as the city. If the soul compared Amsterdam to London and Paris, it could be said to be in all three cities at the same time. The soul could encompass the size of the entire earth with one thought, Bekker declared, and many souls could be in one small place if they all thought about that place. Thus it was that the souls of many of his countrymen accompanied William of Orange in his triumphal procession across the channel to become king of England in 1689, Bekker noted. With this somewhat ecstatic profession of the power of the human mind Bekker overstepped the boundaries of Cartesianism and gave his orthodox opponents ammunition with which to attack his larger arguments about spirits. Ibid., 17-19.

thus not a singular one that was half body and half spirit, but rather it was a true double nature. In the same way God could certainly have made a creature that was **neither** spirit nor body. But that creature would have to be known from its actions, and since people understood only bodily or spiritual actions they would have no way of knowing of its existence. So aside from spirit and body (and, of course, God), man could know of nothing existing, Bekker concluded.[55]

The essentially distinct and mutually exclusive nature of body and spirit naturally brought up the question of whether or not these two substances could interact. In humans such interaction certainly took place. God so connected soul and body in man that when the soul thought certain thoughts, certain movements took place in the body, and when certain movements happened in the body, certain thoughts arose in the soul, Bekker explained. The soul acted on the body whenever it caused the body to go, sit, stand, lie, eat, drink, speak, read, write, and many other things. The body acted on the soul by causing it to think as a result of the activities of the five senses: when the senses were affected by external objects they caused the soul to think about those objects. Man could not understand how the body acted on the soul and vice-versa, and it was clear that it was not in the nature of either substance to be united in this way. The combination was miraculous and depended entirely on God.

Bekker next took up the crucial question of whether spirits other than human souls could act on bodies, and the result was the most controversial argument in his entire book. The soul acted immediately on its own body, but it could not act on any other body except through the means of its own body, Bekker argued. How then could a spirit without its own body—an angel or devil—act on a body distinct from itself? It was not even clear, Bekker continued, how a spirit could act on or communicate with another spirit. The human soul could not make its thoughts directly known to other spirits, but had to communicate through the intermediary of bodily language and signs. So how could a spirit without a body communicate its thoughts to other spirits? Nor had it ever been shown how one spirit could act directly on another without the aid of an intermediate body. This was the case even though one spirit resembled another spirit in nature and characteristics more than the human soul resembled its body.[56]

Most writers on spirits agreed with his view that spirits could act on bodies only by means of their own bodies, Bekker asserted. Some held that there were different kinds of body and that spirits had very fine and swift bodies by means of which they could act on people. Joseph Glanville, in his *Considerations on Witchcraft*, held, like some ancient church fathers, that all spirits had very fine and "spiritual" bodies because spirits could not act directly on bodies without the help of an intermediary that shared characteristics of both spirit and body. Writers like Glanville thus recognized that nothing in the nature of spirit itself would allow it to act directly on body, Bekker argued. As a Cartesian Bekker rejected as absurd the notion of a spiritual body. Spirits other than the human soul were defined and limited by the natures that they received from God at creation, he continued, and thus it was highly unlikely that they could act immediately on bodies or perform other bodily functions. The actions of angels and devils on bodies or on other spirits were therefore not confirmed by reason, Bekker added, in what was perhaps the single most explosive conclusion in his book.[57]

[55]Ibid., 35-38.
[56]Ibid., 38-42.
[57]Ibid., 38-41.

Bekker presented more questions than he did answers when dealing with what reason could say about the actions of spirits. His critics, on the other hand, insisted on exactly those points that Bekker refused to admit without proof: that angels and devils could act on bodily creatures as well as on each other. But Bekker pointed out that the party who asserted something bore the responsibility for proving the assertion, and therefore people who claimed that angels and devils could act on bodily creatures had to prove that this was the case. The burden of proof was not his, Bekker insisted. He simply pointed out the lack of evidence and rational proof for popular claims about the temporal activity of spirits.[58]

The Cartesian arguments relating to the temporal activity of angels and devils that Bekker brought into the spirit debate became one of the focal points for the controversy that swirled around *The World Bewitched*. Bekker was the first to introduce into the debate the specifically Cartesian conception of the relationship between spirit and body, and with it came all the controversy that had engulfed Cartesian metaphysics since its introduction into Dutch intellectual life some 50 years earlier.[59]

Nevertheless, Bekker's Cartesian arguments end here, at chapter seven, page 49, of volume two of what was to be a four-volume work. There were 29 more chapters and 143 more pages in volume two. Volume one had contained 24 chapters and 146 pages, while volumes three and four made up 59 chapters and 515 pages. Clearly, even though Bekker's Cartesian metaphysical ideas were controversial, they were not the center point of his work or his thinking in his extensive treatment of spirits.

The end of chapter seven does, however, provide a natural breaking point in Bekker's overall argument. Just as he had done in his book on comets, Bekker divided volume two of his book on spirits into two parts: what reason could establish about spirits and what could be known about spirits from Scripture. Having finished with what reason could teach, Bekker was ready to move on to an investigation of biblical accounts of spirits. By devoting so much more time and space to his scriptural investigation Bekker indicated that it was biblical exegesis rather than Cartesian metaphysics that most fully engaged his interests, and by extension, those of his critics.

---

[58]Ibid., 40-42.
[59]Knuttel, 195-204; van Bunge, "Balthasar Bekker's Cartesian Hermeneutics," 55-80; van Sluis, 23-24.

CHAPTER FOUR

The Friesian Hercules

As Bekker moved to the second part of his argument about spirits and their temporal activities, he left behind the realm of metaphysical speculation and entered perhaps the most dangerous mine field of late seventeenth-century intellectual discussion: biblical exegesis. To successfully bring home his overall argument about spirits, he had to deal with scriptural accounts of spirit activity. And deal with them he did.

Bekker's methods of biblical exegesis, employed in bold fashion in the final 29 chapters of volume two of *The World Bewitched*, made up by far the most extensive part of his argument against spirit activity and provoked an outraged response from the confessional wing of the Reformed church. In his discussion of scriptural passages dealing with the actions of angels and devils and with spirit possession, Bekker adopted an exegetical position that undermined biblical literalism by fully embracing the doctrine of accommodation. Despite the smoke created by his use of Cartesian dualism in earlier chapters, it was Bekker's exegesis that was the most radical part of his thought. It was here that he struck the nerve of Dutch Reformed confessionalism, and it was here that his ideas closely followed those of the most radical Dutch Cartesian of them all: Benedict Spinoza.

I

In his investigation of biblical passages relating to spirits, Bekker's goal was to show that Scripture did not say nearly as much about the powers and activities of spirits—especially evil spirits—as was commonly believed. Because of problems with the translation of biblical terms, many of the actions traditionally ascribed to spirits in scriptural stories were more correctly attributed to human or natural activity, Bekker argued. He thus reinterpreted many biblical places in a distinctly non-literal way.

Although Scripture confirmed that there were spirits called angels distinct from the human soul, Bekker argued, it never explained what they were, it said little about what they did, and it never explained what was meant by the term "angel." But this was not, after all, what the Bible was for. The purpose of Scripture was to show people the way to salvation, and the nature of spirits had little bearing on that. For this reason, Scripture only discussed angels when they were involved in man's relationship to God. Even the name "angel" had nothing to do with angelic nature but referred instead to their function as messengers.[1]

To make matters even more difficult, the Bible did not consistently use the words "angel" and "devil" to refer to spirits, and thus it was hard to interpret passages where these terms appeared. The Dutch translators of the Bible believed in the temporal activity of angels and devils, and they interpreted the original Greek and Hebrew words as referring to spirits in many places where this translation was not really justified. For example, the angels of Judas 6 were really human messengers sent by Israel to spy on the land of Canaan. Similarly, when the Bible used the word usually translated as "spirit," the Hebrew original could also be rendered as "wind," "breath," or even as an inclination to do something. An example of the difficulties that this caused was what David said of God in Psalm 104:4, which was usually translated as "he makes his angels spirits, his servants to a flaming fire." But since the Hebrew word "ruach," usually rendered as "spirit," could also be translated as "wind," and since the word translated as "angel" could also be rendered as "messenger," the passage could just as legitimately be translated as "he makes the winds his messengers." The task, then, was to decide which of the two translations better fit the biblical context. Since Psalm 104 spoke generally of God's miracles done in the course of nature, the latter translation seemed preferable. Thus one of the key scriptural passages used to support traditional belief in angels did not really speak of spirits at all.[2]

The Bible said very little about the strength and powers of spirits, Bekker continued, and what it did say was difficult to interpret. The strength of angels was clearly great: in Psalm 103:20 David called them God's mighty heroes, and in II Peter 2:10-11 the disciple said they were much stronger than men. But Scripture did not explain of what their strength consisted. It was in the nature of spirits that they did everything through their will, Bekker explained, but how much could angels act on bodies and other spirits in this way?

Scripture also said little about the knowledge possessed by angels. Matthew 18:10 said that angels always saw the face of God. This was certainly more than Moses ever did, and it would not happen to man until after death, so it was clear that angels knew many things that people did not. And good angels suffered from no corruption of their will or darkening of their understanding like men did: they were as intellectually pure as when God created them, and they therefore had very great understanding. But despite their great knowledge, angels could not know or control the thoughts of people, as some suggested. There were no examples in Scripture of spirits knowing men's thoughts or putting any ideas into people's minds without the mediation of a body. Only God could do this, as II Corinthians 28:9 testified.[3]

Just as the Bible said little about the nature and powers of angels, what it said about their actions was very hard to interpret, Bekker continued. While Hebrews 1:14 called angels "serving spirits" ("*dienstige geesten*") that honored God and served his people, the name of divine servant was applied in Scripture not only to angels but also to the sun, moon, stars, fire, hail, and any other means that God used to carry out his will. And although there were places in the Bible that told of angels doing miracles in God's

---

[1]Balthasar Bekker, *De Betoverde Weereld, Zijnde een Grondig Ondersoeck van 't gemeen gevoelen aangaande de geesten, deselver Aart en Vermogen, Bewind en Bedrijf, als ook t' gene de Menschen door deselver kraght en gemeenschap doen...*(Amsterdam, Daniel van Dalen, 1691), II, 43-49.

[2]Ibid., 43-52.

[3]Ibid., 57-60.

service, many more passages that showed men doing great deeds in God's service: Moses turned water to blood in Egypt, parted the Red Sea, and brought darkness by stretching out his arm. In each case it was really God who did these things, Bekker added.[4]

And it was the same with angels. According to the catechism angels fought for people, carried people, led people, plagued evil doers, and the like. But, Bekker added, "...of course all of this work is really done by God."[5] In Genesis 19:24, angels proclaimed the destruction of Sodom, but it was God who brought down fire from heaven to destroy the city. The Bible said that an angel slew 70,000 people by plague in David's time, but it was God who really did this. Luke 22:43 said that an angel strengthened Jesus in his suffering, but this passage, too, showed what God did, not what an angel did through its own nature, Bekker argued.

There were a number of other scriptural passages that supposedly spoke of the bodily actions of angels: in Exodus 12 an angel was said to have killed the firstborn of Egypt, in II Chronicles 19:35 and Isaiah 37:36 an angel was said to have killed 185,000 men in the Assyrian army, in Acts 12:23 an angel was said to have killed Herodes Agrippa, and in Daniel 3:25 an angel was said to have entered a burning oven to protect three young men. But Scripture spoke figuratively in these places, Bekker declared, attributing the work of God to angels in order to show the "pomp and ceremony" befitting divine activity. Angels were employed by Scripture in these and other instances as signs of divine majesty, but the honor of these works should be kept strictly for God, Bekker stressed.[6]

Angels were said by Scripture to protect and to help men in just the same way that they were said to eat: figuratively. The Bible called manna a food worthy of the angels in order to praise it, without really meaning that angels ate it, Bekker argued. Likewise, when the Bible said that angels fought for believers, it only meant that God considered man worthy of being defended by heavenly bands. Why was it necessary to infer more from such passages?[7] When angels proclaimed the help (or punishment) of God to man, the certainty of their word made it seem as if they actually brought the help themselves, but in fact the help came from God.[8]

Sometimes those that the Bible called angels were really humans sent by God as messengers or missionaries, and other times the outward signs of God's presence were called his angels. The angels who appeared to Abraham and Lot were men called angels because of their mission, Bekker argued.[9] Biblical references to the angels who delivered God's law on Sinai and the angel that led the people of Israel through the wilderness were simply symbolic language meant to indicate God's majesty.[10] Anticipating objections to the seemingly diminished role that he assigned to angelic spirits, Bekker added:

> You might say that I take away all the angels' work and make them useless in the world, and that this will finally lead to the conclusion that there are no angels. But

[4]Ibid., 61-62.
[5]Ibid., 64-65.
[6]Ibid., 59-61, 65-70.
[7]Ibid., 64-65.
[8]W.P.C. Knuttel, *Balthasar Bekker: de Bestrijder van het Bijgeloof* (Groningen-Castricum, 1979), 207-208.
[9]Bekker, II, 85-90.
[10]Ibid., 90-94.

this is not true. Just because I say that I do not see what the angels and devils do, this does not mean that I think there are none. It also does not follow that angels do nothing just because God does not let us know what they do....Does God give no work to angels that he does not tell us about? It is a very arrogant idea for us to think that the noble angels exist only for our sake....When you consider the whole extended plenum with all that God has created in the universe, the earth is but a point. And on that tiny point that men make do with, people want to know precisely all that happens in the whole wide world, and whatever they cannot learn about in their tiny corner they pretend does not exist. I think that this is pretty evidently ridiculous.[11]

Concerning angels, then, Bekker concluded that: 1) reason could not demonstrate whether or not they existed; 2) neither could reason prove that angels acted on other spirits or on bodies, nor could it explain how they might do so; 3) the Bible confirmed that angels existed but said very little about their nature; 4) actions that the Bible figuratively attributed to angels were really the actions of God, with angels often serving merely as signs of God's majesty; 5) actions that the Bible attributed to angelic spirits were often really the actions of man or nature; and 6) angels might well do other things that men do not know about.

II

Bekker presented strong arguments against the temporal actions of angelic spirits but he did not rule out such actions as impossible. When it came more specifically to the devil and evil spirits, however, Bekker was uncompromising in his claim that such spirits could not act on people on earth. Scripture had little to say on the subject of evil spirits, but what it did say was clear. II Peter 2:4 said that the devil and his evil angels were cast by God into hell and chained there in darkness to await the Last Judgement, Bekker noted, while Genesis 49:26 declared that the bonds placed on the devil were eternal. This proved, Bekker claimed, that the devil was God's prisoner in hell and could not harm people on earth.

Other scriptural passages, such as Jude 6 and Matthew 25:41, supported this interpretation. There was nothing in the Bible to support the popular belief that God needed evil spirits to torment people. Scripture often reported that believers were tortured by bad people, but the Bible was not so clear when it came to the activities of evil spirits.[12] People who believed that devils were free to plague people on earth distorted the Bible to support their own preconceived ideas, Bekker maintained.

In Bekker's view, Scripture did not speak as broadly about the devil and his power as many people assumed. The word "diabolos" used in the Greek New Testament had been translated in various places in various editions of the Bible not only as "devil" but also as "slanderer," "enemy," "evil one," "accuser," "deceiver," "rogue," and "damager," Bekker pointed out. The word "diabolos" was often used in Scripture to refer to bad people. For example in Matthew 13:39—"the enemy who sowed them is the devil; the

[11]Ibid., 64-65.
[12]Ibid., 52-54.

harvest is the end of the world; and the reapers are the angels"—the word "diabolos" could also be translated as a slanderer who opposed sound teaching with abuse much as the unbelieving Jews did in Acts 13:35.

"Now…one cannot be certain what Scripture teaches us about the devil without being sure that it is indeed the devil that Scripture discusses," Bekker continued. He thus recommended a full investigation of all biblical passages in which the word "diabolos" appeared. "In each passage one must see what sense the circumstances and the thread of reason require—this is the common rule of right interpretation," Bekker declared, laying out his basic rule of scriptural exegesis.[13] Taking up Ephesians 4:27— "Give no place to the devil"—Bekker argued that this passage could better be rendered as "Give no place to the slanderer" because Paul urged Christians to live lives that would give their opponents no cause for slander. In Ephesians 6:11 "The poisonous wiles of the devil" could better be translated as "The cunning diversion of opponents" because Christians had many opponents in Ephesus. In I Timothy 3:6-7, "The judgement of the devil" had been rendered by a number of translators (and even in a marginal note of the States Translation) as "The judgement of slanderers," evil-speaking men ready to slander a young and inexperienced teacher. Indeed, Bekker concluded, the word "diabolos" was used in so many different ways in the New Testament "that it applies better to men than to the chief of the evil spirits."[14]

The case with the Hebrew word "Satan" was similar, Bekker argued. Although "Satan" was used 22 times in the Old Testament and 34 times in the New Testament,"in the Hebrew text where the word is at home, since it is originally Hebrew, it never occurs in such a way that it must apply to the devil."[15] Nevertheless, in most places (such as Job 1:6-9, 12, and 2:1-7; Psalms 109:6; and Zacharia 3:1-2) the Dutch translators had rendered the word as "devil," although in a few places (Numbers 22:22 and 32; II Samuel 29:4; I Kings 5:4 and 11:14, 23, 25) they translated it as "enemy" or "opponent." But to Bekker it was unclear why the translators had rendered the word sometimes as "devil" and other times as "opponent" in places where the sense was very nearly the same.[16]

Bekker conceded that in a few places (Matthew 25:41; Revelations 12:9; John 8:44, 13:2; I John 3:10; and Hebrews 2:14) Scripture did clearly refer to Satan and his angels as evil spirits. But, he continued, "as far as the word 'Satan' goes, aside from these places I do not find many others where the word clearly means the devil."[17]

In order to interpret the many passages where the word "Satan" did not clearly refer to the devil, Bekker proposed four basic exegetical rules: 1) scripture always speaks truly and to the honor of God. It often uses well disguised reasons, but it never ascribes anything absurd to God, who is himself its author; 2) individual Scripture passages may not be understood in a way that contradicts the consistent thread, style, and content of the whole of Godly Scripture; 3) when different stories applied to the same thing or person appear to contradict each other when they are interpreted literally, both or at least one must be interpreted figuratively. "Because it cannot be that the mouth of truth says something literally in one place and in another place says something else that contradicts it;" and 4) the devil as a creature may not be compared to God, but only to his fellow creatures.[18]

---

[13]Ibid., 98-101.
[14]Ibid., 100-102.
[15]Ibid., 101-102.
[16]Ibid., 101-104.
[17]Ibid., 104-105.
[18]Ibid., 104-106.

Bekker inclined to figurative interpretation of most biblical passages speaking of the devil: "All of this leads me to say that all that which is said of the devil cannot be understood literally," he declared. It was not the purpose of Scripture to teach what the devil did, but rather what the corruption of man caused. In a certain sense it could be said that the devil did all the evil that people did because people's evil actions came from the corruption of human nature originally caused by the devil. Those who murdered or lied did the devil's work, and it was in this sense alone that the Bible spoke rightly of the works of the devil.[19] "Don't you see, reader, as clear as the day, that the devil's works are the sins that evil people as children of the devil commit?" Bekker implored.[20]

God controlled and limited the evil that resided in man, Bekker added. This was the meaning of scriptural passages that referred to God's binding of the devil (Revelations 20:1-2, 7). After the devil deceived the first man in paradise there was no further evidence that he personally had done anything more to people, nor was there any indication that he could do so, Bekker argued.[21] Because God had bound and chained the devil in hell, his influence over people remained limited to the effects of original sin, Bekker argued, in a sweeping denial of demonic power.

The battle between the archangel Michael and the devil in Revelations 12:7-8 could not be understood literally, Bekker held. "Who can imagine that this really happened?" he exclaimed. The battle was said to take place in heaven, but the devil had no place in heaven after his fall.[22] The "depths of Satan" in Revelations 2:24 were the deceits of men trying to bring others into error; the "power of Satan" in Acts 26:18 was the inborn evil in man that opposed his spiritual state; the "working of the devil" in II Thessalonians 2:9 was the working of sin that originally came from the devil; when Revelations 2:9-13 said the devil had his people at Smyrna and Pergamus, this meant that godlessness had triumphed there; when the devil was said to be in Judas (Luke 22:3, John 13:27) and Ananias (Acts 5:3), this meant that evil was in those two men; when I Thessalonians 2:18 said the devil hindered Paul on his trip, it meant that the enemies of the Gospel hindered him; and when Revelations 12:9-10 called the devil "the accuser of our brothers before God," this had to be understood figuratively as well because the devil, a prisoner in hell, could not accuse anyone before God in heaven.[23]

Bekker had his most difficult task in explaining the devil's role in the fall of man as reported in Genesis 3, John 8:44, and II Corinthians 8:44. He did not doubt scriptural testimony that the devil did indeed cause the fall of the first humans, but he was mystified about how the devil had done this (although several of his followers were not equally at a loss to explain the fall). What could the devil do to the heart of man to move him to such sin? Bekker asked.[24] He was certain that the devil had not spoken through a snake to cause the fall of man, even though both Paul and Moses said that the snake deceived Eve with its cunning. How could a snake, with no understanding, having "neither tongue nor lung" capable of sound, much less speech, be cunning and deceive Eve? And Scripture nowhere specifically said that the devil spoke through the snake. Interpreters had made this assumption because Revelations 12:9 called the devil

[19]Ibid., 108-110.
[20]Ibid., 111.
[21]Ibid., 116-117.
[22]Ibid., 115-116.
[23]Ibid., 111-115.
[24]Ibid., 117-118.

"the old snake." Why did the devil not choose a parrot for this work of deception? Bekker asked. At least parrots could imitate speech. And on top of this, Paul and Moses did not even mention the devil in their accounts of the fall of man.[25] These passages simply could not be taken literally, Bekker concluded, whether one applied them to the devil or to a snake. "We have clearly seen," he added, "that the story taken literally cannot be true. Could Moses write something that was not true? Far from it. It must be understood in a sense that can be true.... One must understand something other than what the words at first appear to say."[26] This type of statement was the worst fear of a biblical literalist.

While Scripture affirmed that the devil was the origin of sin, it did not say whether this happened through bad advice, bad example, or in some other way, Bekker continued. He confessed that he did not believe that the devil had acted directly on the human soul or body, but he added that even in his own day many people sinned because of someone who did not act on them directly with words, deeds, or thoughts.[27]

Bekker treated the biblical account of the devil's temptation of Christ in a similar fashion, declaring that it could not be interpreted literally. The world was round, Bekker argued, so how could the devil show Jesus all the kingdoms of the world in one instant? Here Christ was figuratively describing his own inner strength, not speaking about the devil's power.[28] The rest of Bekker's exegesis proceeded in a similar fashion.

After devoting a chapter to a more detailed discussion of the biblical account of the battle between the archangel Michael and the devil, and another chapter to David's encounter with the devil, Bekker took up Biblical accounts of spirits that told the future. I Samuel 28 described Saul's visit to the witch of Endor, a favorite story for demonologists and witch hunters. Some Protestant theologians claimed that it was not Samuel's spirit but the devil that appeared to Saul, but Bekker pointed out that the passage said nothing about the devil. Scriptural stories about Job and Paul being plagued by the devil could not be interpreted literally either, Bekker maintained.[29] In short, almost all scriptural passages which appeared to describe the power of the devil and the devil's actions on earth could, when properly interpreted, be understood as not referring to the devil at all.

III

Bekker next took up New Testament accounts of spirit possession and attempted to explain them in the light of his views on the devil and evil spirits. This difficult task led Bekker into his most controversial biblical exegesis. First he pointed out that in the various stories of spirit possession the Greek text always spoke of demons (*daimones*) not devils (*diaboli*), although the States Translation sometimes rendered "*daimones*" as devils. According to the common interpretation of these scriptural passages, when one or more of these demons possessed a person's body they made the person speak

[25]Ibid., 120-127.
[26]Ibid., 127-128.
[27]Ibid., 127-129.
[28]Ibid., 117-138.
[29]Ibid., 138-172.

strangely or brought terrible sickness, pains, even frenzy and insanity. Jesus healed many of these possessed people, saying that he cast the demons out of them, and he gave the disciples the power to do the same. This casting out of demons was taken to be a sign of the Lord's divinity and the authenticity of his mission, since only divine and supernatural power could break the hold that the devil had over people.[30]

But a closer investigation of these passages revealed a different interpretation, Bekker continued. It was important to notice that in the New Testament when mention was made of possession by an "unclean spirit" this was always done in the context of a discussion of mental and physical illnesses. For example Matthew 4:24 said "...and they brought unto him all sick people that were taken with divers diseases and torments, and those which were possessed with devils, and those which were lunatic, and those that had palsy; and he healed them." Matthew 8:16, Mark 1:32, and Luke 6:18 and 7:21 spoke similarly. From this Bekker concluded that spirit possession was simply a name for one of the illnesses current in biblical times. In Acts 1:38 Peter said of Christ that he had been "healing all who were overcome by the devil." If Peter had meant possession by an evil spirit rather than a simple sickness he would have said "saving" rather than "healing."[31]

Illness was often called a spirit in other places in the Bible, Bekker continued. The woman in Luke 13:11 was said to have "a spirit of sickness" for 18 years. Furthermore, the casting out of demons was nowhere foretold by God's prophets, but when Matthew 8:16 said that "they brought unto him many that were possessed with devils: and he cast the spirits out with his Word, and healed all that were sick," verse 17 added that this was a fulfillment of the prophecy of Isaiah 53:4 ("Surely he hath borne our griefs and carried our sorrows: yet we did esteem him stricken, smitten of God, and afflicted). And, Bekker added, in the original Greek text of Matthew 8:16 one read not "possessed with devils," but merely "possessed," thus revealing another example of the Dutch translators acting to "shove the devil into places that he had nothing to do with."[32]

The Bible also related how unbelieving Jews who were shocked by the things that Christ said attributed these to an evil spirit that possessed him, again showing that people in biblical times "often ascribed a demon or impure spirit to those not in their right mind." For the unbelieving Jews it was "the same thing to say that he was crazy or possessed by an evil spirit," Bekker argued, adding:

> From all this it seems to me that one can well decide that this race of demons, evil or unclean spirits ...were certain bad sicknesses which afflicted the brains and through them the inward senses, especially the imagination. In time these got worse like fever, often being mixed with fever and convulsions,leading to frenzy and insanity.[33]

If spirit possession was simply a way that biblical people spoke of mental illness, how could one explain the Bible passages in which the Lord himself, by his words and deeds, seemed to believe that he was in fact dealing with cases of spirit possession? This extremely difficult question brought Bekker to the crucial point of his exegesis. The problem that he faced was to explain why Christ, who knew that the people he

[30]Ibid., 172-173.
[31]Ibid., 173-175.
[32]Ibid., 175.
[33]Ibid., 176.

healed were not possessed by evil spirits but were instead mentally ill, did not openly explain this but rather left people with the erroneous belief that he had cast out demons.

In order to interpret these passages in a way consistent with his ideas about spirit possession, Bekker held that Scripture did not teach natural knowledge, a position that flowed from the Dutch Cartesian separation of religion from philosophy, and he also de-emphasized the Bible's role in teaching religious doctrine. Both claims infuriated the confessional party within the church, the latter especially striking at the heart of the confessional party's assumption that doctrine could be drawn from the Bible and used as the material of belief in confessional documents.

When Jesus was on the earth, Bekker began, he "never let it appear that he had come to teach man the natural causes of things nor the errors in the conception of things, but only to better those things pertaining to morals and religion."[34] Not only did the Lord not teach about natural things, Bekker continued, he did not even teach much about "the things of belief. It is always about morals." The only teachings of Christ touching doctrine were his declaration that he was the promised messiah and three Scripture texts (Matthew 22:23, Mark 12:18, and Luke 20:27) in which he discussed the resurrection. There were no special scriptural chapters discussing such things as the creation, angels, election, justification, hereditary sin, or even Christ's satisfaction for man's sins, Bekker argued. Sometimes Christ touched on one or another of these things but only in passing, never saying enough to give a full and complete treatment of any doctrine. "These doctrines had to be gotten from somewhere else," Bekker declared.[35]   .

One could see from Christ's actions and teachings, Bekker continued, that he intended while on earth to use these means primarily to make himself known: "What further pertained to doctrine he left to his disciples to do after his ascension," when he sent them the Holy Spirit to enlighten their understandings, enabling them to comprehend and teach doctrine. And even though Christ intended his disciples to teach people doctrine, he did not instruct them in doctrine while he was on earth. So "how do you expect him to have wanted to teach the great mass of the people who had neither ears to hear nor eyes to see and who could not understand mysteries?" Bekker asked. To these people the Lord spoke figuratively ("*door gelykenisse*").[36]

Not only did these exegetical ideas directly attack the biblical authority of Reformed confessional documents and Reformed theology, on this point Bekker's argument showed striking similarities to Spinoza's discussion of biblical interpretation in the *Tractatus Theologico-Politicus*. Like Bekker, Spinoza held that Christ's teachings in the Bible were directed toward moral instruction and did not deal with religious doctrine except in a tangential way. Spinoza wrote: "Scripture teaches only very simple doctrines and inculcates nothing but obedience, and...concerning the nature of God it teaches only what man can imitate by a definite code of conduct."[37]

When Bekker turned to the question of why Christ had left people in error about spirit possession, his exegesis became even more radical. It was not surprising, he continued, "that Jesus did not declare himself against various errors that were in fashion at the

[34]Ibid., 181.

[35]Ibid., 183.

[36]Ibid.

[37]Benedict Spinoza, *Tractatus Theologico-Politicus*, trans. by Samuel Shirley (Leiden, 1989), 214; See also Andrew Fix, "Bekker and Spinoza," in *Disguised and Overt Spinozism Around 1700*, ed. by Wim Klever and Wiep van Bunge (Leiden, E.J. Brill, 1996), 23-40.

time among the Jewish people, even when a specific opportunity to do so presented itself to him, and his silence seemed to be silent agreement." And this was not just the case with spirit possession. In John 9:2-3 his students asked Christ about a person born blind: "Who sinned, him or his parents?" Jesus merely answered "Neither him nor his parents: it is so God's work will be revealed in him." But Christ did not mention, much less correct, either of the two errors that gave rise to the question—the Pythagorean idea of the transmigration of souls and the popular belief that a child could sin in its mother's womb.

Even to so great a question as "What shall I do to inherit eternal life?" Christ only answered "Uphold the commandments" in Matthew 19:16-17 and Luke 10:25-28. He did not explain that salvation had nothing to do with doing anything, nor did he mention the inborn corruption in man that made it impossible for him to follow God's commands, Bekker pointed out.[38] On many such weighty points of belief, even concerning his own divinity, Christ left people in error until he went to heaven and sent down the Holy Spirit to the disciples.

More to the point, Bekker went on, "about spirits themselves and their affairs the Savior spoke in such a language that, taken literally, sounds very absurd." It was not his purpose to correct the errors that people showed in their speech, and "indeed, he himself made use of errors to shut up his opponents with their own words," Bekker claimed.[39] "The style of great masters has been not only to leave people in errors for a time, but also to accommodate themselves to that language which in part arose out of such misunderstandings" Bekker argued. Christ had good reasons for doing this. "The people were still rough and uncivilized" and were dominated by old ideas. For this reason it was much easier to convince them of the corruption of their morals than of the errors of their ideas. So Christ started by teaching them morality, since fear of the Lord is the beginning of all wisdom. Then, when peoples' hearts had become truly pious, they would be more prepared and eager to "investigate the knowledge of more Godly things."[40]

Christ could not have spoken in any other way than in the language of the people in order to be understood, Bekker added. He gave sick people the names that they had among the masses so that everyone would know to whom he was referring, and his moral teaching would be successful. But by using the common names Christ did not indicate that he believed in the errors that the names embodied.[41] Such an interpretation took nothing away from Christ's work, Bekker added. The wonderful strength to heal the worst of illnesses was indeed a powerful weapon against the devil's work of sin, from which all human misery since Adam's fall had arisen. The fact that Christ had not actually cast out evil spirits made little difference to the message his healing was meant to deliver: that belief in Christ was the remedy for the real evil spirit that man was born with.[42]

By arguing that in accommodating his teaching to the limited understanding of the people Christ had left many in error about the truth of things, Bekker again closely approached a controversial part of Spinoza's exegesis. In the *Tractatus*, Spinoza argued that many biblical stories were adapted to the understandings both of the authors

[38]Bekker, II, 185.
[39]Ibid., 185-187.
[40]Ibid., 187-189.
[41]Ibid., 187, 188-190.
[42]Ibid., 188, 191-192.

who related them and the audience for whom they were intended. The object of Scripture was not to teach either natural or supernatural truth, but rather to instill piety and obedience in people. Scripture used the language "most effective in moving men—and particularly the common people—to devotion. That is why it speaks of God and events in terms far from correct, its aim being not to convince on rational grounds but to appeal to and engage men's fantasy and emotion."[43]

Spinoza thus made the extraordinary claim that the writers of the Bible had made mistakes. While Bekker did not argue that biblical authors were in error, he did hold that Christ had knowingly perpetuated popular errors by not correcting them. While Spinoza saw the Bible as essentially a rhetorical text the truth content of which was irrelevant, Bekker did not go that far. Like Spinoza, Bekker did de-emphasize the role of Scripture in teaching true knowledge while stressing instead its role as a moral guide. On the crucial point of whether or not the Bible as a whole was divinely inspired, however, the two men parted ways, Bekker insisting that it was, while Spinoza held that such an assumption was an obstacle to accurate interpretation of the text.[44] On other points there was much less distance between the exegetical positions of the two men, an issue that did not go unnoticed by Bekker's opponents. Bekker himself, with his critical treatment of Spinoza's exegesis in his 1685 work on ecclesiastical history, was surely aware that comparisons would be made between his methods of biblical interpretation and those of Spinoza.

Bekker next proceeded to analyze several biblical stories in which Christ cast out demons in order to show that these texts could be interpreted in such as way as to support his own view. The first was the story related in Mark 1: 23-27:

And there was in their synagogue a man with an unclean spirit; and he cried out, Saying, Let us alone; what have we to do with thee, thou Jesus of Nazareth? Art thou come to destroy us? I know thee who thou art, the Holy One of God. And Jesus rebuked him saying, Hold thy peace, and come out of him. And when the unclean spirit had torn him, and cried out with a loud voice, he came out of him. And they were all amazed, insomuch that they questioned themselves, saying, What thing is this? What new doctrine is this? for with authority commandeth he even the unclean spirits, and they do obey him.

For Bekker this unclean spirit was "...a spirit of insanity, corrupting the strength of imagination," and thus making the man in the synagogue think that he was an enemy of God.[45] The man was frightened when he saw Jesus, whom he had heard was the messiah, and he cried out because he believed that he was an unclean spirit. Jesus cured the man in the same way that he cured Simon's mother-in-law from fever, as reported in Luke 4:39. Bekker added that in his pastoral duties he had met people like this who thought they were God's enemies.[46]

The next case that Bekker took up was the hardest to explain. It came from Matthew 8:28-34, Mark 5:1-17, and Luke 8:26-39, and was the story of a man possessed by demons that Christ cast out and drove into a herd of pigs. Mark wrote:

And they came over unto the other side of the sea into the country of the Gadarenes. And when he was come out of the ship immediately there met him out of the tombs

[43]Spinoza, 134.
[44]Ibid., 135-136.
[45]Bekker, II, 193.
[46]Ibid., 193-194.

a man with an unclean spirit, who had his dwelling among the tombs; and no man could bind him, no, not with chains: Because that he had often been bound with fetters and chains, and the chains had been plucked asunder by him, and the fetters broken in pieces: neither could any man tame him. And always, night and day, he was in the mountains, and in the tombs, crying, and cutting himself with stones. But when he saw Jesus from afar off,he ran and worshipped him, And he cried with a loud voice and said, What have I to do with thee, Jesus, thou Son of the most high God? I adjure thee by God, that thou torment me not. For he said unto him, Come out of the man, thou unclean spirit. And he asked him, What is thy name? And he answered, saying, My name is Legion: for we are many. And he besought him much that he would not send them away out of the country. Now there was there nigh unto the mountains a great herd of swine feeding. And the devils besought him, saying, Send us into the swine, that we may enter into them. And forthwith Jesus gave them leave. And the unclean spirits went out, and entered into the swine: and the herd ran violently down a steep place into the sea (they were about two thousand) and were choked in the sea. And they that fed the swine fled, and told it in the city, and in the country. And they went out to see what it was that was done. And they came to Jesus, and saw him that was possessed with the devil and had the legion, sitting, clothed, and in his right mind, and they were afraid...

According to Bekker the actions of the possessed man gave proof of "insanity, as bad as it can be." One could find such people in the Amsterdam madhouse, he added. The inmates of the asylum might say that they could break chains, and they often escaped and ran around in the wilderness, so it was not surprising that Christ should meet one such among the tombs. When escaped insane people met other citizens they would often fall down before them as a sign of respect and plead to speak, just as this man ran up to Jesus and "worshipped" him, which in the original Greek meant he bowed down before Jesus. Bekker said that this had happened to him many times, most recently when he met a Jew who had twice broken out of the asylum.

When Jesus told the unclean spirit to depart from the man, he was granting the man what he imagined tormented him so that he could save him from it, Bekker continued. He might just as well have said "evil torment, leave this man." Christ also wanted to show that he had enough power to command an evil spirit if one actually did possess a man. The man was afraid of Jesus because he believed that damned spirits were in his body, and he behaved as if that were indeed the case. Bekker reported a similar incident from his pastorate in Franeker. A woman believed that she had sinned so badly against God that she no longer had to pray, read the Bible, or go to church. She felt damned and robbed of all Christian traits, and she believed it would give her particular pleasure to drown her small children. Bekker was able to prevent the murder of her children and to get the woman to care for her family only by convincing her that such things were fitting for a damned person.[47]

Returning to the biblical story, Bekker explained that the poor man begged the Lord to let the evil spirits go into the swine because he believed that this was the voice of the demons speaking through him, trying to prevent being sent by Jesus back to hell. But it was clear that this was not really the voice of evil spirits, Bekker argued, because as soon as the supposed spirits were allowed into the pigs they drowned them, thus

[47]Ibid., 194-196.

destroying the host that was to save them from hell. These strange events could be easily understood if one considered "the imagination of the hurt brain of this man," Bekker continued. The insane, especially if they had once been religious people, often showed great displeasure at the profanation of religion and taunted and cursed teachers and rulers for not preventing it. This man was upset by the Gadarenes' keeping of pigs because the Jewish law forbade the eating or sacrificing of these animals. In an effort to punish the Gadarenes the man said that the evil spirits should go into the pigs, Bekker argued.

Jesus drove the swine insane and to their deaths in order to heal the man of his insanity by making him believe that the demons had indeed left him and gone into the pigs. This was a supernatural act that only Christ had the power to carry out. "Thus I frankly say," exclaimed Bekker, "away from here with the Devil and let Christ have the honor that thoughtless people give to evil spirits."[48] It was every bit as great a miracle to heal a man from insanity and to make 2,000 pigs insane as it would have been to cast out thousands of demons, Bekker insisted.[49]

If anyone objected that Jesus, by speaking with the evil spirits, appeared to believe that they existed, Bekker reminded his readers that:

Jesus, speaking with the common people, accommodated himself to the language that they understood, until the time that they became more truly enlightened and could learn a higher language. What wonder is it that this wise master, speaking to one who was entirely out of his mind, did not speak as one would with intelligent people? It is foolish to want to speak wisely with fools."[50]

To further explain this story, Bekker compared it with another case in his personal experience. He once knew a man in Franeker who was not all that different from the one in the Bible story. He was an intelligent but greedy man who lived at first in the countryside but who later came to Franeker in search of profit. There he operated a shop, but the profits were not what he had hoped for, and this failure combined with his greed drove him into a rage and frenzy. He believed that he had wasted his time in an unrecoverable fashion and that he was lost. He further believed that he no longer had entrails in his body and that all that he ate and drank fell into and out of his hollow body without providing him with any nourishment. He shut himself up in a small barn behind his house without a bed and with only a few blankets. He wore only a shirt and shirt-coat, wounded himself with his nails, and pinched off pieces of his rectum in an effort to prove that he was hollow inside. When he heard someone coming, he moaned in a most pitiful way because he thought that was fitting for one damned as he was.

Bekker related that he had once been in the man's house when he emerged from the barn and came into the house, naked except for a bloody and dirty shirt. He spoke with Bekker like an intelligent and coherent person, more intelligent than a common farmer, but afterwards he resumed living like a beast. After some time his wife sent him to a "certain master" in Workum who had had success in treating cases like his. The man placed himself under the complete control of this master during the course of his treatment. He behaved like a mature and intelligent person and wrote very coherent letters home to his wife advising her on the marriage of their daughter.

[48]Ibid., 198.
[49]Ibid., 195-200.
[50]Ibid., 199-200.

One could say that this man was possessed by an unclean spirit because of his unclean life, Bekker commented, and one could also refer to him as the "man with no entrails." But this would not mean that one really believed that the man was possessed by an evil spirit or that he actually had no entrails.[51] Likewise, there were people who stubbornly believed that they had a living animal inside of themselves, and for this reason one might refer to such a person as "the man with the animal in his head" without believing that he actually had an animal in his head. It was the same in the Bible when Christ referred to someone as possessed—it meant only that the person in question, or other people, believed that to be the case, Bekker concluded.[52]

Bekker analyzed in similar fashion several other biblical texts commonly believed to tell of spirit possession. In each case he showed that what had been believed to be the effects of demons were in fact instances of mental illness that Christ had cured while accommodating his language to the understanding of the common people. In the concluding chapters of volume two, Bekker discussed the phenomenon of "moon sickness" or lunacy, which he said had nothing to do with evil spirits or the moon. He also dealt with several additional Scripture texts commonly thought to report the activity of the devil but which, when properly translated and understood, spoke only of evil men.[53] Bekker concluded that he had shown that the devil was not really mentioned in many biblical passages where it had previously been believed that he appeared. This was proof, he maintained, that the devil did not haunt the world and appear to people in dreams or waking life.[54] Having thus exposed as fraud the great power and wisdom of Satan, Bekker declared the devil removed from his mastery over the earth, a mastery incompatible with true Christian belief.[55]

Bekker's publisher, Hero Nauta, must have been aware of the potentially explosive—and thus profitable—impact of such arguments. The full text of the first two volumes of *The World Bewitched* had been delivered by Bekker to Nauta early in 1691, but severe winter weather interrupted the proofreading. The delivery of copy from Bekker in Amsterdam to Nauta in Leeuwarden experienced delays, and problems developed between author and publisher over the correction process. As a result, Bekker began considering a change of publishers, hoping to find one closer to Amsterdam. Nauta, foreseeing the promising commercial future of the book, began to sell separately the parts of the book that he had already printed. To Bekker's great consternation, incomplete and partly uncorrected copies of both of the first two volumes appeared for sale in Friesland, and people began talking about the book even before Bekker himself had seen a copy. Bekker then decided to entrust the reprinting of volumes one and two and the printing of the rest of the work to Daniel van Dalen in Amsterdam. He made revisions in the first two volumes in response to criticism that he had received from readers of the Leeuwarden edition, and the revised and corrected first two volumes were available in Amsterdam by the summer of 1691, where they sold well and demand quickly outran supply.

The first two volumes of *The World Bewitched* did indeed give rise to a storm of controversy, and for this reason Bekker was not able to finish volume three for two more years. The need to further explain his initial ideas and to defend himself against

[51]Ibid., 200-201.
[52]Ibid., 196-197.
[53]Ibid., 202-213.
[54]Ibid., 213-217.
[55]Ibid., 228-262.

the attacks of his critics left him little time for the difficult task of completing his extensive work on spirits. By 1693 he was at last ready with the next installment of the work. Having laid the theoretical groundwork in the first two volumes for his contention that the devil could not act on people on earth, Bekker proceeded in the later volumes to expand upon this argument and to apply it to the case of sorcery. In the final two volumes Bekker was less original than he had been in book two, largely relying on arguments against witchcraft and sorcery taken from earlier writers such as Johannes Weyer, Abraham Palingh, Antonie van Dale, and Reginald Scot.

Because of his beliefs regarding evil spirits, Bekker rejected as fraud all manner of witchcraft and sorcery. Many people believed that sorcery, conjuring, and fortune-telling were done by those who had given themselves over to the devil, Bekker pointed out. According to this belief, witches concluded pacts with the devil in order to use his power against people, mumbling unintelligible words, reading from a book, or using words outside of their usual meanings while adding all sorts of gestures in order to get a devil or familiar spirit to do their bidding. When this was done to get information from the devil that would otherwise be hidden from man, it was called fortune telling. But it was irrational to believe that evil spirits had these kinds of interactions with people, Bekker argued, and he held that it was especially mistaken to believe that the devil had bodily contact with people.[56]

When the Bible referred to sorcery, magicians, or wise men, it did not mean people who worked with the cooperation of evil spirits or the devil, but rather simple tricksters who seldom accomplished anything. Scriptural accounts of sorcery were really tales of idolatry, Bekker declared. Different translations of the Bible varied in the ways that they treated the question of sorcery. Where the Dutch Bible spoke of "devil magicians," other translations called the same people astrologers or augurs. Predicting the future from the flight of birds as some ancient augurs did had nothing to do with the devil or evil spirits. And while the States Bible said that the witch of Endor in I Samuel 28 had a "fortune-telling spirit," the original Greek text called her a "*engastrimuthon*," or a "ventriloquist," Bekker continued, following Scot. While the text itself never mentioned the devil, later commentators and translators added him to the story.[57]

The sorcerers of the Old Testament were priests, augurs, fortune-tellers, dream interpreters and the like, but the Bible nowhere said that they got help from evil spirits. The laws given to Israel that spoke of sorcery were directed against idolatrous practices, Bekker argued.[58] Sorcerers in the Bible never made pacts with the devil. References to sorcery in Deuteronomy 18 never mentioned demonic pacts because such pacts would contradict God's covenant with man, Bekker declared.[59] The very idea of the pact was impossible and absurd, and although it came originally from the pagan poets even Protestant theologians had believed it. To believe that the devil had such power insulted God's honor and was a Manichean idea, Bekker repeated.[60]

What little the Bible did say about the devil was exaggerated and embroidered by people who read into the holy text ideas that they already held, Bekker continued. Voetius had produced a series of "proofs" of the reality of sorcery and the activities of

[56]Bekker III (Amsterdam, 1693), 1-18.
[57]Ibid., 19-43.
[58]Ibid., 54-66; Knuttel 219.
[59]Bekker, III, 67-99; Knuttel 219.
[60]Bekker, III, 129-136.

the devil in his *Disputationes*, Bekker noted, adding that many of Voetius's arguments were taken from Catholic sources. In his work Voetius referred to scriptural passages without explaining their context, language, or terms, Bekker objected, in a direct criticism of biblical literalism. The Bible taught nothing about the power of the devil, and belief in demonic power was against the Reformed catechism and true piety as well, Bekker argued in concluding volume three.[61]

In volume four, Bekker examined the causes for commonly held beliefs about the devil, evil spirits, ghosts, and sorcery. He found prejudice and fear of things that could not be understood to be the primary causes of such beliefs, which also arose from deception of the senses.[62] Man's incomplete understanding of nature and its phenomena often made things seem supernatural when in truth they were not, Bekker explained, echoing Spinoza's argument about miracles in the *Tractatus Theologico-Politicus*. In addition, a great deal of sorcery was simply deceit and slight of hand.[63] Bekker then related a number of incidents that he himself had observed or that had been reported to him in order to show that what seemed to be sorcery could be found to have natural causes.[64]

Cases of spirit possession could also have many causes, Bekker argued. People often faked such phenomena in order to make money, and people suffering from melancholy often believed themselves to be possessed, an argument that Bekker took from Weyer. Some people were simply so vain that they imagined themselves attacked by the devil because of their great piety. Sometimes symptoms displayed by people thought to be possessed were in fact caused by physical disorders. Bekker next discussed several possession cases that he had researched where the victims proved to be faking.[65]

In the closing chapters of his final volume, Bekker discussed reports of sorcery from heathen, Moslem, Jewish, and Catholic sources, arguing that they were the result of superstition and could easily be explained as natural occurrences.[66] Moving on to Protestant sources, Bekker treated their stories in a similar way. The miracle healing of Knight Digby, the strange story of a bricklayer in Bolsward, the piper of Hamlen, the devils of Macon and Tedworth, and the ghosts of Annenberg and Lausanne were all frauds.[67] None of these stories of sorcery and witchcraft really involved the devil or evil spirits.

Bekker finished by attacking the cruelty and irrationality of witch trials, arguing that foolish testimony had led judges to pass death sentences on innocent people, a sentiment that was widely shared in the Dutch Republic by the 1690s, even among the judges themselves.[68] It was evident that popular beliefs about sorcery and witchcraft were mistaken because these things simply did not exist, Bekker declared. He called on the authorities of the church, schools, and courts to take the lead in putting an end to such un-Christian beliefs.[69]

[61]Ibid., 162-173; Knuttel 214-222.
[62]Bekker, IV, (Amsterdam, 1693), 1-7.
[63]Ibid., 16-25.
[64]Ibid., 43-91.
[65]Ibid., 43-49.
[66]Ibid., 99-129.
[67]Ibid., 130-203.
[68]Ibid., 204-276; Knuttel 222-224.
[69]Bekker, IV, 282-287.

IV

Beginning with the appearance of the first two volumes in 1691, *The World Bewitched* lit a firestorm of controversy. The debate over Bekker's view of spirits was most intense from 1691-1693, and it made the *Vaste Spyze* controversy pale by comparison. This was the moment that Bekker's enemies had waited 20 years for.

Bekker's Cartesian arguments in the first third of book two proved highly controversial, as did his method of Bible interpretation and his criticism of the States Translation, which the Reformed church considered divinely inspired. Reformed preachers accused Bekker of attacking the foundations of the faith, while many theologians called his biblical exegesis arbitrary and designed to support his philosophical arguments. His opponents charged that he mocked God, showed disrespect for the States Bible, opposed the doctrines of the Reformed church, distorted Scripture, and gave reason too much power in religion. Bekker was also accused of following the "arch-heretics" David Joris, Thomas Hobbes, and Benedict Spinoza. By the time the final two volumes of Bekker's work appeared in 1693, the controversy was already burning itself out, so they did not attract as much attention from opponents as book two did.

In the debate that took place around Bekker's book, more voices were raised against his position than in support of it. By the end of the seventeenth century, Cartesianism was well established in Dutch universities and among the educated public of Holland, and modern science found a home in the Republic nearly as congenial as the one that it found in England. Nevertheless, belief in the temporal activity of spirits continued to be defended even by some Cartesians and empirical scientists. Nearly a century after the last death sentence for witchcraft was handed down by a Dutch court, and despite the fact that the practical implications of spirit belief had therefore diminished considerably in the United Provinces, the intellectual controversy over spirits still raged and spirit belief still found defenders.

Spirit belief was still such a controversial topic even as the issue of witchcraft was fading in importance in part because the question of spirits was interlocked with other controversies that were still very much a part of the Dutch religious landscape. Disputes over the relative authority of the Bible and confessional formulas, along with the debate over scriptural interpretation surrounding Coccejus and the sabbath question, were set against the larger question of the nature of the Dutch Reformed church itself. Bekker's ideas on spirits necessarily involved him in the dispute over biblical exegesis, and thus in this whole web of controversies, and it was largely for this reason that his position on spirits touched a nerve that vibrated violently throughout the entire structure of the Dutch Reformed church.[70]

Incomplete copies of the first two volumes of *The World Bewitched* were in circulation by the spring of 1691, and the complete first two volumes would appear in Amsterdam that summer. In June of 1691, the Amsterdam church council, probably with an eye on Bekker, ruled that all members of the classis had to have their books inspected by church authorities before they could be published. Bekker immediately agreed to submit his first two volumes for inspection, and meanwhile to delay publication

[70]Knuttel, 224-268, J. van Sluis, *Bekkeriana: Balthasar Bekker biografisch en bibliografisch* (Leeuwarden, 1994), 31-33.

of volume two. A commission of the church council consisting of three preachers and two elders was appointed to review the book and report back to the council. The commission's report stated that parts of *The World Bewitched* appeared to contradict the Reformed church Formulas of Unity, and as a result the church council condemned the book in late June, while Bekker was out of town on a trip to Friesland.

The commission's criticism focussed not on philosophical points but rather on Bekker's exegesis. The reviewers accused Bekker of misinterpreting certain scriptural passages, insulting the States translators, being arbitrary in his exegesis, and denying the power of the devil, thereby undermining belief in God. Despite Bekker's protests, the Amsterdam classis voted in July to require him to submit his book to a group of inspectors who would purify it of the "errors" found by the commission. Bekker appealed this decision to the Synod of North Holland and meanwhile proceeded with the printing of volume two.

In August 1691, the Synod of North Holland met at Edam and presented seven objections to Bekker concerning his book: 1) his ideas about spirits, and especially those about the devil, contradicted the Formulas of Unity of the church; 2) he appeared to deny that the devil caused man's fall; 3) his interpretations of a number of Bible places were "unheard of" and possibly slanderous to God; 4) he accused the church of error in the matter of spirits; 5) he did not respect the States Bible; 6) he mocked church interpretations of the Bible; and 7) he accused Jesus of leaving the Jews in error about spirits. As a result of these objections, the synod, too, condemned the book. For his part, Bekker protested that he was not being accorded the respect due a doctor of theology and pastor of 35 years experience.

Meanwhile, in an effort to end the controversy, a commission of the Amsterdam church council drew up a list of 13 points reaffirming the church's position on spirits and asked Bekker to sign it. Among the points on the list was an admission that the complexity of biblical languages permitted certain scriptural places to be interpreted in the way that Bekker had done, but added to this was an insistence that there was no need for such "tortured" interpretations because standard versions maintained the honor of God and the doctrine of salvation. The document also declared that biblical passages could not be interpreted in a way contrary to the catechism and confession of the Reformed church, a hallmark statement of confessionalism. Among the other points was a promise by Bekker to write an open letter recanting the beliefs contained in his book, and another promise not to preach or write anything against the church's Formulas of Unity. Bekker did not object to the points that dealt specifically with spirits, but he objected to other points and refused to sign the document because he felt that such an action would be an admission of guilt.

In reply to the council, Bekker declared that his book had been an attempt to purify the church from all remnants of "Catholic superstition." He said that he believed that there were good and bad angels as reported by Scripture, and he further declared that he had not intended for his book to contain anything contrary to the Formulas of Unity. He admitted that some biblical passages could be interpreted in ways other than the way that he had rendered them, and he said that he had no desire to contradict the doctrines of the Reformed church. He also promised not to press his ideas further and not to publish volumes three and four without the prior approval of the church. But he stood by the central thesis of his book that the devil was imprisoned in hell and thus powerless on earth. For this reason, his other concessions were not enough to satisfy the church council, and once again the matter was referred to the classis.[71]

At the classis meeting on November 20, 1691, a will to compromise was present on both sides, but the meeting was not satisfied with Bekker's concessions and urged him to sign the 13 articles presented by the Amsterdam church council. Despite some calls by conservatives for Bekker's removal from office, negotiations continued. Bekker finally gave in to the extent of saying that his view on the devil was simply his personal opinion, not a formal doctrine, and was therefore open to modification. He took a similar stand on other of his scriptural interpretations that differed from standard church exegesis, but the classis pressed for an admission of guilt and recommended to the church council that Bekker be suspended from office and barred from communion for two months to think things over. A commission was appointed to talk to Bekker in order to bring him back to "sound ideas." The Amsterdam church council refused to bar Bekker from communion but did suspend him from office for two months to think over his position. Bekker's enemies on the church council then passed a resolution to be read in the churches of Amsterdam asking the congregations to continue to tolerate Bekker's service while efforts were made to bring him to "sounder" views. Bekker bitterly protested this resolution, and the city government forced the church council to alter it significantly in order to avoid an open breach within the church.

At the end of the two-month period, on January 22, 1692, Bekker made further concessions to the classis and specifically recanted his claim that by believing in the powers of the devil one insulted God and was a Manichee. But he still maintained that the devil was chained in hell. The majority of the classis seemed at last satisfied, and it was decided to let Bekker continue as pastor. But, to mollify his enemies, Bekker's suspension was continued until April, and the classis also asked that his concessions be published.

The whole affair might well have ended with this resolution within the Amsterdam church. Bekker's critics outside of Amsterdam, however, did not want to see him re-admitted to the service of the church. The Rotterdam church council sent an open letter to other church councils in Holland protesting the decision of the Amsterdam classis, and the church council of Utrecht sent a letter of protest to its counterpart in Amsterdam. Bekker's opponents on the Amsterdam church council used these protests to revive efforts against him and requested that the classis not reinstate Bekker before the next synodal meeting without a full recantation. At a tense meeting on April 8, 1692, the classis refused these new demands, but Bekker himself responded to great pressure by deciding not to resume his duties before the next synod. He spent the intervening time in Friesland working on the final two volumes of *The World Bewitched* and replying to some of the works written against his ideas. Meanwhile, opposition to him mounted.[72]

The classis of Hoorn added its voice to those protesting Bekker's possible reinstatement by imploring the classis of Amsterdam to repudiate its settlement with him, and the Amsterdam body began to back down from its earlier position as a result of this growing opposition. The entire compromise reached between Bekker and the classis now came unraveled. The classis said that it was not, after all, satisfied that Bekker could return to church service, and it turned the matter over to the synod of

[71]Knuttel, 270-284; van Sluis 23-26.
[72]Knuttel 284-306; van Sluis 26.

North Holland, which met in Alkmaar during August of 1692. The synod drew up a full recantation of Bekker's views that he was asked to sign, but Bekker protested that his case had been settled and that the synod could not re-open the matter. Bekker told the synod that he was ready for friendly talks aimed at resolving the difficulties some still had with his ideas, but he refused to submit himself again to church judgement. He presented the synod with a printed *Remonstrantie* (Remonstrance) complaining of injustices in the procedure against him, and then he left the meeting early so as not to hear it render a judgement that he felt it had no authority to make. Upon Bekker's refusal to sign the recantation, the synod officially deposed him as pastor. Bekker, however, was determined to ignore the synod's decision, which he considered illegal, and fully intended to resume his duties as preacher.

In response to the synod's actions, the Amsterdam church council forbade Bekker from preaching, and the dispute was then taken to the city government. The burgomeesters feared the turmoil that would result within the church if Bekker tried to preach, so they instructed him not to resume his duties even though they were not in favor of the church's action in his case. The magistrate continued to pay Bekker's salary and promised him protection from further attacks as partial compensation for barring him from preaching. The church council next voted to exclude Bekker from communion, and when he declared that he would attend anyway the council again called on the burgomeesters for help. The city government had little sympathy for the way that the classis, synod, and church council had treated Bekker. When the synod appealed matters to the States of Holland and requested that it ban *The World Bewitched,* the deputies refused even to discuss the matter after receiving a long defense of free speech and press written by Bekker. The civil authorities could not force the church to readmit Bekker to communion, however, and the result was a stalemate between church and state.

In 1693, the Synod of South Holland drew up a list of "heresies" in Bekker's book that included his claim that spirits were unable to act on each other or on bodies, as well as his insistence that the devil and his evil angels were locked up in hell where they could not deceive or tempt people. The synod also condemned Bekker's contention that biblical stories about evil spirits were to be understood as referring to bad people and illnesses, and his claim that scriptural stories about good angels referred to good people or were a symbolic way of discussing God's behavior toward people. If church ideas about the power of spirits were mistaken, the synod declared, how could one prove that Jehovah was God, that Jesus was the messiah, or that the Bible was the word of God?[73] These questions adequately summed up the fears of many conservatives in the church regarding Bekker's ideas and helped to explain the continuing pursuit of him by the church hierarchy.

The classes of North Holland were not in full agreement with the "heresy test" applied to Bekker's book by the Synod of South Holland, but the Synod of Gelderland adopted the South Holland document for use in training its clergy. The North Holland synods at Amsterdam in 1694, Enkhuizen in 1696, and Edam in 1697 repeatedly failed to convince the States of Holland to ban *The World Bewitched.* The burgomeesters of Amsterdam blocked efforts by the church council to fill the vacancy created by Bekker's dismissal and continued to pay him his full salary. Bekker's book became a best seller, and translations were made into French, English, German, and other languages. To the

---

[73]Knuttel, 308-327; van Sluis 26-27.

great irritation of many in the church, Bekker's ideas continued to spread, and the final two volumes of *The World Bewitched* appeared without any prior permission from the church.

Bekker tried on several occasions to take part in Reformed communion but he was refused both in Jelsum in his native Friesland and in his former congregation at Weesp. Beginning in 1694, Bekker wrote out and distributed to his friends and followers the sermons that he would have given from the pulpit had he been readmitted to his post as pastor. In 1696, he published a series of sermons that discussed the Reformed confession, maintaining that it was not an unchanging rule of belief and that it was certainly of lesser authority than the Bible, a position that harkened back to what he said about funeral orations in his doctoral disputation. For his unflinching opposition to Dutch Reformed confessionalism and for the fighting spirit that he displayed throughout his life, especially during the great debate over spirits, Bekker earned the nickname "the Friesian Hercules" from Johannes Duikerius in his philosophical/ theological novel *Het Leven van Philopater* (The Life of Philopater).[74] Bekker died of pleurisy in June of 1698 at the age of 64 and was buried in Jelsum. The following lines penned by Hendrik Miering could well have served as his epitaph:

Dit is dien Schriftdoorlerde Bekker
Dien heil en toovery ondekker,
Die, hoe getrapt, geterght, noch stil
Zich onderwerpt zyns Heeren Wil
Een man gesont in leer en leven:
Hoe meer verdrukt, hoe meer verheven.[75]

— Hendrik Miering

This is the biblical scholar Bekker,
Of salvation and sorcery the unmasker.
Who, however kicked, provoked, silent still,
Subjected himself to his Lord's will.
A man solid in doctrine and life,
The more oppressed, the more exalted.

[74]Johannes Duijkerius, *Het Leven van Philopater* (Groningen, 1691), modern edition ed. and trans. by Gerardine Marechal (Amsterdam, 1991), 49.
[75]Knuttel, 302-303.

PART TWO

Reaction to Bekker's Ideas

CHAPTER FIVE

Bekker's Opponents:
Confessionalism under Siege and Cartesianism in Crisis

The earliest and most heated opposition to *The World Bewitched* came from the conservative, confessional wing of the Reformed church. Heirs of Gomarus and Voetius, these dogmatic Calvinists saw the Bekker controversy as an important battle in their campaign to protect the Reformed faith from the corrosive influences of Cartesian philosophy and the exegetical methods associated with it. The confessionalists targeted Bekker's biblical exegesis for their harshest criticism, arguing that his figurative interpretation of scriptural passages dealing with spirits cast into doubt the veracity and authority of the entire Bible. They also attacked Bekker's Cartesian ideas and charged that it was his allegiance to the new philosophy that led him into his exegetical errors. In their assault on Bekker's ideas conservatives armed themselves with the biblical literalism that formed the intellectual foundation of Dutch Reformed confessionalism. Again and again they mustered biblical passages that they believed showed the devil's power and the actions of spirits on bodies. Any attempt to interpret passages in a context larger than that provided by the words themselves was anathema to the confessionalists, and violent verbal assaults on Bekker often accompanied these arguments.

While confessionalist opposition to Bekker's position was predictable, criticism that he received from another quarter was more surprising. Bekker's views on spirits also came under attack from a number of theologians who were themselves inclined toward Cartesianism. Although Bekker's use of Cartesian dualism aroused angry opposition to his position on spirits, Cartesian metaphysics ultimately proved to be a two-edged sword in the spirit debate, used both by critics and defenders of traditional belief.

Cartesian dualism appeared to many clerics to be a serious threat to orthodox doctrines concerning spirit belief and divine intervention in the temporal world, but as Cartesianism evolved as a philosophical system the Cartesian distinction between spirit and matter gave rise to serious epistemological and causal difficulties that produced a split within the ranks of Dutch Cartesians. Some adopted a modified version of dualism that avoided these problems and at the same time seemed more compatible with traditional religious belief, including belief in spirits. Others rejected dualism altogether, along with other points of Cartesian metaphysics that were seen as dangerous for religious orthodoxy. A few, like Bekker, retained an unmodified dualism. This internal Cartesian controversy effectively blunted the threat that dualism, and much of the rest of Cartesian metaphysics, posed for traditional religious belief and provided a modified version of dualism for Cartesians to use in defending traditional spirit belief.

Like Bekker's other opponents, his Cartesian critics opposed his scriptural exegesis, but unlike more conservative clerics they did not see Cartesianism as the root of Bekker's errors. While they criticized the way that Bekker used some Cartesian ideas, these critics believed that the new philosophy could be used to support traditional spirit belief. Bekker's Cartesian opponents thus demonstrated that it was not Descartes' metaphysics, Bekker's unique contribution to the spirit debate, that posed the real threat to spirit belief; rather it was Bekker's exegesis that proved the more serious danger for traditional belief and for the biblical literalism that was the underpinning of Dutch Reformed confessionalism. These opponents made it clear that being a Cartesian did not automatically assure one's support for Bekker's cause.

I

Among the most vociferous of Bekker's confessionalist critics was Everhardus van der Hooght (1642-1716). Van der Hooght studied philosophy and theology at the university of Utrecht before becoming Reformed pastor at Knollendam, Marken-Binnen, and Nieuwendam. While he was in Utrecht he was influenced by the sermons of Voetius, Jodocus Lodenstein, and Johannes Teellinck, three leaders of the *Nadere Reformatie*. His own sermons, which were published in 1701 under the title *De Saligheyd der Vreedsaame* (The Salvation of the Peaceful), were influenced by Lodenstein, and in 1697 van der Hooght published ten of Lodenstein's sermons along with a biographical sketch of him entitled *Geestelijke Opwekker* (Spiritual Awakener). While he was pastor at Nieuwendam, van der Hooght spent much time studying and teaching Biblical Hebrew, writing a short Hebrew grammar, and composing a grammatical commentary on the Hebrew text of Psalms 1-10. In 1691-92 van der Hooght published a series of seven letters under the pseudonym Haggebher Philaleethes attacking Bekker's ideas on spirits and accusing him of ignorance of theology and Hebrew.[1] In the fourth letter van der Hooght addressed the question of the nature and actions of good and evil spirits.

According to van der Hooght, the controversy surrounding Bekker pointed out the dangers of making natural reason the interpreter of Scripture. Divine miracles and revelation could not be tested by reason and science. The Bible had to be recognized as a true historical account and interpreted literally or else Scripture would become a mere device to be used for the purposes of others.[2]

When van der Hooght discussed the question of spirits and whether they could act on bodies he argued that the action of spirit on body required a direct touching of the body by the spirit. But spirits were immaterial and thus could not themselves touch

---

[1]D. Nauta, *et. al.* (eds.), *Biografisch Lexicon voor de Geschiedenis van het Nederlandse Protestantisme* (Kampen, 1983), II, 256-257.

[2]Everardus van der Hooght, *Vierde Briev van Haggebher Philaleethees Geschreven aan zijnen Vriend N.N. Over het Weesen, Denken, Willen, Vermogen, ende de Plaats der Engelen, in het gemeen, ende der quade Geesten, in het byzonder. Item, van des menschen Ziele, en hare Werking, hetzij Afgesonderd, ofte ook vereenighte met het Lichaam, ende hoe verre de quade geesten op de selve konnen werken* (Amsterdam, 1691), 59-60.

bodies. For this reason, between the will of the spirit and the body it acted upon there had to be a moving agent, which van der Hooght called the *Tactus Spiritualis ad Corpus*—a "spiritual touching of the body." Using this agent spirits did indeed act on bodies, he asserted, following a Scholastic argument first presented by Thomas Aquinas. They acted on other spirits as well, either by moving them or by speaking to them, van der Hooght continued. Pursuing this line of argument he noted that the Scholastics had several opinions about how one spirit could speak to another. Some said that spirits shared a "natural affinity" and could thus call forth inborn forms or species in each other, while others believed that communication happened in other ways. But even though it could not be known exactly how spirits communicated with each other, biblical passages such as Luke 2 made it clear that such communication did indeed take place, van der Hooght insisted.[3]

Van der Hooght next took up the vexed question of whether spirits could occupy a place. Bekker had denied that spirits could physically be in a place because they were not extended or material things. Van der Hooght, on the other hand, held that spirits could be said to be in a place, although not a bodily place. Spirits could not be in a bodily place because they had no extension, and it was this inability to be in such a place that distinguished spirits from bodies. But if a spirit was in the world it had to be in some place. Although a spirit could not be said to be in a place in the sense of filling it up, it could be said to be in a place in the sense of being limited to it: a spirit could not be in two places at once. Thus a spirit could be said to be in a place "definitively," van der Hooght argued, again following a standard Scholastic distinction. To be in a place definitively a spirit did not have to have a body. This was clear from Augustine's *De anima*: the saint wrote that all that was finite had to be limited to, or defined to be in, a certain place.

It was also clear from the Bible that spirits could be in a place, van der Hooght continued. Scripture often said that spirits moved from one place to another. Bekker had suggested that a spirit could only be said to be in a place with regard to its actions, but how could action in a place occur without the spirit being substantially present in that place? van der Hooght asked. Even though the actions of spirits were as spiritual as their natures, both could be said to be in a place.[4] The question of whether unextended and thus immaterial beings could occupy space touched on the very nature of immateriality itself, and by implication on the question of whether an immaterial being could have contact with and act on a material being. If an immaterial being could occupy space like an extended being then it might share other characteristics of extension as well, and it might thus be able to contact an extended thing.

Moving to a discussion of angels, van der Hooght questioned Bekker's Cartesian assumption that the essence of an angel was thinking. How could an action be the essence of an independently existing thing? he asked. A being's actions were properly considered separate from its nature, van der Hooght continued, again making a Scholastic distinction. Thinking thus had to be considered as distinct from the essence of a spirit. In addition, an angel's essence had to be unified and unchanging, but thinking was manifold and transitory. When God created angels he created more than just thought because angels were the causes and authors of thinking. And van der Hooght added that Scripture distinguished between the essence of angels and their actions in

[3]Ibid., 68-70.
[4]Ibid., 70-72.

such passages as Colossians 1:16, Psalm 104:4, and Hebrews 1:4-7.[5] By rejecting the Cartesian definition of spirit van der Hooght hoped to weaken dualism in order to allow for the activity of spirits on bodies.

When van der Hooght came to the question of the temporal activities of the devil his attack on Bekker sharpened. Bekker gave the appearance of banning Satan from the world, he wrote, but in fact his ideas helped Satan's kingdom to grow and increased the number of atheists. Bekker held that Satan was a spirit—a thinking being—and that he was tightly bound in hell. But how could a being without a body be bound? van der Hooght asked.[6] Although the devil's powers were limited, he could do a great deal on earth, van der Hooght argued. The devil could act on matter distinct from himself through a direct act of local motion or by using an intermediary. With God's permission the devil could make bodily material obey him, and in this way he often worked through other creatures. The devil could do more than people could because he knew more about the hidden powers of nature. His knowledge had grown through long experience, and he had learned a lot from divine revelations when God used him as a tool, for example in Job 1:22.

The devil could correctly guess some future events but he had no supernatural power to foretell the future, nor did he have the supernatural ability for knowledge that the blessed got from God's grace, van der Hooght continued. Angels and prophets knew the future from divine revelation, but the devil did not. And the devil could not know the thoughts or will of angels or men, present or future, with any certainty—he could only guess at this. God alone knew the heart, van der Hooght insisted. Nor could the devil control the human will—again, only God could do that. Finally, concerning things that depended on God's supernatural power, the devil was ignorant.[7]

Despite these limitations on his power there was still a very great deal that the devil could do. He could act on the human soul by bringing intelligible forms into it, thus revealing things to the soul. In this way the devil could place sinful suggestions and temptations before the most pious person, although the devil could not act on the human will in such a way as to actually cause a person to sin. Satan could communicate things directly to the human understanding whether the person were awake or asleep; this was clear from John 13:2, Acts 5:3, II Corinthians 4:4, Luke 22:3, and many other places. By using examples, appearances, reasonings, sorcery, and temptations the devil could act on what the Scholastics called the "sensate soul," man's internal sense that received messages from the external senses and stimulated the imagination. In this way the devil could affect the imagination and memory of people, van der Hooght argued. Satan acted on the imagination in three ways: he could bring forth forms of feeling from the memory into the imagination, he could cause new ideas to come into the imagination, or he could affect the imagination through the sense organs by local motion. In these ways the devil could make people think that they had seen things that they had not really seen.[8]

The devil could not be wounded or murdered by bodily means because he had no body, van der Hooght continued. For the same reason he could experience no pain or desire for sensuous things, nor could he experience corruption or death. Satan had a

[5]Ibid., 64-65.
[6]Ibid., 74.
[7]Ibid., 60-62, 76.
[8]Ibid., 89-93.

completely free will in that he acted according to prior judgement and rational exercise of the will, and even though many of his actions were dependent on God this did not take away his freedom. But the devil's will was bad and could only do bad things, van der Hooght continued. The devil's corruption far surpassed that of evil men, and his will was so hardened in evil ways that it could never intend good. Any good that Satan did occurred because God chose to use him as an instrument for good.[9]

Bekker was wrong to argue that the Reformed church, with its belief in the devil, really believed in two Gods, van der Hooght declared. Bekker "shamed and blamed" the church inappropriately. He did not care about the authority of Scripture or the honor of God, and he showed this when he criticized the treatment of Hebrew accents, words, and letters in the Dutch translation of the Bible. When one started to deny points, letters, and even words, one soon destroyed the entire text of the translation, van der Hooght argued. Bekker hatefully attacked reputable theologians to advance his own ideas, ideas which had not been taught by any orthodox theologian of the church in 1600 years. The result was the commotion and trials that Bekker's book had given rise to. Even the Cartesians had not supported his book, van der Hooght noted.[10] In the end, van der Hooght found nothing redeeming in Bekker's writing, a position that was fairly common among Bekker's literalist critics.

The profound conservatism of many of Bekker's opponents came through clearly in Henricus Brinck's attack on Bekker in *De Godslasteringen van de Amsterdamsche Predikant Dr. Bekker Ter Waerschouwing van alle Vroome in der Lande, Wederleyd In de Vorreden voor de Toot-Steen der Waarheid en der Meyningen* (The God Slanders of the Amsterdam Preacher Dr. Bekker, Refuted in the Preface to the Touchstone of Truth and Meaning, Utrecht, 1691). Brinck attacked not only Bekker's ideas but the very concept of change itself as it applied to religious belief.

Brinck was born in Franeker, the university town of Friesland, in 1645. Educated entirely in his home town, he was admitted to the Reformed ministry by the classis of Franeker in 1667. After serving in Buitenpost and Joure and as a field preacher appointed by the States of Friesland, he was called to a post in Utrecht in 1687. A tireless fighter for what he considered the central principles of the Reformed religion, Brinck was from early in his career an opponent of the influence of Cartesian philosophy in religion. He was a preacher for 55 years, 36 of those at Utrecht, and during that time he wrote against many thinkers whose ideas he considered damaging to religion, including Coccejus and Bekker.[11] Brinck represented a broad base of conservative opinion within the Reformed church that considered any deviation from traditional ideas concerning spirits to be a threat to belief in the truthfulness of Scripture and thus to the very fabric of religion.

In Brinck's view it was wrong to always be looking for "new and strange things" in religion because this made it seem as if there were no solid foundation to the faith. One should not interpret Scripture in a search for constant change, giving holy writ a different meaning from the one given it by orthodox theologians for centuries. This would lead weak believers and unbelievers to conclude that there was no certainty in God's Word. "That which is oldest is also most true," Brinck asserted, adding that those who

---

[9]Ibid., 62-63.
[10]Ibid., 73-74, 95-97.
[11]J.P. de Bie, J. Loosjes, *et. al., Biografisch Woordenboek van Protestantsche Godgeleerden in Nederland* (The Hague, 1903-1949), I, 615-618.

despised the well-known paths often erred. People who sought out the new often fell
into dangerous confusion, so it was much better for Dutch congregations not to abandon the firm and well-tested old belief for the unproven, new paths of Coccejus and
Descartes, Brinck declared.[12]

Brinck saw Bekker as a threat to religion because he was a purveyor of dangerous
novelties. Bekker used the principle of reason to interpret the Bible and thus "dis-
graced the Reformed church in unheard of ways," Brinck declared. Anyone with a
spark of true Christianity and respect for the authority of Scripture was obliged to
reject *The World Bewitched* because Bekker's "excesses" in the book amounted not
simply to errors but to heresies, blasphemies, and slander against God. Bekker openly
rejected scriptural passages that clearly described the temporal activities of angels and
devils, saying that these things could not have happened the way the Bible related
them because the stories contradicted reason. To remove all credibility from such
passages Bekker mocked the Bible in the same way that heathens like Julian the Apos-
tate and Porphry had done in earlier times. Bekker claimed that he was upholding the
honor of God by pointing out that God really did the things that Scripture ascribed to
angels and devils, but God's infallible word clearly stated that angels themselves did
much, and devils not a little, with God's permission, Brinck argued.[13]

In Brinck's view Bekker had held opinions damaging to the Reformed church from
the very beginning of his service to that institution. Many were apprehensive when
Bekker obtained the doctorate in theology before the age of 26 with an inaugural disputation containing theses that contradicted the divine authority of Scripture, Brinck
noted, recalling Bekker's earlier clash with confessionalists in Friesland. In 1670, Bekker
published his adult catechism, the *Vaste Spyse der Volmaakten*, a work that caused
great turmoil in the church because of the dangerous ideas that it contained, Brinck
asserted. In 1671, the Friesian Synod of Bolsward judged that the book contained
novelties, unscriptural ideas, and dangerous opinions unsuited to a catechism intended
to promote unity in the church, Brinck wrote.[14]

In his other works Bekker sought to delude believers into accepting damaging new
ideas, chief among which was his assertion that created spirits could not act on bodily
things. Bekker argued that angels and devils had no bodies and thus had no way to act
on bodily creatures, that they had little knowledge of temporal things because they
possessed no bodily eyes with which to see, and that they could not communicate their
ideas to each other like people did. Bekker ignored the fact that Scripture was full of
stories of the temporal missions, appearances, and actions of angels and devils, Brinck
insisted. Some of these stories Bekker interpreted as referring to men and not spirits,
and still others he claimed could not be interpreted literally because they were written
in a language accommodated to the ignorant prejudices and erroneous opinions of the
common people in biblical times. Despite these assertions, however, Christians seeking to build the salvation of their souls on God's holy word would recognize that
biblical stories of angels and devils could only be understood literally as referring to
good and evil spirits that acted on temporal things, Brinck declared.[15] Any pious

---

[12]Henricus Brinck, *De Godslasteringen van de Amsterdamsche Predikant Dr. Balthasar Bekker Ter
Waarschouwing van alle Vroome in der Lande, Wederleyd In de Vorreden voor de Toet-Steen der Waarheid
en der Meyningen* (Utrecht, 1691), pp. 1-3.

[13]Ibid., 21-23.

[14]Ibid., 24-27.

person could easily see that if Bekker were able to show that biblical stories about the appearances and activities of angels were not true, the next step would surely be to doubt scriptural accounts of the immaculate conception, birth, death, and resurrection of Christ.[16] Brink thus made clear that the central issue involved in the spirit dispute was not the actions of spirits as such but the larger question of the meaning and authority of Scripture.

In Hebrews 1:14 Paul called angels spirits sent to serve those who would be saved, Brinck noted. If angels were sent to serve people, it followed that they would be able to act on the souls and bodies of people. For example, in Luke 1:26-37 the angel Gabriel told Mary of the immaculate conception of Christ. Gabriel was a spirit sent by God who took visible form in order to be seen by the Virgin. The two spoke together and Gabriel gave Mary many reasons in an audible voice. Luke 2:9-15 provided the best history of the birth of Christ, and there it was reported how an angel appeared to the shepherds and a heavenly host of angels sang praise of God. In Matthew 28:2-7 an angel came down from heaven and removed the stone from the door of Christ's tomb, and Acts 1:10-11 described how the Lord ascended into heaven accompanied by two angels in shimmering clothes.

These texts proved beyond a doubt that spirits called angels were sent down among men, assumed bodily form so that they could appear to people, and both knew and spoke with people, Brinck asserted. If it pleased God their voices could be heard over the entire earth and they could show strength beyond that of men. Although spirits did not have the kind of bodies that people used to act, to speak, and to know, the Bible testified that they could do, and indeed had done, all of these things. Bekker provided no good reason to interpret such scriptural places differently, Brinck added. It was clear that these texts were all historical accounts with nothing parabolic about them.[17]

Brinck next took up Bekker's denial of the devil's temporal activities. Just as it could be shown that angels acted among men, Brinck argued, it was easy to prove that devils did so as well. Genesis 3:1-6 told of the temptation of Adam and Eve by the snake, whom the devil made to speak in an audible voice so as to convey treacherous ideas to the first humans. Anyone who understood the Bible knew that this story was an historical account of what actually took place, Brinck asserted. Indeed, the entire book of Genesis was a history of the creation of the world and of man, and of man's fall. Many New Testament writers referred to Genesis as history and said that it was the devil acting through the snake that caused man's fall, Brinck continued. But Bekker tried to throw doubt on the historical accounts written by Moses by finding contradictions in them and by saying that it was neither a snake nor the devil who tempted Eve because snakes by their nature could only hiss and the devil did not have the power to make them talk.[18]

As evidence for his contention that the devil was active among people Brinck referred to a number of Scripture passages: in I Peter 5:8-9 the devil went among people like a roaring lion; in Revelations 2:10 Jesus told the angel of the Smyrna congregation that the devil would imprison and tempt several members of that congregation; in Revelations 12:7 Michael and his angels fought the devil and his angels; in I Corinthians 7:5 it was said that Satan could tempt people; in Acts 26:18 Paul was said

[15]Ibid., 31-32.
[16]Ibid., 36.
[17]Ibid., 33-36.
[18]Ibid., 36-39.

to be under the power of Satan; II Thessalonians 2:9 spoke of the workings of Satan and the coming of the Antichrist; in Acts 19:15-16 an evil spirit was said to jump on people; and Hebrews 2:14 said that the devil had the violence of death.[19] And of course there was also the story of Job, Brinck pointed out. Bekker could not deny that this story spoke of the devil but he tried to distort the text by saying that the devil was mentioned only because he was the origin of all temptation. Bekker also tried to distort the discussion of the devil in Zacharia 3:1-2 by using his very tenuous knowledge of Hebrew, Brinck continued, but Dr. van der Hooght had revealed Bekker's errors of translation in that case.[20]

Bekker painted fear of the devil as an irrational and negative superstition, Brinck continued, but that same fear had often caused people to choose the side of God. If one took away any reason to fear the devil, as Bekker tried to do, some people would not be moved to convert to Christ. Bekker maintained that there was only one devil and that he was chained in hell, and that even if the devil were among people he could not do anything to them because he had no body. With this argument Bekker mocked God, who in his holy word repeatedly told of the appearances and actions of evil spirits. Bekker even claimed that the Reformed church was guilty of the old Manichean heresy because its belief in the power of the devil reduced the omnipotence of God and amounted to belief in two gods. This argument was a slanderous lie, Brinck declared, because no theologians in the Reformed church gave the devil omnipotence or omniscience. They only followed the Bible in recognizing that God allowed evil spirits to be present and to act in the world. Spirits could act on bodies, the devil could do things to help evil people and to harm others, and there could be ghosts and sorcery in the world if God allowed it, Brinck argued. Bekker would never be able to disprove these things because Scripture, reason, and experience were all against him.[21]

Although Bekker pretended to believe in angels and a single imprisoned evil spirit, Brinck charged, he really believed in neither and was secretly a Saducee.[22] Bekker denied the many biblical accounts of spirit possession, devising all sorts of reasons why these things could not have happened the way Scripture said they did. But if one could bully the text in this way then he could make it say whatever he wanted. In order to distort biblical passages to fit his own opinions, Bekker held that Scripture spoke in the erroneous language of the common man, and he also argued that Jesus had thought it best not to tell the Jews that their ideas about spirit possession were wrong. But Christ was an almighty teacher who would never lie to people in this way, Brinck objected. Many Coccejans took a position similar to Bekker's on these issues, he added.[23]

If all Biblical stories mentioning the activities of spirits were put down as concessions to the erroneous understanding of the common people and interpreted in another way by the learned, what would then happen with all the rest of the Bible? Brinck asked. To believe that all the writers of the Old Testament described the activities of spirits in a way that did not actually happen, and to believe that Jesus left in ignorance those who wrongly believed that they were possessed by spirits, contradicted the holiness and sincerity of God upon which human salvation depended, Brinck declared. A true Christian would be horrified even to think such things.[24]

[19]Ibid., 48-50.
[20]Ibid., 52
[21]Ibid., 67-74, 86-87.
[22]Ibid., 84.
[23]Ibid., 89-90.
[24]Ibid., 64-65.

Bekker's ideas were not reconcilable with the authority of Scripture, and if one followed them all sorts of blasphemies would result, Brinck argued. Following Bekker's method of exegesis one could hold that biblical stories of Christ's suffering and death were composed according to the understanding of the masses in order to get them to love God even though God never really had a son who suffered. Even if Bekker maintained that only passages about spirits were written to accommodate the ignorance of the masses and that all other scriptural passages were trustworthy, biblical stories about spirits were often combined with accounts of the life of Christ. Thus, to disbelieve stories about spirits was not far from destroying the authority of the entire Bible, Brinck declared.[25]

By arguing with the Dutch translations of the Bible's Hebrew and Greek words for Satan and the devil, Brinck complained, Bekker put the entire States Translation in doubt, preventing people from basing their salvation on the vernacular text. After all, if the translators had made some mistakes they could have made many others. If the Bible were as seriously questioned as Bekker threatened to do, it could open the way for a return to the kind of heathenism that had been absent from Europe for over a thousand years. Brinck added that Bekker followed in the army of the "cursed Spinoza" who denied God and saw everything as *pars corporis*.[26]

Bekker's exegetical errors arose from his devotion to Cartesian philosophy, Brinck continued. Bekker made reason into an idol, and where Scripture did not agree with his rational ideas he forced it to do so. It was his own mission, Brinck asserted, to "open the eyes of those brothers of Coccejan and Cartesian studies in the church" in order to show them how seriously they erred with such novelties.[27] Reading Holy Scripture had to be done with a faithful respect, accepting whatever interpretation was "indicated by the words in their clearest and simplest sense" ("als de woorden in haare duidelijxste en meest eenvoudige sin komen aan te wijsen"). All orthodox scriptural interpreters followed this path, Brinck added, but Coccejus and his Cartesian friends were not satisfied with this approach.[28] They used human reason to come up with ideas that clearly contradicted what the Bible said, and they tortured and forced God's Word to fit the concepts of their reason, thus giving Scripture a strange new sense. [29]

II

Despite the fact that his confessionalist critics saw Cartesianism as one of the primary sources of Bekker's errors, several of hi s most effective opponents were themselves Cartesians. Cartesianism added new issues to the already complex web of controversy surrounding the temporal activity of spirits, and Cartesians could be found arguing against Bekker's views as well as for them. In addition, Bekker's interjection of new philosophical elements into the spirit debate during the 1690s partially changed the conceptual vocabulary with which issues were formulated and debated.

[25]Ibid., 69-78.
[26]Ibid., 51-72.
[27]Ibid., 87-89.
[28]Ibid., 5-7.
[29]Ibid., 4-10.

The division in the ranks of Cartesians on the issue of spirits reflected the extremely complex relationship that existed between the new philosophy and traditional religious belief. The split on the issue of spirits was also an extension of a divisive philosophical debate among Dutch and French Cartesians concerning the nature and implications of metaphysical dualism, a debate prompted by a powerful critique of Cartesian metaphysics by the French academic skeptic Simon Foucher (1644-1696). Foucher's critique built upon problems with dualism recognized by earlier thinkers, including French philosophers Louis de la Forge and Geraud Cordemoy as well as Dutch Cartesians Johannes Clauberg and Arnold Geulincx. Foucher highlighted serious difficulties of both a metaphysical and an epistemological nature arising from one of the central tenets of Descartes' philosophy, producing a crisis within Cartesianism that threatened its viability as a philosophical system.

In working through this crisis moderate Cartesians developed philosophical positions modifying the Cartesian distinction between spirit and matter, and this modification of dualism in turn became a very effective tool for Cartesians who opposed Bekker's views on spirits. Two of the most lengthy and effective criticisms of Bekker's work came from Cartesians: the *Pneumatica ofte Leer van de Geesten* (Pneumatica or Teaching on Spirits, 1692) by Henricus Groenewegen, and the *Zedige Aanmerkingen Waar in de Gronden en de daar op gebouwde redeneringen van de Wijtberoemde Heer Dr. Balth. Bekker Nopende den Aard en Werkingen der Geesten aan Gods Woort en de Reden getoetst Worden* (Modest Remarks in which the Grounds and Reasonings of the widely-known Dr. Balth. Bekker Concerning the Nature and Actions of Spirits are tested by God's Word and Reason, 1693) by Johannes Aalstius and Paulus Steenwinkel. Both works attacked Bekker's ideas on spirits by modifying Cartesian dualism to support traditional beliefs concerning angels and devils.

Dualism had presented serious religious and philosophical problems for Dutch Cartesians at least as early as Regius's break with Descartes in 1647-1648. Regius held that he could not clearly and distinctly conceive of mind as a substance separate from body, and he suggested that the soul was a modification of body. Regius ended with a broad rejection of Cartesian metaphysics, as did Johannes De Raey. Regius and De Raey nevertheless upheld Cartesian physical theories and other parts of Descartes' philosophy. For both men the philosophical problems of dualism were compounded by the threat to religious orthodoxy that such a distinction implied.

After 1650, the philosophical difficulties arising from dualism became increasingly apparent to those who were concerned with the overall viability of Descartes' thought as a philosophical system. During the 1650s and 1660s French thinkers Louis de la Forge and Geraud Cordemoy, along with Dutchman Johannes Clauberg (who studied with De Raey in Leiden in 1648-1649 before moving on to teach in Germany), began to wrestle with problems arising from Descartes' conception of the relationship between spirit and body. Shortly thereafter these problems exploded in dramatic fashion in France in a controversy that rocked the very foundations of Cartesian philosophy.

Among the difficulties that emerged within Cartesian metaphysics in the 1660s was the problem that dualism of mind and matter could not easily be reconciled with the existence within Cartesianism of epistemological and causal likeness principles derived from Scholasticism. While the likeness principles held that a cause had to be substantially like its effect, a representation substantially like the thing represented, dualism seemed to make this impossible.[30]   This internal contradiction within Cartesianism was dramatically pointed out in 1673 by Simon Foucher, whom historian Richard Watson has called "an eccentric and obscure skeptic." Foucher originated a series of powerful epistemological criticisms of Cartesianism that were to prove a serious problem for the new philosophy, significantly effecting its later evolution as an intellectual system.[31]

Foucher argued that Cartesians who held dualism could give no intelligible account of how the human mind could know the material world. Cartesians believed that ideas were modifications of mind, but according to the likeness principle a representation had to be substantially like the object it represented. How could a mental idea be substantially like the material object it represented when, according to dualism, mind and matter were essentially distinct? Cartesians could not explain how ideas represented objects that they in no way resembled, and yet experience seemed to testify that such non-resembling representation did indeed take place because the mind did have knowledge of the material world.[32]

The contradiction between dualism and the likeness principle presented tremendous problems for Cartesians, and eventually several solutions emerged within the Cartesian camp. The most philosophically radical solution was represented by Spinoza's monism, but the dangerous theological implications of the resulting pantheism prevented this idea from gaining wide acceptance. Two other solutions proved more popular. One was presented by French philosopher Nicolas Malebranche (1638-1715) in his *De La Recherche de la Verite* of 1674, which called upon the power of God to solve the Cartesian crisis. For Malebranche, God was the source of all ideas. God created the material world according to the ideas of material things that he had, and he allowed people to know the material world by sharing these ideas with them. Thus people knew the world only through the mediation of God. In this system ideas were no longer modifications of mind but rather divine archetypes, and human knowledge of the world resulted from God's power and intellect.[33]

More moderate Cartesians developed a different solution to the epistemological problem. Retaining dualism but rejecting the likeness principle, they claimed that non-resembling representation was indeed the basis of human knowledge of the world. But these thinkers also had to appeal to God's power to explain how this was possible. As French Cartesian Robert Desgabets (1605-1678) explained it, it was only through the power of God that an idea that was ontologically unlike its object could still represent it.[34] These revisionists also argued that despite the restrictions placed upon the interaction of spirit and body by dualism, God often miraculously caused the two distinct substances to interact.

The problems of Cartesian dualism and the various solutions to these problems were discussed at length by Dutch thinkers as well. Even before Foucher published his landmark critique the Dutch Cartesian Arnold Geulincx (1624-1669) focussed specifically on problems of causation raised by dualism in his *De virtute et primus eius*

---

[30]Richard A. Watson, *The Downfall of Cartesianism 1673-1712: A Study of Epistemological Issues in Late Seventeenth-Century Cartesianism* (The Hague, 1966), 1-2.

[31]Ibid., 2.

[32]Ibid., 3-4.

[33]Ibid., 49-64; Michael E. Hobart, *Science and Religion in the Thought of Nicolas Malebranche* (Chapel Hill, 1982), 122-125.

[34]Watson, 66-67.

proprietatibus, published in 1665 and translated into Dutch in 1667 as *Van de Hooft-Deuchden; De eerst Tuchtverhandeling* (On the Chief Virtues; The First Treatise on Ethics). Geulincx had become interested in the problems surrounding dualism from discussions he had held with Guilelmus Philippi, his teacher at Leuven University, and from reading the works of De Raey and Clauberg. In his writings Geulincx focussed chiefly on causal rather than epistemological problems raised by dualism.

Dualism held that spirit and matter did not interact, but experience seemed to testify otherwise. Like Malebranche, whose doctrine came to be known as occasionalism, Geulincx believed that God not only knew everything in the world but caused everything in the world as well. For Geulincx, the unbridgeable gap between spirit and matter expressed by Cartesian dualism ruled out any interaction between those two substances even in man, where Descartes allowed it. The human soul was merely an "onlooker" (*toeschouwer*) upon events, having no power to cause any activity or movement in the material world, even in its own body. The soul's willing, itself caused by God, was merely the occasion upon which the Almighty caused the desired movement to occur in body.[35] Thus God was the direct cause of all that happened in the world, and there was no need for secondary causes.

On some points Geulincx's ideas were different from Malebranche's occasionalism. Cornelis Verhoeven has suggested that a better name for Geulincx's philosophy might be "Parallelism," because Geulincx believed that God had arranged the world so that he would not have to intervene on every occasion that something took place. God adjusted the world machine to create a perfect parallelism between the will of spirit and the movement of body, both of which he caused. Geulincx used the analogy of two clocks running parallel—the clock of the will striking when the soul wanted to speak, and at just the same time the clock of the body striking to set the tongue in motion.[36] Geulincx saw the human soul as an observer watching a play written and directed by God, unable to effect the course and operation of events set in motion by God in a kind of intellectual counterpart to Calvinist predestination. Man could only accept life as it was with Stoic resignation.[37]

Because Geulincx was one of the few seventeenth-century authors who wrote philosophical prose in Dutch, his ideas had influence among Dutch Cartesians, especially among those non-professional philosophers outside of the university structure who had limited access to works in Latin. It was precisely this kind of thinker who brought into the spirit debate ideas about dualism similar to those of Geulincx and other Cartesian revisionists. The occasionalism and parallelism of Malebranche and Geulincx seemed to resolve the epistemological and causal problems posed by dualism, at the same time effectively neutralizing dualism as a weapon against various kinds of spirit/matter interaction. For this reason occasionalism and parallelism were ideally suited for Cartesian opponents of Bekker who disagreed with his views on spirits.

Henricus Groenewegen (1640-1692) used a version of occasionalism to argue against Bekker's position on spirits. As a theology student in Leiden, Groenewegen studied under Johannes Coccejus, and at Utrecht he studied under the Cartesian Franciscus

---

[35]Arnold Geulincx, *Van de hoofddeugden: De eerste tuchtverhandeling*, ed. C. Verhoeven (Baarn, 1986), 17-20.

[36]Ibid., 19-20.

[37]Ibid., 21-39.

Burman. From 1667 until his death in 1692 he served as Reformed pastor in Lier, Delfshaven, Enkhuizen, and Utrecht. He led a party of Reformed theologians known as the "Leidse" or "Groene" Coccejans, who prided themselves on following the pure doctrine of Coccejus, as opposed to another group of Coccejans led by D. Fludd van Giffen who favored a more emotional and pietistic preaching similar to that of Voetius. Groenewegen and his followers were known for their learned sermons and allegorical Scripture interpretation, but despite his links to Cartesian and Coccejan circles Groenewegen became a staunch opponent of Bekker's ideas on spirits.[38] His position shows that even among some Cartesians and Coccejans traditional ideas died hard. In his *Pneumatica*, Groenewegen dealt with the problems posed by dualism in much the same way as Geulincx and other Cartesian revisionists had, using these arguments to support traditional beliefs about the temporal activities of angels and devils.

Like both Descartes and Bekker, Groenewegen held that spirits were substances essentially distinct from matter, but he nevertheless argued that spirits and bodies "can, in a certain relative respect, act on each other" (zij door een zeker relatie opsight...op malkander kunnen werken).[39] He then went on to explain how this interaction was possible.

Groenewegen began by arguing that the likeness principle did not really explain causation. When one body collided with and seemed to move another body, it was assumed that movement was transferred from the first body to the second by the natural application of like substance to like substance. Spirits, then, could not move or affect bodies because the two were unlike in substance. But Groenewegen argued that the likeness principle did not really explain what caused a body to move when another body contacted it. Was it the actual substance or extension of the first body that caused the second to move, or was it some quality of the first body, or was it perhaps something else? For Groenewegen there was only one possible explanation for what caused one body to act on another body: the power of God. And it was likewise the power of God that allowed spirits to act on bodies. God was the first and only mover of all things, Groenewegen held.[40] Spirit did not act on body directly, through its substance, as indeed neither did body. Rather, a spirit acted on a body through its will. "Between this will and its object God has established such a relationship that upon the will of the spirit a movement follows in the body," Groenewegen wrote.[41] "Out of the strength of God's will come all actions," he declared.[42]

Even though God himself had nothing essential in common with body, he acted on body, Groenewegen argued. Just as God's power made it possible for him to act on body, so too this power could cause any created spirit to do likewise. In fact it was not even true that spirit and body had nothing in common: "They are both creatures of God, regulated toward each other by God and standing in a closely-bound relationship to each other."[43]

When he turned to the question of angels and devils Groenewegen argued that angels "can act in a miracle that happens in bodily nature."[44] Concluding that both good and

---

[38]D. Nauta, *et. al.*, eds., III (Kampen, 1988), 151-154.

[39]Henricus Groenewegen, *Pneumatica, ofte leer van de Geesten, Zijnde Denkende en Redelijke Wesens, in Welk Bewesen word, dat de zelve Geesten, en wel bijsonder Engelen, zoo Goede als Quade, Oefenen dadelike werkingen, volgens haren natuur, op Lichamen* (Enkhuizen, 1692), vol. III, 20-22.

[40]Ibid., 28-34, 72.

[41]Ibid., 34-41.

[42]Ibid., 41-42.

[43]Ibid., 42-43.

[44]Ibid., 72.

bad angels acted on humans by way of divine miracles, Groenewegen set himself in
opposition to Bekker. Some people of "erroneous learning" poked fun at miracles and
the actions that Scripture ascribed to angels, he continued. They said that the Bible
spoke only figuratively when it said that angels acted on human beings. But if spirits
really could not act on bodies it would make a mockery of scriptural testimony that
angels were created to serve man and honor God, and it would make a liar of the Bible
where it spoke of the actions of angels toward men.[45] It was God's normal practice to
make good and evil spirits act on each other and on bodies because spirits were instruments of divine grace and punishment toward man.[46] Satan was not shut up in the
abyss of hell in such a way that he could not act on people on earth, Groenewegen
argued. Many places in the Bible showed the active working of the devil and evil
spirits on people to tempt or to distress them, he added. [47]

A work similar to Groenewegen's was the *Zedige Anmerkingen* of Johannes Aalstius
and Paulus Steenwinkel. Aalstius (1660-1712) was a Reformed pastor at Hoornaar
who had studied at Leiden and who later taught philosophy in Middelburg. He was
much influenced by the ideas of Geulincx, and his writing and teaching were instrumental in the spreading of Cartesianism in The Netherlands. Steenwinkel (1662-1740)
was a Reformed minister at Schelluinen who had studied theology at Utrecht. He was
an important Cartesian/Coccejan who was nevertheless opposed to Bekker's ideas on
spirits.[48] Together, Aalstius and Steenwinkel wrote their book not only to refute Bekker's
Cartesian arguments about spirits but also to maintain that Bekker was not a true Cartesian, again linking the spirit debate to internal Cartesian controversies.

Aalstius and Steenwinkel agreed with Descartes and Bekker that spirits were beings
entirely distinct from matter, but they rejected Bekker's claim that spirits could therefore not act on bodies. There were many occasions reported in the Bible on which
angels visibly appeared to people, they noted. When angels appeared to people they
did so in bodily form, because people could not see that which had no body. This
meant that when an angel appeared it must have taken on a body to do so, and thus for
a time the angel controlled and acted on a body. But how could pure spirits act on
bodies? Aalstius and Steenwinkel asked.

Spirits could act only through their will, and it was not an easy thing for the will of
a spirit to affect a body. The human soul acted on its body only because God allowed
it to do so, and it was the same with angels and devils: the ability of a spirit to act on a
body was a miracle of God.[49] God caused actions in bodies to follow upon the will of
spirits, Aalstius and Steenwinkel argued. For this reason, the actions that the Bible
ascribed to angels could be called their actions in the same sense that the actions of
people were called their actions. In support of this argument Aalstius and Steenwinkel
referred to ideas and passages from the work of Geulincx. Bekker's "errors" showed
that he was no true Cartesian, they added.[50] Indeed, Aalstius and Steenwinkel insisted
that they had used "true" Cartesianism to refute Bekker's ideas.[51]

[45]Ibid., 73-76.
[46]Groenewegen, vol. II, 1.
[47]Groenwegen, vol. III, 1-32.
[48]Nauta, Vol I, 26, 359-360.
[49]Johannes Aalstius and Paulus Steenwinkel, *Zedige Aanmerkingen waar in de Gronden en de daar op
gebouwde redeneringen van de Wijtberoemden Heer Dr. Balth. Bekker, Nopende den Aard en Werkingen der
Geesten aan Gods Woort en de Reden getoetst worden* (Dordrecht, 1693), 151-159.
[50]Ibid., 162-167.
[51]Ibid., 171-175.

When they turned to biblical accounts of the actions of angels and devils, Aalstius and Steenwinkel disagreed with Bekker's claim that such accounts often had to be interpreted figuratively. All of the actions that the Bible ascribed to angels could justly be called their actions so long as it was remembered that these actions were only possible through the intervention of God. "There is no reason to shut angels out of this world and rob believers of help," they continued, adding: "We believe that angels do not only honor God in heaven, they also serve men on earth through their will and God's help."[52] As for the devil, Aalstius and Steenwinkel did not agree with Bekker that he was forever harmlessly chained in hell. How could chains hold spirits? they asked, echoing van der Hooght. And if the devil was bound in hell, who tempted Eve? To deny the devil's actions on earth went against all accepted ideas, they declared, adding that Bekker had no real proof to back up such a claim.[53]

Arguments such as these did not catch Bekker by surprise. The eclectic nature of Dutch Cartesianism and the need of its adherents to prove their religious orthodoxy created a situation in which division of opinion among Cartesians was natural on issues far less sensitive than spirit belief. Bekker was thus prepared for the arguments against his position presented by his Cartesian opponents, and in replying to these arguments he entered in a limited way into the internal Cartesian debate over dualism.

In chapter seven of book two of *The World Bewitched*, a chapter that he added during the summer of 1691 specifically to reply to criticisms such as those made by Groenewegen and Aalstius/Steenwinkel, Bekker rejected the revisionist argument that God miraculously caused spirit and body to interact even though this was otherwise impossible. [54] It was wrong to believe that spirits could do something simply because God could make them do it by giving them special powers above and beyond the nature that they were created with, Bekker argued. In a discussion concerning the actions of spirits it was simply beside the point to argue that God could do things in or through spirits that spirits themselves could not do. When one considered the capabilities and activities of creatures such considerations had to be based on the nature that God had created in them. It was not helpful to appeal to miracles in such cases. If the question were whether or not a horse could fly, Bekker continued, it would not be helpful to answer yes because God could make it fly. The question at issue was not what God could do, but what a horse could do. It would be the same with the question of whether an ass could speak. Just because God might once have made an ass speak this did not mean that asses spoke. When scientists investigate nature, Bekker argued, they do not investigate how God's power could change it: how he could make trees grow on the sea or ships sail on mountains. Scientists examine how nature operates according to the laws that God created in nature, because:

The influence and pairing of God's power with that of secondary causes maintains and directs each creature according to its nature. God created everything with its

---

[52]Ibid., 176-223.

[53]Ibid., 70-97

[54]In a reply to Aalstius and Steenwinkel published in 1693, Bekker said that he had added a chapter between chapters VI and VII of book two in order to directly address the actions of spirits. See Balthasar Bekker, *Brief van Balthasar Bekker S.T.D. en Predikant tot Amsterdam Aan twee eerwardige Predikanten, D. Joannes Aalstius tot Hoornaar Ende D. Paulus Steenwinkel tot Schelluinen Over derselver Zedige Aanmerkingen Op een deel des tweeden Boex van sijn Werk genaamd De Betoverde Weereld* (Amsterdam, 1693), 6-7.

own nature, and he maintains everything according to its own nature. This we daily see in the direction of divine providence, according to which God calls forth rain and sunshine upon the earth to make it ready to bear fruits and sustain men and beasts....If you want spirits to act on other spirits or bodies, you have to ask whether their nature and inborn essence allows this.[55]

Bekker thus maintained that God worked through the ordinary laws of nature, and active secondary causes ("werkende onderoorzaken") such as spirits had to have a nature that would permit them to do what people claimed that they did. Like many English Newtonians, Bekker stressed the regularity of the laws of nature and de-emphasized the possibility of divine intervention that could miraculously abrogate those laws. For him it made little sense to say that the nature of spirit and body made their interaction impossible, but God caused them to interact anyway. God did not produce contradictions, Bekker maintained: he would not make something both black and white, both light and dark at the same time. Likewise, God would not produce something with a defined nature and then cause it to act contrary to that nature. Thus Bekker rejected the avenue taken by Cartesian revisionists to deal with problems posed by dualism. By appealing to the traditional Dutch Cartesian device of separating reli-gion from philosophy Bekker tried to remove the whole issue of divine power from the debate over dualism and the actions of spirits. It was a strikingly naturalistic, even secularistic, argument.

Bekker made it clear, however, that he was not questioning God's omnipotence. God could indeed work through all creatures, and he of course had the power to make anything happen. But just because something was possible did not mean that God would necessarily do it. Thus while Bekker did not rule out miracles, he put little stress on God's providence operating outside of the ordinary laws of nature.[56]

When Bekker discussed the actions of angels as described in the Bible, he at times approached the position that God was the direct cause of all. When he considered Genesis 33:29-32, where an angel was said to wrestle with Jacob, and Genesis 19, where God used an angel to destroy Sodom and Gomorrah, Bekker held that these passages had to be interpreted figuratively because they really described actions done by God, not by angels. The same was true of other passages where angels were named in God's work, Bekker argued, explaining that he wanted to preserve the honor of these actions for God.[57] It is not clear from these passages whether Bekker believed that God acted in these instances through angels as tools or directly, in place of the interaction of spirit and body, as occasionalists believed. The fact that in other places Bekker rejected God's miraculous intervention to cause the interaction of spirit and body would seem to indicate that he tended toward the latter position. He did not, however, expand upon or generalize from these few examples.

By rejecting the argument that spirit and body interacted through a miracle of God, Bekker dismissed his critics' appeal to divine power to uphold traditional ideas about spirits. He also rejected the charge that he was not a true Cartesian. In a reply to Aalstius and Steenwinkel published in 1693, Bekker maintained that he was indeed a true

---

[55]Balthasar Bekker, *De Betoverde Weereld, Zynde een Grondig Onderzoek van 't gemeen gevoelen aangaande de Geesten, deselver Art en Vermogen, Bewind en Bedrijf; als ook 't gene de Menschen door deselver kraght en gemeenschap doen* (Amsterdam, Daniel van Dalen, 1691), II, 39-40.

[56]Ibid., 38. Margaret Jacob, *The Newtonians in the English Revolution* (Ithaca, NY, 1976), 61-107.

[57]Bekker, *De Betoverde Weereld*, II, 60-61, 64-65.

Cartesian even though he deviated on some points from the teachings of the master. To follow Descartes completely on all matters would itself not be Cartesian because it would be contrary to the basic principles of rational inquiry that lay at the heart of Descartes' philosophy, Bekker argued ("Doch dus hard Cartesiaansch te zijn is niet Cartesiaansch").[58] Bekker had been an advocate and defender of Cartesian ideas since early in his career. Nevertheless, his refusal to use the mechanism of divine intervention to uphold traditional religious ideas as other Cartesians did might be considered surprising coming from a minister of the Reformed church. It showed, perhaps, that Bekker was less willing than other Cartesians to discount dualism or to attempt to explain away its logical consequences. It also shows that Bekker's chief interest in Cartesian metaphysics did not revolve around its viability as a philosophical system but rather its usefulness as a weapon against Dutch Reformed confessionalism.[59]

III

A more radical Cartesian critic of Bekker was the Amsterdam merchant and philosopher Willem Deurhoff (1650-1717). Deurhoff used arguments drawn from occasionalism to defend belief in the temporal activity of spirits, but his ideas were so unconventional that many conservatives believed that he actually favored Bekker's position. Deurhoff's ideas were attacked by the Cartesian Willem van Blyenberg, who criticized his positions both on spirits and on the relationship between body and soul in man. The disagreements between Deurhoff and van Blyenberg showed that the two men stood on different sides of the Cartesian debate over dualism as well as at opposite extremes of the spirit controversy. Deurhoff's ideas were also attacked by several conservative Calvinists who believed that his Cartesian arguments were simply an indirect effort to defend Bekker's position. So controversial were some of Deurhoff's more radical claims that his ideas became a second focal point of the spirit controversy. Rather than welcome Deurhoff as a supporter in the struggle against *The World Bewitched*, Bekker's confessionalist critics saw him as a threat nearly as dangerous as Bekker himself, a fact that highlighted the ambiguous role that Cartesianism played in the spirit debate.

Deurhoff was more controversial than most Dutch Cartesians in part because his thought and his career were very different from those of the typical academic Cartesian. He was by profession a merchant whose interest in philosophy and theology arose from family connections as well as from his own intellectual curiosity, but Deurhoff had no formal training in either field. Nevertheless, he read and wrote widely in both areas, collected a group of followers, and developed a number of radical positions. Unlike most Dutch academic Cartesians, he made no effort to separate religion from philosophy, which itself made his work highly controversial.

Deurhoff was born in Amsterdam in 1650 and was brought up in his father's business. Although his parents never encouraged him to get any formal education, he had family links to the world of intellectual life that fostered in him an interest in ideas. His

---

[58]Bekker, *Brief*, 7.
[59]See Andrew Fix, "Hoe Cartesiaans was Balthasar Bekker?" *It Beaken: Tydskrift fan de Fryske Akademy* 58: 2-3 (1996), 118-135.

mother's brother was Arnold Senguerd, teacher of philosophy in Utrecht and later in Amsterdam. Arnold's son Wolphard Senguerd taught philosophy at Leiden University for 19 years until his death in 1724. Deurhoff's early interest was in history and po-etry, but later in life his interest turned to philosophy and theology.[60]

Although Deurhoff was interested in the ideas of Descartes, he had an independent mind that would not allow him to accept Cartesian doctrine in its entirety without thorough examination. In 1682 this examination led him to write his first book, a commentary on Descartes' *Meditations*. In the years that followed Deurhoff wrote a number of his own works on philosophy and theology, six of which were published by Jan ten Hoorn in Amsterdam between the years 1684-1701. In these works Deurhoff created his own philosophical system by combining ideas from Descartes, Spinoza, Geulincx, and other thinkers, adding his own interpretations and nuances. While it perhaps cannot be said that Deurhoff mastered the complex and often intricate philo-sophical systems of these thinkers, he did creatively combine many of their ideas into a unique philosophy capable of winning its own adherents.[61]

Despite his interest in philosophy, Deurhoff made his living not from writing or teaching but from operating his father's shop. Even while he was busy in the shop, however, he did not abandon his intellectual pursuits. He wrote almost all of his pub-lished works at the business counter of his shop. When customers, friends, or neighbors visited the shop they found him hard at work on his writing, and he often kept right on with this work as he talked with them about business matters. One can hardly resist the image of Deurhoff behind his counter, showing his wares as he tells his customers about the essential difference between thought and extension.[62]

Over the years Deurhoff collected a group of friends and family who met together with him once a week at his home to study and discuss philosophy. In the early years the group usually met on Tuesday evenings, and Deurhoff and his friends took turns giving talks on theological or philosophical topics. It soon became apparent, however, that Deurhoff was progressing much faster than his friends in the understanding of difficult philosophical problems. It was therefore not long before Deurhoff came to dominate the meetings with his own ideas and personality, and the practice of giving the talks was handed over entirely to him. Soon, his friends had become his disciples.

In 1692 Deurhoff became involved in the Bekker controversy when he received a letter from Willem van Blyenberg, Dordrecht city councillor and correspondent of Spinoza, asking for his opinion of Bekker's ideas. The correspondence between the two men that resulted was published the same year by Jan ten Hoorn under the title *Klaare en beknopte verhandeling van de natuur en werking der menschelijke zielen, Engelen en Duivelen* (Clear and brief Discussion of the Nature and Actions of Human Souls, Angels and Devils). In his first letter to van Blyenberg, Deurhoff expressed dismay over the uproar surrounding Bekker's book. According to Deurhoff, many of the writings both for and against Bekker had been "trifling," and as a result much confusion had arisen about spirits and their temporal activities. His own ideas on spirits were different from those both of Bekker and his opponents, Deurhoff pro-claimed, and he proceeded to outline those views.[63]

[60]Koningklijke Bibliotheek manuscript #128, G1,II; part two, 7.
[61]Ibid, 8.
[62]Ibid., 69-70.
[63]Willem Deurhoff and Willem van Blyenberg, *Klaare en Beknopte Verhandeling van de Natuur en Werking der Menschelijke Zielen, Engelen en Duivelen* (Amsterdam, 1692), 3-4.

Deurhoff saw God as the sole cause of all actions in the universe and he considered all creatures to be effects of God without power to be causes. It was impossible for one creature to act on or cause something to take place in another creature. From this Deurhoff concluded that a spirit, be it an angel or a devil, could not act on anything outside itself.[64]

Like Bekker, Deurhoff began his examination of spirits with the human soul, but with very different results. Despite the fact that experience seemed to prove that the human soul did indeed act on its body, Deurhoff argued that an investigation into the nature of body and soul would show this not to be the case. The soul was an immaterial thing that consisted of "consciousness" ("meewustheid"), while bodies had a nature consisting of length, breadth, and depth. Movement was not part of the nature of body because body was entirely passive and did not act on or cause anything. Thus the motions of the body were caused by God. The soul, on the other hand, did not even exist independently but rather depended on God for its very being. But the soul did have the ability to know the body and the "imaginations and reflections" of the body, and it was the soul's knowledge of the body that united body and soul in man. It was clear, however, that body and soul could not act on each other or be united in any other way, Deurhoff argued. The immaterial soul could not be in a place nor touch any body. One could only figuratively say that the soul moved the body, for in reality all movement of bodies was caused by God.[65] Deurhoff thus adopted an extreme monotheism similar to Bekker's and an occasionalism much like that of Geulincx, but with his own ideas added.

Deurhoff explained the interaction of bodies in a similar fashion. When a body moved close to and touched another body, it was assumed that the first body was the cause of movement or changes in the second body. Thus the sculptor was called the cause of the statue, and all movements that resulted from the contact of human parts were attributed to man as cause. Man was said to speak, to stand, to go, and the like. But in reality all bodies were passive and could not act on each other, Deurhoff reiterated, in an argument resembling that of Groenewegen. All bodily movements depended directly on God.[66]

Deurhoff departed from other occasionalists when he claimed that it was because man's soul knew the activity of the body that such actions could rightly be ascribed to man. Deurhoff argued that if he struck a man with a sword, that action was his only in so far as his soul was aware of it and approved it. Without this awareness and approval the action was not his. The soul was thus said to do good or bad things only insofar as it knew the activities of the body and approved of them, Deurhoff maintained.[67]

When he turned to angels and devils Deurhoff argued that because they were spirits like the human soul they could be said to act in the same way that the soul acted, not by causing effects in bodies but rather by knowing the activity of their own bodies. Angels and devils possessed bodies, although not bodies of flesh like human bodies, he continued. They knew the "imaginations and reflections" of their bodies and they were aware of and approved or rejected the actions that God caused in their bodies. Thus they could be said to be the authors of these actions in the same way that men were said to be the authors of their actions. It was this argument that led many conservatives to conclude that Deurhoff actually defended Bekker's views.

[64]Ibid., 6-7.
[65]Ibid., 7-11.
[66]Ibid., 13-14.
[67]Ibid., 13-14.

When Eve was deceived by the snake in Eden the devil knew and approved of those actions, Deurhoff argued. The devil's knowledge and approval of the snake's actions made Satan the tempter and deceiver. Deurhoff took another case in point from II Chronicles 19:35, the story of the angel that the Lord sent to strike down 185,000 soldiers of the Assyrian army. All of these soldiers really died of a plague that came from a certain condition of the air, Deurhoff argued. As the angel in its body moved toward the army it pushed part of the pestilential air in front of it and the air surrounded and killed the soldiers. God arranged this combination of events but the angel knew and approved, and thus it could be said that the angel struck down the soldiers. Angels and devils did the things that the Bible ascribed to them in just the same sense as humans did anything. Indeed, to deny that spirits acted on things outside of themselves was clearly against the word of God, Deurhoff concluded.[68]

In his reply to Deurhoff, the more orthodox Cartesian Van Blyenberg upheld dualism of spirit and body but also insisted that the two substances interacted in man. Souls as thinking beings were completely different from bodies as extended beings, he argued, but nevertheless the soul received thoughts from the body and moved the body.[69] Van Blyenberg agreed with Deurhoff that God was the ultimate cause of everything and that creatures were only effects, but he argued that God sometimes worked through secondary or intermediate causes. While Deurhoff maintained that creatures could only be effects and never causes, van Blyenberg argued that this would mean that the soul could not be said to think independently from God. Thus while he agreed with Deurhoff that creatures could never be first causes independent of God, van Blyenberg insisted that the human soul as well as other spirits could act on each other and on other creatures as secondary causes.[70]

Van Blyenberg rejected Deurhoff's contention that the union of body and soul consisted only in the soul knowing the ideas and sensations of the body. It seemed impossible, he argued, that the soul could know the ideas and sensations of the body without acting on the body. If one considered the soul and body in the abstract and according to their natures—the one as material, the other as immaterial—they did not seem to have anything in common with each other nor any relationship to each other. But experience taught the contrary, van Blyenberg insisted. The fact that the soul had knowledge of the body was evidence that the soul did indeed act on the body, he contended.[71]

Van Blyenberg also took issue with Deurhoff's claim that all human actions were done by God and were only called man's actions because his soul knew and approved them. This would mean that when a murder was committed it was God, not man, who killed. How could a judge punish anyone for murder under these circumstances? van Blyenberg asked. If a person's soul knew and disapproved of a bad action carried out by its body, was the person still to be punished for that act? And if a person's soul knew and approved of a bad act carried out by someone else was the first person also guilty of that act? If the soul was simply a "passive observer" of deeds that God carried out, what place was left for reason and morality? van Blyenberg asked.[72]

[68]Ibid., 15-16.
[69]Ibid., 19-20.
[70]Ibid., 23-25.
[71]Ibid., 31-35.
[72]Ibid., 36-38.

Van Blyenberg strongly disagreed with Deurhoff's contention that the devil deceived Eve because he knew and approved of the actions of the snake. Where did the deceit come from? he asked. Surely not from the body of the snake, since body could not make intelligible utterances. The deceit came from the devil, a spirit, who merely used the snake body as a tool. John 8:44 said that the devil was a murderer and liar from the beginning, not that he simply knew and approved of murders and lies. The devil clearly acted on Eve as the originator of this deceit, van Blyenberg insisted.[73]

In reply to van Blyenberg, Deurhoff again denied that the human soul could move its body. He stated that even though the will of the soul preceded the movement of the body this did not mean that the soul moved the body. Both will and movement were caused by God, Deurhoff asserted, completing the occasionalist equation. He rejected van Blyenberg's contentions about secondary causation, insisting that God was the one and only cause and that every creature was totally dependent on him.[74] "Neither human souls nor angels and devils can act on any body or spirit distinct from them," he declared, a statement that misled some to believe that Deurhoff actually agreed with Bekker despite his claims of opposition to *The World Bewitched*.[75]

Responding to van Blyenberg's questions regarding morality, Deurhoff said that when a person's body committed murder and the soul knew and approved of the action, the person and not God was guilty of the murder even though God was the ultimate cause of it. This was because the guilt rested not with the action itself but with the moral evil of the approving soul. Deurhoff went on to make the stunning claim that if a person's body killed another person but the soul disapproved, the person was not guilty of murder. He also maintained that a person was guilty of murder if his soul approved such an act by another person or even if it enjoyed a person's death.[76]

Deurhoff concluded by reminding van Blyenberg that passages in the Bible that appeared to show the soul and other spirits acting on bodies had to be interpreted in a figurative way. God intended Scripture to be the salvation of all people, both educated and uneducated, Deurhoff wrote, and for this reason Scripture often used language that ordinary persons could understand. Passages that could be understood literally should be taken as the key for deciphering the figurative meaning of other passages, Deurhoff claimed, making use of the doctrine of accommodation much as did Bekker.[77]

Deurhoff's use of the doctrine of accommodation, as well as other of his Cartesian-inspired ideas, aroused the anger of Bekker's opponents even though he used occasionalist arguments to criticize Bekker and uphold traditional spirit belief. Even though some of Bekker's opponents charged that Deurhoff actually supported Bekker, it was clear from a letter written by Deurhoff to the Utrecht Reformed minister Henricus Brinck in 1693 that Deurhoff himself believed that his ideas were opposed to Bekker's position on spirits. In the letter he argued that his ideas properly limited the activities of created spirits according to their natures whereas Bekker did not do so because he believed that the human soul really acted on its body.[78]

---

[73]Ibid., 38-40.
[74]Ibid., 46-50.
[75]Ibid., 51.
[76]Ibid., 60-61.
[77]Ibid., 58-59.
[78]Willem Deurhoff and Henricus Brinck, *Vervolg van de Klaare en Beknopte Verhandeling van de Natuur en Werking der Menschelijke Zielen, Engelen en Duivelen* (Amsterdam, 1693), 43-44.

Nevertheless, the hypersensitivity of the confessional party to exegetical issues and to what they perceived as the threat of Cartesianism led Brinck and others to pounce on Deurhoff. In a letter written to Deurhoff in 1692, Brinck complained that it was not clear from Deurhoff's correspondence with van Blyenberg whether Deurhoff agreed or disagreed with Bekker's views on spirits. Brinck accused Deurhoff of giving himself over to the new philosophy of Descartes even though he understood "better than most" the dangerous consequences of that philosophy.[79] Even those who opposed Bekker's ideas while at the same time upholding Cartesianism were guilty of serious error, Brinck charged, because they maintained that the soul acted on the body and that other spirits acted on things outside themselves only because God coordinated the thinking of the spirit with the movements of the body. This idea "robbed the soul and other spirits of all reality and activity" Brinck charged.[80]

Scripture refuted Deurhoff's claims that creatures were only effects that could not act or cause anything, Brinck asserted. In many places the Bible clearly said that creatures acted: the sun was said to spread its light, many real actions were attributed to the animals of the earth, and the Bible often spoke of the actions of good and evil spirits. God put the strength of movement in creation and the creatures that possessed this strength caused changes that took place in other creatures. Scripture ascribed many actions to man: he built the earth's surface (Genesis 2:5), spilled human blood (Genesis 9:6), built the tower of Babel (Genesis 11:5), made offerings (Leviticus 5:4), and much more. Thus it clearly contradicted Scripture to maintain that all things that men were said to do were really done by God through the human body, and that the human soul had no role in these actions except being conscious of them, Brinck wrote. The Bible said that the human soul blessed another (Genesis 27:4-9), cleaved to another in love (Genesis 34:7, 44:30), left the dying (Genesis 35:18), refused another counsel (Genesis 49:6), and sinned (Leviticus 4:2, Numbers 15:27).[81]

Brinck especially took issue with Deurhoff's use of the principle of accommodation in Scriptural interpretation. There were many biblical texts that clearly showed that the soul acted on the body. It was not acceptable to dismiss these passages by saying that they employed the language of the common people and thus could only be understood figuratively. All Christians who had ever read Scripture agreed that the soul acted on the body. On the other hand, Brinck continued, no scriptural support could be found for denying the activity of the soul and all secondary causes, as Deurhoff did. Genesis said that God made all creatures with the power to live and to grow, and thus also to act, Brinck declared.[82]

Brinck also rejected Deurhoff's claim that because God caused all action without the cooperation of secondary causes the soul merely had knowledge of the "ideas and imaginations" of the body. When the soul had this knowledge, whose action was it? he asked. Was the soul's act of knowing not the action of a secondary cause? Or was the soul an independent cause like God? And if the immaterial soul could not act on the body nor the body on the soul, as Deurhoff claimed, then how could the soul have

[79]Ibid., 6-7.

[80]Ibid., 7-8. Surprisingly, however, Brinck implied that Deurhoff himself did not hold these occasionalistic ideas. He claimed instead that Deurhoff recognized the absurdity of this position and therefore denied that angels and devils acted on things outside themselves. Brinck thus vented his anger toward Cartesianism by casting Deurhoff on the same side of the spirit controversy as Bekker.

[81]Deurhoff and Brinck, 8-10.

[82]Ibid., 11-13.

knowledge of the body? Brinck asked, echoing Foucher's criticism. "Your new philosophy has really gotten you into a mess," he wrote to Deurhoff. "You deny that the soul acts on body, but when you say it gets knowledge from the body you must agree that the body acts on the soul."[83]

In Job 30:19 and Proverbs 6:26 the Bible called man's soul noble and valuable, Brinck continued, but Deurhoff discounted the soul by claiming that it was only "an observer." Deurhoff said that the soul was noble for what it knew, Brinck added, but in Deurhoff's view the soul could not even stop the body from doing a bad deed. In Deurhoff's theory it was hard to see how a man did anything, Brinck added. Could an action really be attributed to a man simply because his soul knew and approved it? Then a man could be said to have done everything that he knew! This was also the way Deurhoff ascribed actions to angels and devils, Brinck continued, but such ideas "offended the true and simple meaning" of the Bible and contradicted the truths of belief. If immaterial things could not act on bodies then God, who was a spirit, could not act on bodies. On the other hand, if God really did all things that bodies seemed to do this would make God the author of sin. And if a person were only guilty of a bad action if his soul knew and approved of it, how could the government punish the wrongdoer who said that God made his body do the action and his soul only approved of it before he knew that the action would have a bad outcome? Brinck asked.[84]

No Christian doubted that God was the highest cause, Brinck concluded, but God made creatures to act in accordance with the nature and power that he gave them. Deurhoff ruled out all secondary causes and thought that his ideas were so great that only he could save the world from error, Brinck chastised. In this way Deurhoff was "just like Bekker, who entitled his book *The World Bewitched* and assumed that only its arguments could un-bewitch the world." Deurhoff called his opponents slanderers, Brinck added, but if Deurhoff believed his own ideas it was not his critics but God who wrote against him![85]

Thus the tremendous bile that moved the confessional party to bitter opposition against Bekker spilled over even onto critics of Bekker's views if those critics threatened biblical literalism or showed sympathy for Cartesian dualism. In his letter of 1692, Brinck accused Deurhoff of holding Socinian ideas, and in 1693 Brinck took this charge against Deurhoff to the Reformed church council of Amsterdam. Deurhoff appeared before the council to defend himself against the charges of Socinianism in December of 1693, and again in January, 1694. Guilhelmus Anslaar, an ally of Deurhoff who had influence on the council, managed to convince his fellow members not to take action against Deurhoff, but after Anslaar died in July of 1694 Deurhoff's enemies brought the matter before the council once again. Over the next five months Deurhoff presented no fewer than three separate written defenses of his ideas to the church council, but the members were not satisfied. Angry and frustrated, in June of 1695 Deurhoff resigned from the Reformed church. Later in 1695 he published an account of his dealings with the council entitled *Geloofs-onderzoek van de Eerw. Kerkenraad van Amsterdam; de goede zaak van Willem Deurhoff* (Faith Examination of the Honorable Church Council of Amsterdam; the Good Case of Willem Deurhoff).[86]

---

[83]Ibid., 14-18.
[84]Ibid., 19, 22-24.
[85]Ibid., 25-30.
[86]Ibid., 20-26.

Deurhoff's troubles with the Reformed church council formed an ironic parallel to Bekker's confrontation with the church during the same years. It was a measure of the extreme fear that conservative Calvinists had for Bekker's exegetical and philosophical ideas that this fear moved them to action even against Deurhoff. Cartesian defenders of Reformed orthodoxy who used revisionist arguments to criticize Bekker's position on spirits thus found themselves in an ambiguous position in the spirit debate. Their arguments were often met with suspicion or even with open hostility on the part of conservative clerics.

Cartesian metaphysics supplied arguments to both sides in the spirit debate, and at the same time drew criticism from many quarters. Cartesians were divided among themselves about key issues such as dualism and spirit belief, and the cohesion of Cartesianism as a philosophical system seemed in danger. Nevertheless, the confessional party felt increasingly besieged by the new philosophy and the exegetical methods often associated with it, and especially on the exegetical issues they were prepared to fight to the last man. In his attacks both on Bekker and on Deurhoff, Brinck repeatedly appealed to what he called "the plain text" of the Bible, for it was on this position that Dutch Reformed confessionalism would ultimately stand or fall.

CHAPTER SIX

Cats Not to be Touched Without Gloves:
Eric Walten and Other Supporters of Bekker

In the wide public controversy that surrounded *The World Bewitched*, few voices were raised in Bekker's defense, and those that were raised were uniformly more radical than Bekker himself. These voices drew harsh criticism in their turn. If Bekker's book marked a decisive turning point in the spirit debate as some historians have suggested, why was the work received with such nearly uniform hostility? Why was there so little evidence of minds changed by *The World Bewitched*?[1]

This apparent lack of moderate support for Bekker's ideas was explained by Eric Walten (1663-1697), an outspoken pamphleteer who was without doubt Bekker's most radical supporter. According to Walten, it was largely a matter of discretion, if not of fear. Many people read Bekker's book and were convinced by its clear reasoning but they lacked the courage, love, and zeal to speak out in Bekker's defense, at least until the initial controversy had passed.[2] While Bekker's supporters were perhaps a minority, they were the most learned and decent of Christians, and many were of high rank in government, Walten argued. Although they did not dare to speak out publicly, they often expressed sorrow to each other privately over the attacks made upon Bekker. Walten added that he had heard high government officials in The Hague privately declare themselves in favor of Bekker's ideas.[3]

While Bekker's supporters were educated and concerned Christians, his opponents were the "Sohorry Morry," the rabble, "the kind of people who read no books nor want to read, and imagine that all they hear from the pulpit is true," Walten continued. Decent Christians were increasingly irritated by the actions of their preachers who attacked Bekker despite the fact that he "so heroically, zealously, stout-heartedly, and with such strength of reason and proof defended God and his honor and truth."[4] But, Walten added, in Amsterdam Bekker's supporters outnumbered his detractors and many

---

[1]Robin Attfield, "Balthasar Bekker and the Decline of the Witch Craze: The Old Demonology and the New Philosophy," *Annals of Science* 42 (1985), 383-395; G.J. Stronks, "The Significance of Balthasar Bekker's *The Enchanted World*," Marijke Gijswijt-Hofstra and Willem Frijhoff (eds), *Witchcraft in The Netherlands from the Fourteenth to the Twentieth Centuries* (Rotterdam, 1991), 149-156.

[2]Eric Walten, *Aardige Duyvelary, Voorvallende in dese dagen. Begrepen in een Brief van een Heer te Amsterdam, geschreven aan syn Vrienden te Leeuwarden in Vriesland* (n.p., n.d.), 10.

[3]Eric Walten, *Brief aan een Regent der Stad Amsterdam, Behelsende een Regtsinnige uytlegginge, en redenmatige Verklaring, van de Articulen die D. Bekker op den 22 Januari 1692 heeft overgeleverd aan de Classis van Amsterdam, wegens syn uytgegeven Boek, genaamd de Betoverde Wereld...* (The Hague, 1692), 133.

[4]Walten, *Aardige*, 40.

who appeared to oppose him really did not, but only pretended opposition to divert suspicion from themselves. The numbers of Bekker's supporters grew daily so that in the end his case was sure to triumph, Walten assured his readers.[5]

In the relatively tolerant atmosphere of the Dutch Republic, a wide range of views on many different topics regularly appeared in print without official repercussions, and within the Reformed church dissent from official views was not uncommon and was rarely severely punished. Nevertheless, Bekker was excluded from Reformed communion, a punishment that indicated the sensitivity of the confessional nerve that his work had touched, as well as the radical potential his ideas possessed. The silence of many of Bekker's supporters might well have been accurately explained by Walten, and the extremism of Walten and others who did speak out in Bekker's defense clearly showed the dangerous directions in which his ideas could be taken by those less moderate than he. Walten was so harsh in his criticisms of Bekker's clerical opponents that he ended his life in jail. The spirit debate in Holland thus exposed the limits of Dutch toleration and showed just how heated the conflict around Reformed confessionalism had become.

The extreme views of Bekker's defenders would seem to offer support for suggestions made by historians Margaret Jacob, Wiep van Bunge, and Silvia Berti that a radical and partly clandestine branch of the early Enlightenment in Holland, until recently little known, developed Cartesian and Spinozistic ideas in an extreme direction under the influence of thinkers such as Adrian Koerbagh and Lodewijk Meyer.[6] Walten was considerably influenced by the ideas of Koerbagh. If the number of Bekker's supporters was as large as Walten indicated, this might point to the existence within the Republic of a large and radical underground intellectual movement.

Among the voices raised in support of Bekker, Walten, the Collegiant Herman Bouman, and the mysterious writer J. Pel put forward the most serious philosophical arguments. They not only defended Bekker's ideas, especially his arguments based on Cartesian dualism, but they also built on these foundations to produce a more thoroughgoing critique of traditional spirit belief than Bekker himself had proffered. Pel adopted a materialistic position, while Bouman and Walten extended Bekker's dualistic arguments to rule out most of the activities of good angels as well as devils. Together these men offered chilling proof of the radical potential in Bekker's position.

I

About J. Pel so little is known that even his Christian name remains a mystery. Upset by Brinck's attacks on Bekker, Pel wrote *De Wonderdaden des Alderhoogsten* (The Miracles of the All-highest) in 1693, an examination of the actions of spirits that

[5]Walten, *Brief aan een Regent*, 10; *Aardige*, 10, 40; *Brief aan Syn Excellentie de Heer Graaf van Portland. etc., etc. Rakende de person en het gevoelen van Dr. Bekker. en 't geen tegen hem, by eenige van syn Partyen, word verwagt, en uytgestroyd...*(The Hague, 1692), 14.

[6]Wiep van Bunge, "Eric Walten (1663-1697). An Early Enlightenment Radical in the Dutch Republic," in Wiep van Bunge and Wim Klever (eds), *Disguised and Overt Spinozism Around 1700* (Leiden, 1996); Margaret Jacob, "Radicalism in the Dutch Enlightenment," in Margaret Jacob and Wijnand Mijnhardt (eds), *The Dutch Republic in the Eighteenth Century: Decline, Enlightenment, and Revolution* (Ithaca and London, 1992), 224-240; Jacob, *Living the Enlightenment: Freemasonry and Politics in Eighteenth-Century Europe* (New York, 1991); Silvia Berti, "The First Edition of the *Traite des trois imposteurs* and its Debt to Spinoza," Michael Hunter and David Wootton (eds), *Atheism from the Reformation to the Enlightenmemt* (Oxford, 1992), 182-220; Berti, "Jan Vroesen, autore del *Traite des trois imposteurs?*", *Rivista storica italiana* 103 (1991), 528-543.

targeted Brinck's criticism's of Bekker. In 1694 Pel published *De Leeringe der Duyvelen Verwoest: Synde ook een bevestiging van myn Boekje De Wonderdaden des Alhoogsten* (The Doctrine of the Devil Destroyed: Being also a Confirmation of my Book The Miracles of the All-highest) to defend his own views against critics who had attacked his first book. In *De Leeringe...* Pel called Christian beliefs about the devil "old wives' tales" that "poisoned men's understanding of the Bible and religion," leaving "leprous marks" in their hearts. The Reformed church held that there were fallen angels who misled man, but reason did not confirm this idea nor did the Bible teach it, Pel declared. He assured his readers that he did believe in angels because the Bible was full of them, but he added that he did not mean the kind of angels that most people believed in. God was Lord over all, Pel continued, echoing Bekker, and there was thus nothing that God could not use as a messenger or as a means of carrying out his will.[7]

Pel attacked traditional belief on a wide front by denying that angels were created by God when he created the world, by denying that angels ever fell from grace, and by denying that the fall of man was caused by a deceiving spirit. This last idea especially did violence to the true sense of the Bible, Pel declared, but people simply did not know how to understand the fall of man without attributing it to a spirit. For this reason, Pel continued, theologians had tried to show how the devil had moved the tongue of the snake to make sounds. Bekker, however, saw that these ideas had no foundation and he tore them down. Unfortunately, Pel added, Bekker did not then tell how it really was that man had fallen because he believed that the Bible did not explain this. Pel himself would not be so inhibited.

Pel admired Bekker's ideas and thought little of those of Bekker's Cartesian opponents. Aalstius and Steenwinkel explained the actions of spirits on bodies not as natural occurrences but as miracles of God, Pel continued. Following this reasoning it was God who caused the snake to tempt Eve and therefore it was God who was the deceiver, Pel continued, adding that this made God the cause of sin. .

Pel rejected the idea that body could not naturally act on the soul and vice-versa. The body of an object appeared to the human soul through the senses, and this appearance then became a human thought. In this way an outside object acted on the soul. The variety of objects that acted on the senses created a variety of thoughts in the soul. The link between soul and body was further shown by the fact that many people sweated in their sleep because of the terrible thoughts that they had in dreams.[8] Thus Pel pointed out the problems with dualism that underlay Foucher's criticisms of Cartesianism.

God was certainly the highest cause of the movement of extended things, Pel declared, but at creation he gave creatures their own powers of movement. The ideas of Aalstius, Steenwinkel, and Geulincx ignored the natural power that creatures had and led to the absurd conclusion that God did not give creatures enough power to move their own tongues.[9] It was beyond all reason to maintain that every movement of our bodies was a supernatural act occurring through the will and power of God. And if God caused what the devil willed to come to pass that made God a servant of the devil. On these points Pel claimed that his views and those of Bekker were about the same.[10]

---

[7]J. Pel, *De Leeringe der Duivelen Verwoest: Synde ook een Inleyding over Matt. 4, met een nader Bevestiging van myn Boekje De Wonderdaden des Alderhoogsten* (Amsterdam, 1694), 2-3.

[8]Ibid., 3-5.

[9]Ibid., 48-49, 71.

[10]Ibid., 43-69, 77.

The reason that some people believed in devils, sorcerers, and witches was that they could not separate their dreams and imagination from their natural senses and perceptions, Pel continued. Those who did not distinguish their dreams from their waking thoughts had fearful visions and imagined that they saw things such as the shadows of dead people and spirits. But this happened mostly to people who were superstitious, and if such superstitious fear of spirits were taken away people would understand Scripture much better.

It was a completely unsupported presupposition that there was an evil spirit called the devil who put evil and deceitful thoughts into people, Pel added. Papists used the idea of the devil for their own advantage, selling people incantations, holy water, and all sorts of other things supposedly to prevent diabolic evil. Others claimed that devils were thinking substances, acting through their intellect and will, creatures whose natures were not subject to measurement or movement. For his part, Pel took the daring step of denying both the "reality and the essence" of devils.[11]

There was no devil in the Garden of Eden who tempted man to fall, Pel argued. Man was forbidden to taste the tree of wisdom, but it reflected light in such a way that it affected the eyes and brain of the onlooker and caused him to imagine fruit. These powerful imaginations confused man's reason and caused him to think that by eating the fruit his finite understanding would be made infinite. It was this idea resulting from the action of the tree on man's senses that tempted man to eat the fruit. Sin and deception, therefore, were in the idea that tempted man to eat from the tree. Thus sin occurred when human knowledge missed the goal that God set for it: Adam and Eve fell by not using the knowledge that God gave them for the purpose that God intended.[12]

Pel went on to consider the opinion of some who held that man could not have fallen unless some spirit had tempted him, because if man had strayed without being tempted this would mean that his spirit was already corrupt before he sinned. But then what about the angels? Pel asked. They fell without being tempted by anybody, yet God had created them good. When preachers discussed scriptural passages that mentioned a deceiver they always brought in the heathen doctrine of the devil, a hellish spirit who fell and then supposedly deceived man into doing the same. But neither Scripture nor reason supported this view, Pel declared. Even Bekker had assumed that since Eve's sin did not come from herself she must have been tempted by the devil, although he did not know how this had happened. But even while man was created good he was created with a limited understanding, Pel argued, and it was this limitation that led to sin. Man willingly sinned, but he did so out of ignorance. The forbidden tree created such disturbances in man's senses that he left the path of reason and love of God. The Bible gave the name of the snake to the erroneous idea that the tree created in man simply in order to find an expressive way of describing something irrational, Pel argued, using the kind of exegetical license that conservatives feared most.[13]

Pel listed several more reasons why he did not believe in devils. In the first place, the essence of such creatures was beyond reason; in the second place, Scripture did not prove that devils existed, remaining relatively silent on this point; and finally, when Scripture spoke of spirits in general it did not discuss their characteristics.

In fact, Pel continued, when the Bible used the word spirit it really meant something material. God could easily create a material being that could do all the same things that

[11]Ibid., 7-8.
[12]Ibid., 5-6.
[13]Ibid., 9-17.

a spirit could do: it would be an eternal and independent being that thought, willed, and judged but yet was measurable and existed in a place. Pel thus attempted to give spirits material characteristics just as some of Bekker's critics had, although for a different reason. "There are no unbodily substances created in the work of creation called angels," he insisted, "no spirits that are in no place, that appear to be something and yet are nothing" (derhalven soo zijnder dan geen onlichaamelijke selfstandigheden geschapen in 't werk der schepping, dewelke Engelen worden genaemt...dat is, Geesten die in geen plaats of die nergens zoude zijn, of die iets soude schynen en inderdaad niets wesen).[14]

God had three kinds of material creatures in his service as angels, Pel continued; the first two kinds had heavenly bodies, and the third kind had an earthly body. The first kind were creatures made of purest heavenly material, formed in heaven and sent from there to appear on earth as rational creatures. In Matthew 28:2 the Bible called these "angels who descended from heaven." Then there were the souls of holy people taken by God into his service after the death of their bodies and given by God new heavenly and quick bodies so that they could appear to people on earth. They often brought messages to saints on earth. Both of these first two kinds of angels had bodies made of a fine, light material that moved but could not act contrary to reason, so these angels could not sin. Their bodies were immortal, they could not suffer or lose their strength, and they did not need to eat or drink. The third kind of angel included Christian rulers, teachers, and other human ambassadors of Christ on earth who served God and his people.[15] In addition to these three kinds of angels there were also bad "spirits" who were deceivers, but these were "spirits" of flesh and bone, Pel argued. One need not seek for them in hell, for they were right here on earth, Pel continued—these were the followers of the Pope. Heathens had believed in devils, demons, spirits, demigods, and the like, and the religion of the Papists continued these heathen beliefs. Thus Papists were called deceiving "spirits" although they were bodily.[16]

Pel interpreted biblical passages referring to spirits much as Bekker did. Many references to spirits were figurative, he argued. God made the wind, clouds, fire, light, hail, thunder, and lightening his angels and messengers in numerous biblical passages. In Genesis 49:38 Pharaoh referred to Joseph's wisdom as a spirit of God. In other scriptural places uncommon heroism was called a spirit of God.[17] The doctrine of the fall of the angels was clearly impossible because it contradicted reason and could not be found in Scripture. How could such holy things as the angels fall? Angels did not have the limited understanding or the desire for material things that led to man's fall, and thus they had no inclination or ability to sin. Some tried to prove the fall of the angels with the passage I Timothy 3:6: "Not a novice, lest being lifted up with pride he fall into the condemnation of the devil." But in this passage the word devil did not mean a fallen angel, Pel claimed. It referred to a man who was so called because of his evil heart. In other places in the Book of Timothy the apostle called those who were arrogant about their knowledge devils, and indeed the Greek word for devil, *diabolos*, meant slanderer. Those arrogant about their own knowledge slandered the truth. The doctrine of the fall of the angels was invented by the heathen Pope for his own purposes, Pel concluded.[18]

[14]Ibid., 26.
[15]Ibid., 28-29, 42.
[16]Ibid., 29-30.
[17]Ibid., 18-24.
[18]Ibid., 31-61.

Despite some similarities in their arguments, Pel's claims were much more sweeping than Bekker's. Not only did he deny the earthly activity of the devil as Bekker had, he went beyond that to deny the temporal activity of angels and even the very existence of angels and devils as Christians commonly conceived of them. He denied that angels were thinking substances distinct from man, by nature immaterial and created by God in the work of creation.[19] Certainly God could have created spiritual angels, Pel argued, but if God had made everything that he could make, then he would have made thousands of things that he did not make. Neither the supposed nature of angels as spirits nor their alleged activities offered any proof of their existence, Pel argued, and the Bible supplied no more definite evidence. To believe something that was contrary to both reason and Scripture was simple superstition. As long as the understanding had no knowledge that angels as spirits existed, their existence had to be denied, Pel concluded.[20]

Pel's final sweeping denial of angels went well beyond what Bekker had written. He followed Bekker when he held that good men were often referred to as angels in Scripture, but his claims were in other ways much more radical than Bekker's despite his insistence that he and Bekker were generally in agreement. Bekker held that reason could neither prove nor disprove the existence of angels, but he then accepted biblical testimony that angels as spirits did indeed exist and act on people. Pel, on the other hand, did not believe that Scripture provided convincing proof of the existence of such spirits. Bekker, when faced with inconclusive evidence, gave the benefit of the doubt to traditional beliefs. In the same situation Pel placed the burden of proof on traditional belief and rejected it when no such proof was forthcoming. In this way the approaches of the two men differed profoundly, with Bekker adopting a much more conservative position than Pel, who was a true radical. Pel's work showed how secularizing a rationalist/materialist approach to spirits could be.

II

Another thinker who proposed ideas about angels that went well beyond Bekker was Herman Bouman, a member of the radical Dutch religious group known as the Rijnsburg Collegiants. The Collegiants were a group of Protestant dissidents, including Remonstrants, Mennonites, Socinians and others, who were opposed to the confessionalism and the doctrinal rigidity of the Reformed church. Founded in 1620 in the village of Rijnsburg as a result of the ban on Remonstrant preaching issued the preceding year by the Synod of Dordrecht, the Collegiants were initially influenced by the spiritualist ideas of Kaspar Schwenkfeld and Sebastian Franck as well as by millennarianism that reached the movement through its Mennonite members. By the mid-seventeenth century the movement had spread to nearly all of the major cities of the Dutch Republic, where meetings were open to people of any religious faith.

Collegiant meetings featured hymn singing and common prayer as well as reading and free discussion of Scripture, but the Collegiants had no clergy, nor did their meetings have sermons. Discussions at college meetings ranged widely over important

[19]Ibid., 77.
[20]Ibid., 56-57.

issues of biblical interpretation and belief as well as controversial issues of philosophy and theology. Over the course of the seventeenth century Collegiant meetings became centers for heated intellectual debates dealing with the most important theological and philosophical issues of the time, and thus it is no surprise that the question of spirits and their temporal activities was also discussed.[21]

In Amsterdam the college was led by Galenus Abrahamsz, pastor of the city's United Mennonite congregation and one of the most important figures in the Collegiant movement. Not surprisingly, therefore, when the question of spirits came up for discussion in the college Galenus was involved. Bouman was a member both of the Amsterdam college and of Galenus's Mennonite congregation. He read *The World Bewitched* shortly after its appearance and was taken with Bekker's Cartesian arguments. In 1695-1696, Bouman was involved in a number of discussions in the Amsterdam college in which he used Bekker's ideas to reject not only the temporal activity of evil spirits, as Bekker had, but also the actions of good angels. On three occasions during 1695 Bouman debated Galenus and other Mennonites at Collegiant meetings held in the Mennonite church, and on two further occasions in 1696 he discussed the issue of spirits with the Socinian Lambert Joosten during college meetings held in the Collegiant orphanage "De Oranjeappel." After the 1696 debates, Bouman and Joosten published a number of pamphlets and longer writings setting forth their views and detailing the earlier debates.

On May 29, 1695, the college met in Galenus's church "Het Lam" (The Lamb) on Amsterdam's Singel canal. The scriptural text for discussion was Luke 15:1-10, and the group's attention came to focus on verse ten, where Christ said: "Likewise, I say unto you, there is joy in the presence of the angels of God over one sinner that repenteth." Galenus declared that the angels mentioned were "independent heavenly beings who expressed the majesty of God" and were happy over man's conversion.[22] Bouman replied that God's angels were men who were able to convert sinners, not spirits sent from heaven. In Scripture the priests, Levites, pastors, and teachers of the church were often called angels of God, he continued, but these were clearly men, not spirits sent by God. The Bible often referred to men as "spirits," Bouman continued, but the idea of angels being heavenly spirits was "dark and confused" and not to be found in Scripture.[23]

Clearly disturbed by Bouman's ideas, Galenus accused him of ignoring biblical evidence when he interpreted scriptural accounts of spirits as reports of human activity. Bouman replied by declaring that he knew of no place in the Bible where angels were called unearthly spirits. He added that while the Bible did not suggest that angels were independent spiritual beings, the Bible did refer to the prayers of the apostles as angels that ascended to God with their messages.[24] At this point the meeting broke up with Galenus still dissatisfied with Bouman's explanation even though the latter had not yet put forward his principal Cartesian arguments.

The college next returned to the subject of angels on July 17, 1695, again at a meeting in "Het Lam." This time the text under discussion was Luke 16:22: "And it came to pass that the beggar died, and was carried by the angels into Abraham's

[21]On the Collegiants see J.C. van Slee, *De Rijnsburger Collegianten* (Haarlem, 1895); C.B. Hylkema, *Reformateurs: Geschiedkundige Studiën over de Godsdienstige bewegingen uit de nadagen onzer gouden eeuw* (Haarlem, 1900), 2 vols.; Leszek Kolakowski, *Chretiens sans eglise: la conscience religieuse et le lien confessionnel au XVII siecle* (Paris, 1969); Andrew Fix, *Prophecy and Reason: The Dutch Collegiants in the Early Enlightenment* (Princeton, 1991).

[22]Herman Bouman, *Disputatio van Verscheyde Saaken...* (Amsterdam, 1695), 5.

[23]Ibid., 16.

[24]Ibid., 16-19.

bosom: the rich man also died, and was buried." Galenus again insisted that the angels mentioned were independent spiritual beings, and Bouman again objected, saying the angels that carried the beggar into heaven were his patience and his faith. Bouman then proceeded to outline his central argument. The Bible never used the word "angel" to mean an independent spiritual being distinct from the human soul, he argued. Scripture said that God sent his angels as messengers to people, but all messages to humans had to be sent through bodies because humans could only receive messages by way of their bodily senses. Spirits having "neither flesh nor bone" could not appear to the human senses, and therefore people could not get messages from them. "Thus it is only rational to conclude," Bouman argued, "that all of God's angels are bodily"—men, not immaterial spirits.[25] Galenus continued to point out biblical passages that he believed proved that angels were spiritual beings.

Bouman made it clear to the meeting that he did believe in the existence of "independent, thinking, immaterial beings," but he did not believe that these beings existed on earth. The souls of the righteous, separated from the body at death, lived on in heaven at the right hand of God. But on earth all angels had human bodies, including those that appeared to people in dreams and visions. When people saw angels in dreams, Bouman continued, they saw them not as spirits but as bodily creatures, because "no message can be comprehended other than in a bodily-pictorial way."[26]

Bouman held his last debate with Galenus at a college meeting on August 7, 1695. Spirits were not the primary topic of discussion as the meeting opened. The text was Luke 17:5-11, with verse five reading: "And the apostles said unto the Lord, increase our faith." Galenus maintained that the apostles had asked God for the power to do miracles, but Bouman declared that God could not give the apostles or any other of his creatures this power because it would make them omnipotent like God was. God could not make a creature omnipotent like himself because one omnipotent creature would necessarily limit the power of the other. Thus God performed miracles through the apostles, but the apostles did not themselves have such power.[27] This argument, which was similar to the one that Bekker had made about the powers of angels, angered Galenus and he accused Bouman of denying the existence of angels. Bouman then replied: "All whom God sends are his angels: pestilence, hunger, rain, men, and any other way God speaks to man."[28] The meeting ended abruptly as Galenus walked out.

After his debates with Galenus, Bouman's views on spirits became well known in Collegiant circles. These views were challenged during meetings the following year when the Socinian theologian Lambert Joosten attacked the Cartesian basis of Bouman's position. At a meeting held on March 18, 1696, the text under discussion was II Corinthians 12:7-8: "And lest I should be exalted above measure though the abundance of the revelations, there was given to me a thorn in the flesh, the messenger of Satan to buffet me, lest I should be exalted above measure. For this thing I besought the Lord thrice, that it might depart from me." Joosten declared that the messenger of Satan was an evil spirit, but Bouman argued that before Joosten could prove that there were evil spirits he had to show that there were good spirits or angels that had fallen to become evil. And even if he could prove that such spirits existed in heaven, Bouman

---

[25]Ibid., 20-21.
[26]Ibid., 21.
[27]Ibid., 7-8.
[28]Ibid., 9-11.

argued, they could not be shown to exist on earth. Godly men like Abraham, Isaac, and Jacob had once been God's messengers on earth, and for this reason the Bible called them angels among men. When they died, their immortal souls went to heaven, where they retained the name of angels. But such spirits did not return to earth as angelic messengers to men, Bouman maintained, because to be such a messenger a spirit needed a body. A spirit without a body could not be observed by people, could not contact or act on people, and could not get a message across to people who had only bodily senses.[29]

Joosten then asked Bouman how he had arrived at these conclusions, and Bouman replied in true Cartesian fashion: "I accept nothing as true except that which I clearly comprehend. Thus I know that that which I accept is true."[30] Bouman added that he would accept as true something that he did not clearly understand only if God's word told him to do so. But neither the Bible nor human reason taught that angels were "intelligent, immaterial beings."[31] Bouman then concluded with an argument even the wording of which was reminiscent of one of Bekker's key points in chapter eleven, Book II, of *The World Bewitched*:

> I cannot understand how God could cause a spirit, created with a body, to act on a body without the help of the body that it was created in. I can lift a hundred pounds with my body, but I cannot see how my spirit could do so only by thinking, using no body. Reason teaches us not to attribute to God powers contradictory in nature.[32]

Joosten, however, refused to give in to Bouman's arguments and continued to insist on his own views. Bouman commented sadly: "I don't know why Joosten acts the way he does. I am afraid that he is stricken with that monstrous torment known as theological hate."[33]

After the Collegiant debates about spirits were over, both sides carried on the discussion in print in an effort to justify their positions. Bouman published a work in 1696 containing several letters of support sent to him by a Collegiant friend whose name he did not reveal. Joosten had maintained, like some early church fathers, that angels had "fine spiritual bodies, like God," and he had further argued that angels "are created by God and exist in their own way and of another rank than men, having no flesh or bones, but bodies of very fine material."[34] Bouman's friend declared in his letter, however, that where the Bible spoke of angels it really meant Godly men. Priests were often called the angels of God because of their high esteem in the eyes of God, and John the Baptist was called an angel of God because he was a person of special worth to God.[35] Bouman's friend criticized Joosten's literal interpretation of Scripture and suggested that in many cases allegorical interpretation was more appropriate.[36]

Joosten had also argued that the reason why angels and even God had to have "spiritual bodies made of very fine material" was that truly immaterial things could not exist. For this reason, Joosten had held that human souls were either themselves bodily or

[29]Herman Bouman, *Brief van Lambert Joosten...* (Amsterdam, 1696), 6-10.
[30]Ibid., 12.
[31]Ibid.
[32]Ibid., 13.
[33]Ibid., 5.
[34]Herman Bouman, *Eenige Nodige Aanmerkingen op Lambert Joosten's Verdediging...* (Amsterdam, 1696), 10.
[35]Ibid., 10-13.
[36]Ibid., 26.

"products of body."[37]   Bouman's friend, however, declared: "We know that the soul does not exist of material because this is not compatible with its powers. But I am certain that it does consist of something because I know that I am, and that I think. I am a thinking thing. My spirit is a thinking thing."[38]

From these exchanges it is clear that Cartesian ideas regarding spirits had come into the college by way of Bouman's reading of Bekker's work, and that these ideas had found defenders there. Bekker's Collegiant supporters took his ideas beyond what he himself claimed when they rejected the temporal activity of good spirits based on rational arguments. While Bekker accepted the temporal activity of good spirits because the Bible reported it, even though reason could not understand how this took place, Bouman believed that reason proved such activity impossible. He thus interpreted Scripture in such a way that all references to angelic activity on earth were merely figurative.

III

The most radical of Bekker's supporters was Eric Walten, a man who styled himself a doctor in theology, philosophy, and law, and who made his living as a physician, solicitor, pamphleteer, and caster of medals. Walten claimed to have been born in Hamm in the Duchy of Nassau, and he perhaps studied in Germany. In 1685 he was detained in a workhouse in Utrecht on charges of vagabondage and begging, and afterwards he lived in The Hague, with a brief stay in Rotterdam. In The Hague Walten worked as a physician and solicitor, in the latter capacity defending the famous engraver and favorite of Stadholder-King William III, Romeyn de Hooghe. During the years 1688-1694 he turned to political pamphleteering as a supporter of the Orangist party, publishing on such topics as the Glorious Revolution in England, the role of the government in church affairs in the Dutch Republic, the 1690 popular uprisings in Rotterdam, and Amsterdam politics. He also became involved in the spirit debate around Bekker.

On the topic of spirits Walten openly admitted that his views were more radical than Bekker's, and his attacks on Bekker's clerical opponents were of unparalleled savagery. He called conservatives devil worshippers and Satanists who wanted to dethrone God and replace him with the devil. After Bekker was deposed as pastor, Walten wrote that the synods of the Dutch Reformed church had become lunatic asylums, a charge that apparently crossed the line of toleration. In 1693 a joint appeal was made to the Court of Holland by the deputies of the synods of North and South Holland requesting that Walten be prosecuted for blasphemy. On March 19, 1694, Walten was arrested in The Hague and jailed in the Gavangenpoort. There he remained for the next three years awaiting trial. In the course of long interrogation it came out that Walten had knowledge of the unsavory role played by de Hooghe and another of the Stadholder's favorites, Govert Bidloo, in the Rotterdam riots of 1690. This attracted the attention of none other than William III himself, who attempted to prevent this information from coming further to light by delaying Walten's trial. Hopeless and desperate, Walten died in prison in 1697, possibly by suicide.[39]

---

[37]Ibid., 27-40.

[38]Ibid., 55.

[39]P.C. Molhuysen and P.J. Blok (eds), *Nieuwe Nederlandsch biografisch woordenboek* (Leiden, 1911-1937), I, 1534-35; van Bunge, "Eric Walten," 1-7.

Walten's radicalism on the issue of spirits was focussed mainly in three areas where he extended Bekker's ideas far beyond what the pastor himself ever intended: 1) Walten insisted that the question of the nature and abilities of spirits was a purely philosophical one to which the Bible had nothing to contribute. In fact, only a thorough knowledge of what philosophy had to say about spirits could enable one to understand scriptural references to them—with this idea Walten approached the position of Lodewijk Meyer in his *Philosophia S. Scripturae Interpres*; 2) Like Bouwman, Walten extended Bekker's dualistic critique of the activities of spirits to a denial of the temporal activities of good angels as well as devils; and 3) Walten's savage attacks on the Reformed clergy approached the level of bitterness found in Adrian Koerbagh's *Een Bloemhof* (1668), a work that impressed Walten so much that there is some evidence that he planned to write a sequel to it.[40] Koerbagh also died in prison, in Amsterdam.

Walten argued that knowledge of the nature, characteristics, and abilities of things belonged to philosophy, and the knowledge of the nature, characteristics, and abilities of spirits belonged to metaphysics. One could not talk about spirits or consider Scripture places that discussed them without first using reason and philosophy to understand the nature of spirits "clearly and distinctly." In fact, the greatest aid to understanding Scripture in general was "the right knowledge of the nature of things," fundamental to which was a "clear and distinct" idea of the nature, characteristics, abilities, and actions of spirits and bodies. This basic knowledge could not come from Scripture, Walten argued. Science had existed in the world for more than two thousand years before Scripture, he added, and the Bible did not speak of scientific matters fully or distinctly. Knowledge of spirits and bodies could only come from man's attentive observation of himself, a compound of spirit and body, from which he would learn the characteristics and abilities of each. It was "the inner light of man's spirit, namely, innate reason," that people used to distinguish truth from error, and it was the same innate reason that man used to understand, accept, and judge Scripture, Walten boldly asserted.[41] Thus Walten actually took a position that Bekker's opponents often accused him of adopting.

The "right knowledge of the nature of things" taught men that spirits were thinking things entirely distinct from bodies in both their nature and activities, Walten declared. The being of spirits consisted of thinking, and the actions and abilities of spirits were limited to thinking. Each spirit could only know its own thoughts, not those of any other, and one spirit could not act on another without the aid of a body. The human soul was the only spirit created by God to work in and through bodies, so only the soul could act on other spirits and bodies, Walten argued.[42]

For these reasons, neither angels nor devils could appear or act in a bodily way on earth, Walten continued. No spirit without a body could act on a body, nor could it obtain a body for itself. God could give any spirit a body to act through if he wanted to, Walten admitted, but where did it appear that God had ever done or would ever do such a thing? God had never revealed that he had given a body to any spirit other than the human soul. Without this evidence one could legitimately conclude that no good or bad angel had ever been paired with a body or appeared or acted in a bodily manner.

God's purpose in creating spirits was not to combine their thinking with a body, Walten continued. If God allowed angels to act in a bodily way he would have to alter their nature, and they would then no longer be angels. God would either have to change

[40]van Bunge, "Eric Walten," 5-8.
[41]Walten, *Brief aan syn Excellentie*, 5-6, 23-24, 79-80.
[42]Walten, *Brief aan een regent*, 23.

the spirit into a body, or unite the spirit with a body, and in either case the actions done by the new creature would not be those of a spirit. God created angels to act only by thinking and he had no desire or reason to change this.

God did not use angels to carry out his judgements, serve the elect, or punish the Godless by acting in a bodily manner. Angels were not created for this purpose, Walten argued. Their nature made them so incapable of doing these things that an ant or a fly would be more help to God in these tasks. Furthermore, to give an angel a body would contradict its righteousness because it would place the angel in peril of being deceived by objects that appear to the bodily senses. God did use the angels to portray his Godly state, Walten added. He revealed part of his divine plan to them as he carried it out and they cheered him in their thoughts, were happy, and glorified him. Angels appeared to the prophets and apostles not in bodily form but in visions and "raptures of the senses" where they were perceived to be bodily even though they were not.[43]

Walten next expanded upon Bekker's rejection of the temporal power of the devil. Bekker clearly proved that God did all, knew all, ruled and governed all, and that the devil was an evil and corrupt creature who could do nothing against God or his people. The devil, a spirit without a body, could only act through thinking and thus was incapable of acting on the bodies or hearts of people, Walten argued. But even if he had a body, the devil could not act through that body in the world because after the fall of Adam and Eve the devil was punished by God and imprisoned forever in hell. God would not let him out even briefly for the purpose of punishing evil people because God had means enough himself to do that. There were enough evil doers in the world with both souls and bodies that God could use if he needed instruments with which to punish or if he wanted to allow evil in the world. These bad people already freely desired to do evil, and God could simply let them follow their evil wills. In this way God was not responsible for the evil done by his earthly instruments, Walten argued.

On the other hand, if God were to use the devil as an instrument of punishment he would have to give him a body to do evil with, and thus God would be responsible for the sins of the devil. And this was, of course, contrary to God's honor and perfection. The common idea that God used the devil as an instrument of punishment Walten thus called baseless and slanderous to God.[44] Furthermore, the devil could not himself create or take on a body to act through. The human soul did not take on its own body; it was paired with a body by a divine miracle. No creature could combine these two contradictory substances, and certainly not the devil, a condemned creature imprisoned in hell, Walten added.

Walten then listed several ways in which bodies might be produced, none of which the devil could accomplish. The first bodies were created by God and given by him an ability to procreate themselves, while all creatures thereafter came from this process of procreation. The devil, having no body, had no way to manufacture a body from pre-existing materials, and of course only God could create a body from nothing. Likewise, since the devil had no body he had no way to generate a body through procreation, nor could he arrange to have one generated for him. Some people said that the devil could make a body by compressing air, but there were no examples of the devil or any other creature making a body in this way. Proponents of the devil claimed that he sometimes took dead people's bodies from the grave or gallows or

[43]Ibid., 24-29, 34-35, 37-39.
[44]Walten, *Aardige Duyvelary*, 5-7; *Brief aan syn Excellentie*, 15-16, 41, 45, 58.

made use of animal bodies. But without eyes to see where the bodies were, feet to approach them, and hands with which to grasp them, the devil could not take an animal body or a dead body. And of course only God could give a dead body life.

The devil's defenders claimed that he could take on not one but many bodies, that he could make his body invisible, that he could use it to enter locked rooms and chests, and that he could travel with it great distances in an instant. But such things were obviously impossible for bodies, Walten pointed out. And even if the devil could some-how get a human or animal body he could not do as much with it as a master could with his slaves or a farmer with his animals. After all, the master controlled his slaves and the farmer his animals through a body, but the devil could not do this.[45]

Another reason for the devil's impotence, according to Walten, was that his knowledge was severely limited. All the knowledge that human souls had they got through expe-rience and the bodily senses, as well as from divine revelation. A spirit without a body and without divine revelation could only know: 1) that he existed as a thinking being; 2) because he was imperfect and finite he concluded that he was created by another; 3) innate reason told him that this creator was omnipotent, omniscient, true, eternal, per-fect, and immutable; 4) he could guess, but not know for certain, that the creator made other beings as well as himself. This was the limit of the devil's knowledge without divine revelation: he knew as much about the world as the soul of a newborn infant.

Before the devil's fall from heaven, however, God did reveal to him certain basic things, and he retained this knowledge in hell. The devil had a general knowledge of the good angels, and thus of good and evil. And he had a general knowledge about Godly people: he knew that there were some and how many there were. God gave the devil this knowledge of Godly people after his fall to increase his pain. But the devil had no specific knowledge of who and where believers were, or of the things that displeased them, so the devil could do believers no harm. Without any specific knowl-edge about believers, and without any eyes with which to see them or ears with which to hear about them, the devil could not even wish them any harm specifically and individually. By thinking about people in a general way the devil (and good angels as well) could be said to act on people, but the devil could not communicate his thoughts to people. Walten added that in this way he himself could be said to act upon the bodies and souls of Reformed believers in Hungary and Savoy and Papists in Rome, even though he had never been to these places and did not know anyone there. And even if God revealed to the devil specifically who and where a believer was, the only harm that the devil could do to that believer would be to wish him ill. This would have about the same affect as when one person wished another a pleasant journey! Walten concluded sarcastically.[46]

People who gave the devil so much power and blamed all their sins on his influence denied the hereditary sin and inborn evil that was the real root of human sin, Walten added. In this way people tried to excuse themselves and escape guilt for their sins. On the other hand, when Bekker denied the devil's power his opponents claimed that by freeing people from fear of the devil he would make them independent, rowdy, and hard to govern. These critics assumed that people feared the devil more than God, an assumption that replaced God the righteous judge with the devil, author of evil. God did not want fear of a bully like the devil but rather love and virtue to cause people to

---

[45]Walten, *Brief aan syn Excellentie*, 29-39.
[46]Ibid., 16, 26-28; Walten, *Brief aan een regent*, 30, 88.

serve and honor him, Walten insisted. It was insulting to Christianity to assume that believers needed a devil to chase them to God and make them pious. Even if one denied that there was a devil at all this would not open the way for Godlessness nor take away eternal punishment, Walten added, because punishment came from God, not the devil.[47]

In Walten's view people sinned of their own free will without the need of a devil to tempt or lure them, and the same was true of the first sin in the Garden of Eden. Neither God nor the devil compelled Adam to sin, and therefore he could still have fallen even had there been no devil. Walten then proceeded to do what Bekker was unable to do: he explained the actual role played by the devil in the fall of Adam and Eve.

God revealed to his angels who and what Adam and Eve were and what God's plans for them were. One angel envied the righteousness and holiness of man and desired that man transgress God's command, become disobedient, and fall. This malignant wish was the sin and fall of the devil, for which God condemned him to eternal punishment in hell. Then God, in order to warn, admonish, strengthen, and test Adam and Eve, revealed to them the devil's evil wish. Instead of heeding God's warning, however, they freely followed the evil wish of the devil and disobeyed God. Thus the devil's only role in the drama in Eden was to set a bad example that Adam and Eve freely followed. The devil in no way compelled them to sin because wishing and willing could not compel a person to disobey God. The first humans sinned without being tempted by anyone, just as the devil had before them, Walten argued.[48]

His explanation of the fall of Adam and Eve brought Walten to the matter of biblical exegesis. Bekker had shown that the scriptural account of the temptation of Eve was not literally true but rather had to be interpreted figuratively or parabolically, Walten noted. The words that the Bible used to describe man's fall had to be interpreted according to the nature of the topic under discussion and the context involved, Walten explained. At various places in the Bible the same words had different meanings according to the topic under discussion, and the Bible often used words borrowed from one context to discuss an entirely different matter.

The Bible said that God came, went, moved, stood, and other such things. But when these words were applied to God, a spirit, they could not mean the same as when they were applied to bodily creatures, Walten argued. Scripture also said that souls sang, spoke, laughed, and even had discussions with themselves, but no soul could do these things in the literal sense. When Scripture used these words with reference to spirits, they all meant "think," Walten claimed. Similarly, in biblical passages that appeared to attribute the fall of Adam and Eve to the temptation of the devil, words such as "speak," "convince," "mislead," and "deceive," when applied to the devil, really meant "think," "will," "desire," and "wish." [49]

All places in the Bible that appeared to ascribe physical actions to the devil had to be interpreted figuratively ("oneigentlijke"), Walten continued. In many of the places where the devil was mentioned the Bible really meant bad people who continued to do the evil work that the devil had originated, Walten argued, echoing Bekker and Bouwman. These people were the devil's followers, or "young devils," he added. Whenever Scripture said that Satan filled someone's heart or was in someone, it really

---

[47]Walten, *Brief aan syn Excellentie*, 59-71.
[48]Ibid., 17-19, 59.
[49]Walten, *Aardige Duyvelary*, 18; *Brief aan syn Excellentie*, 20-22, 25-26.

meant that sin, the work of the devil, was active in someone. Similarly, whenever Scripture spoke of the bodily actions of angels, such passages had to be understood figuratively, or as referring to things perceived in visions or "raptures of the senses." Furthermore, angels were named in many Bible passages that really related the work of God, Walten said, again following Bekker. In these passages, God's works were figuratively ascribed to angels to emphasize God's holy status and majesty.[50]

Like Bekker, Walten's exegesis made use of the doctrine of accommodation. "Anybody who knows anything about the morals, customs, and language of the land in which the Bible's writers lived knows that they...used the words and habits of speech of the people to whom they spoke and to whom their writings were addressed," Walten argued. And he added: "What's more, they sometimes related things not after the truth and characteristics of the things nor even after their own ideas, but according to the erroneous ideas of the people they lived with."[51] With this statement Walten closely approached Spinoza's claim that the Bible's writers had made mistakes. To properly understand the Bible, Walten held, a reader needed a thorough knowledge of the linguistic culture that produced the Bible.[52]

Walten then proceeded to attack the exegetical methods of Bekker's opponents as well as their regard for the States Translation. Those who wanted to restore the devil to power used bad translations and interpretations of Scripture to argue their point, he said. Using the Bible to defend belief in sorcery, ghosts, and the temporal power of the devil could only be done by misuse, bad translation, and bad understanding of the text. The Bible often used words and phrases figuratively, and these could not be interpreted literally as the devil's defenders tried to do, Walten argued.[53]

Bekker's opponents criticized him for attacking the Dutch translation of the Bible, Walten continued. Despite the fact that many Hebrew words had three or four different, and sometimes contradictory, meanings depending on context, and even though different translators differently rendered texts including these words, Bekker's opponents wanted him to accept only the States Translation as accurate despite the fact that he understood the original Hebrew text. Bekker's critics' insistence on the validity of one translation of Scripture was really a weapon against the Coccejans, who "always seemed to draw a better interpretation out of the ground text," Walten declared, indicating that he clearly understood the deeper exegetical and ecclesiastical issues at stake in the dispute between Bekker and his critics.[54]

No sooner had *The World Bewitched* appeared, Walten continued, than "a bunch of bad fellows, who here and there play at preacher" saw that Bekker "blazed a path to properly interpret certain Scripture passages that had up to then been dealt with in a slipshod manner." His critics saw that Bekker's exegesis demanded "more wisdom and understanding...than they possessed," and that "more study was necessary than they had done." They realized that they "might have to go back to school and be disciples again before playing at master, and if they did this they would show the world in what blindness and error they had been." To head off this threat to their pretended mastery, they sided with the devil against Bekker, since they were "too lazy" for further study, Walten hissed.[55] The central importance of exegetical questions in the

---

[50]Walten, *Aardige Duyvelary*, 7-8, 26-27; *Brief aan een regent*, 27.
[51]Walten, *Aardige Duyvelary*, 27,
[52]van Bunge, "Eric Walten," 7.
[53]Walten, *Brief aan syn Excellentie*, 10, 61.
[54]Walten, *Aardige Duyvelary*, 22-24.
[55]Ibid., 8.

spirit dispute was also recognized by the officials who interrogated Walten after his arrest for blasphemy in 1694, and as a result their questioning returned again and again to Walten's view of the Bible.[56]

From exegesis Walten passed on to take up the larger issue of confessionalism. Bekker's opponents in the synod condemned his book because its discussion of spirits deviated from the Formulas of Unity, Walten noted. But the Formulas did not bind preachers to every particular expression, just to the main points. The Formulas should not be exempted from all further improvement arising from the understanding of new truths in Scripture, Walten argued. And no one should persist in evil or error just because he bound himself to it with a signature. When a preacher signed a formula and then found that he had signed error he was not bound by that signature but rather he was obligated to warn everyone of the error. He also had to "attempt to make it disappear through the strength of truth." [57]

Some said that it went against the truth of Scripture to interpret the Bible contrary to the content of the Formulas of Unity because they believed that the Formulas represented the truth of Scripture, Walten continued, penetrating to the intellectual heart of confessionalism.[58]   But he was not convinced of this:

> If you want to make all new discoveries, all clarifications of truth, all increase of knowledge bow before the Formulas without giving any other reason except that there are these Formulas and that they have been signed, then you destroy the word of God with human principles, and you usurp in a Papish way rule over hearts and pretend to a Papal infallibility by saying that the Formula makers, upholders, and defenders cannot err.[59]

If Luther and Calvin had stuck by the Papish formulas and decrees there would have been no Reformation, Walten declared, launching a frontal assault on the principles of confessionalism.

The Formulas were composed by fallible men, but the way that they were revered by Bekker's opponents made it seem that all Scriptural passages contradicting them would either have to be scrapped from the Bible or bent and distorted to fit the contents of the Formulas, Walten scorned. "I...say that no catechism or confession should be made that does not agree with the Bible," he concluded.[60]

It was not Walten's exegetical methods or his radical views about angels that finally drove state authorities to act against him. Rather it was his open scorn for the church's confessional documents as well as his savage and often personal attacks on the Reformed clerics who opposed Bekker. Henricus Brinck he called "One of the foremost and most passionate defenders of the devil," a category in which he also placed Everhardus van der Hooght.[61] The writings of both men "nicely honor the devil and put him on a high throne," Walten charged. The work of Jacobus Schuts, another critic of Bekker, Walten called "so crazy he should be ashamed to sign his name to it."[62]

---

[56]van Bunge, "Eric Walten," 9.
[57]Walten, *Aardige Duyvelary*, 11-13.
[58]Ibid, 17.
[59]Ibid., 17.
[60]Ibid., 17-18, 34-36.
[61]Walten, *Brief aan syn Excellentie*, 75-76.
[62]Walten, *Aardige Duyvelary*, 5.

Critics who claimed that Bekker's ideas on spirits were close to those of the Sadducees and Spinoza either had not read Bekker's book, had not understood it, or intentionally distorted Bekker's views, Walten charged.[63] These opponents could not stand to admit that the devil bore God's righteous judgement and punishment in eternal imprisonment:

> For them it is not enough that sin and desire for evil created by the devil and brought by him into the world rule everywhere. They want to have the devil himself let loose to do still more evil, to spook about throughout the world, to do, to the dishonor of the creator and the sorrow of his creatures, such things as people falsely ascribe to him.[64]

Most members of the Reformed church were so ignorant of God and religion and so permeated with prejudices and errors that "they, in knowledge, life, and conduct, can hardly be called Christians, or even people," Walten declared. Furthermore, "unsuitable and half-dozing men are admitted to the office of preacher, and many teachers are as inexperienced in the Word of Truth as their blind listeners."[65] Bekker's opponents were Papists at heart who wanted to see the Reformed church as an infallible holy mother, Walten boomed, adding this sarcastic advice for his readers:

> so do not read too many books, do not test the spirits, do not explain Scripture or judge what is preached to you. Certainly do not test it by God's Word. The evangelists and apostles who teach you to investigate Scripture (John 5:39, I John 4:1, Acts 1:11, I Corinthians 10:15) know nothing. Have zeal without understanding, believe what the church believes. The church cannot err. [66]

When it came time to confront Bekker about his "errors," his opponents in the synod were not so eager, despite their zeal for the devil, to face him one on one and debate the issues. Even the esteemed and learned Professor Trigland realized that Bekker was "...a cat not to be touched without gloves," Walten smirked, coining a phrase that could just as aptly be applied to him.[67]

When *The World Bewitched* was first published, Walten continued, he had feared that "the ignorance that is still in our land" would create opposition to the work. He had assumed, however, that the learned officials and clergy of Amsterdam would stand up for Bekker. But such a commotion instantly arose around Bekker's book that those in favor of his ideas dared not speak out. Even some Coccejans, who had sympathy for some of Bekker's ideas, attacked him because of remarks he had made in his *Commentary on Daniel* that were critical of Coccejus's prophetic exegesis.[68]

The opposition of the Coccejans grieved Walten because he realized that a fundamental dynamic at work in the controversy around *The World Bewitched* was Bekker's exegetical alignment with the Coccejan party against the biblical literalism of the confessional wing of the church. Walten recognized more clearly than most at the time that the controversy around Bekker's views on spirits was simply the latest episode in

[63]Walten, *Brief aan een regent*, 23.
[64]Walten, *Aardige Duyvelary*, 18-19.
[65]Walten, *Brief aan een regent*, 50.
[66]Walten, *Aardige Duyvelary*, 20-22.
[67]Ibid., 28-29.
[68]Walten, *Brief aan een regent*, 7; *Aardige Duyvelary*, 9.

a long-running battle between Bekker and the confessional party, a battle that went back at least as far as Bekker's publication of his adult catechism in 1670. "All who are against Coccejus and his followers are powerfully embittered against Bekker for his book *De vaste Spyze der Volmaakten*," Walten noted. Many opposed Bekker "because he follows Coccejus in much," Walten wrote, adding that long before Bekker came to Amsterdam he was attacked in Friesland "for upholding the truth."[69]

With these words Walten put his finger on what was in many ways the seminal event in Bekker's career as an ecclesiastical thinker and a primary cause for all of his subsequent troubles with the confessional party of the Dutch Reformed church. When Bekker, in the *Vaste Spyze*, had boldly taken the side of Coccejus and Alting in the controversy over the nature and meaning of the Christian sabbath, he involved himself in complex and highly divisive issues of biblical exegesis. Although more than twenty years had passed since the *Vaste Spyze* had first appeared, the earlier controversy remained Bekker's theological rubicon in the eyes both of his critics and his supporters.

With men like Walten at his back, Bekker's assault on Reformed confessionalism and biblical literalism no doubt seemed even more terrible to conservative minds. While Walten died in jail, Bekker perished in religious exile. He might have been better off without friends who pointed out in such dramatic fashion just how far his ideas could be taken. But when Bekker attacked the authority of the Dutch Reformed church he found out, as Luther had years earlier, that he who takes the first step will not also take the last, nor will he be able to determine where the path will lead.

---

[69]Walten, *Aardige Duyvelary*, 42, 9.

CONCLUSION

The Deep Structure of the Spirit Debate

CHAPTER SEVEN

Most Attacked and Least Defeated:
Confessionalism, Anti-Confessionalism, and
Religious Controversy in the Dutch Republic

The life and work of Balthasar Bekker, from his early conflict with the Reformed church hierarchy over the funeral oration for his first wife to the publication of *The World Bewitched*, stood in marked contrast to one of the most powerful intellectual forces of the seventeenth century: the great transformation of religious ideas and institutions often called confessionalism. It was Bekker's opposition to this thought system, from his early days in Friesland, which in large part defined his own vision of the church and Scripture. Bekker's biblical exegesis, with its rejection of literalism, undermined the intellectual structure of Dutch Reformed confessionalism and provoked heated opposition to his ideas on the part of many church leaders.

Starting from assumptions fundamentally opposed to many of the central ideas of confessionalism, Bekker offered principled opposition to a religious and intellectual system that had come to dominate the post-Reformation churches of western Europe. Bekker's importance as a religious thinker rests as much with his attack on the intellectual structure of Dutch Reformed confessionalism as it does with his critique of traditional spirit belief. When Johannes Duikerius referred to Bekker as "the Friesian Hercules," he no doubt had in mind the size and power of the forces that Bekker was confronting. An examination of the intellectual structure of Dutch Reformed confessionalism and Bekker's principled opposition to it will highlight Bekker's religious and intellectual position in the seventeenth-century Dutch Republic, a position that he himself was quite consciously aware of.

I

The one hundred and fifty years following the death of Martin Luther was a period of intense confessionalization in the religious life of western Europe as the various churches created by the Protestant Reformation strove to set themselves clearly apart from each other and to stake out their own territory in the religious landscape. At the same time, the expanding bureaucratic and military apparatus of early modern states, especially absolutist regimes, sought to use the social and intellectual discipline at the heart of confessionalism for purposes of state power and social control.

R. Po-Chia Hsia has defined confessionalism in this period in Germany as "the formation of religious ideologies and institutions in Lutheranism, Calvinism, and Catholicism." This process involved "the articulation of belief systems...the recruitment and character of various professional clerical bodies, and the constitution and operations of church institutions and systems of rituals."[1] The various confessions used church bodies such as consistory and clerical courts to enforce uniformity in belief, practice, and moral conduct on all of their members. The result was an increasingly rigid religious situation with mutual antagonisms on all sides. Confessions defined and clarified identities at the price of flexibility and compromise.

The spirit debate took place against a background of strong confessionalism within the Dutch Reformed church of the late seventeenth century. On a certain level the spirit debate formed a part of the history of confessionalism and the resistance to it in the Dutch Republic. It was not Cartesianism as such, or even the new philosophy and new science as a whole, that promoted intellectual resistance to confessionalism within the Dutch church. This resistance arose from within the church itself from the days of Arminius onward. It was this resistance, however, which ultimately led to a broader acceptance of the new science and philosophy both within the church, where it was an effective weapon against confessionalism, and in Dutch intellectual life in general.

In the 1960s historian Gerhard Oestreich introduced the concept of social discipline to describe the enforcement of church discipline, the consolidation of confessional identity, and the drive for religious uniformity that were at the heart of confessionalism.[2] Shortly thereafter, Ernst Walter Zeeden used the concept of confession formation to explain the post-Reformation development of the Lutheran, Calvinist, and Catholic churches, arguing that these confessions had structural similarities that included their elaborate doctrinal systems, complex rituals, disciplined personnel, and well-established institutions.[3] Wolfgang Reinhard argued that the Reformation and Counter-Reformation were in many ways parallel rather than opposing phenomena. Both gave birth to a process of confessionalism that rested on the formulation of religious dogma and the use of confessional propaganda, education, discipline, ritual, and language to weld social groups together. The early modern state incorporated the church into the state bureaucracy and used religion to impose social discipline on its subjects, Reinhard argued.[4]   More recently, Heinz Schilling has focussed on the interplay between confessionalism and politics in northwest Germany and the northeast Netherlands,

---

[1]R. Po-Chia Hsia, *Social Discipline in the Reformation:Central Europe 1550-1750* (London, 1989), 5, 123.

[2]Ibid., 1; Gerhard Oestreich, *Geist und Gestalt des fruhmodernen Staates* (Berlin, 1969), translated and altered version Brigitte Oestreich and Helmut Koenigsberger (eds.), David McLintock (trans.), *Neostoicism and the Early Modern State* (Cambridge, 1982).

[3]Ernst Walter Zeeden, *Die Entstehung der Konfessionen. Grundlagen und Formen der Konfessionsbildung* (Munich, 1965); *Konfessionsbildung* (Stuttgart, 1985); Zeeden and H. Molitor (eds.), *Die Visitation im Dienst der kirchlichen Reform* (Munster, 1977); Zeeden and Peter Thaddaus Lang (eds.), *Kirche und Visitation. Beitrage zur Erforschung des fruhneuzeitlichen Visitationswesens in Europa* (Stuttgart, 1984).

[4]Hsia, 2; Wolfgang Reinhard, "Zwang zur Konfessionalisierung? Prolegomena zu einer Theorie des konfessionellen Zeitalters,"*Zeitschrift fur historische Forschung* X (1983), 257-277; "Gegenreformation als Modernisierung? Prolegomena zu einer Theorie des konfessionellen Zeitalters," *Archive for Reformation History* LXVIII (1977), 226-252; "Konfession und Konfessionalisierun in Europa," *Bekenntnis und Geschichte: Schriften der Philosophischen Facultaten der Universitat Augsburg*, ed. by Wofang Reinhard (Augsburg, 1981), 165-189.

arguing that Calvinism was more amenable to the centralization of state power than Lutheranism. Similarly, Richard Gawthrop has examined the role of Lutheran Pietism in the formation of the Prussian state.[5]

Lutheran and Calvinist churches and confessional states relied on a system of visitations, denunciations, and coercion to enforce religious discipline and achieve conformity, but persuasion was also an important tool for uniformity. Confessionalization was more than a process of social discipline; it was also a process of acculturation in which many media were employed to create distinct confessional cultures aimed at reinforcing conformity. Theater, poetry, hymns, catechisms, sermons, legends, and all sorts of books, from biblical, devotional, and prayer books to household guides, almanacs, and histories, were used in a process of acculturation that was critical to the creation of confessional identities.[6]

The process of confessionalization appeared in the Dutch Reformed church during the revolt against Spain and intensified in the first decades of the seventeenth century. In the Dutch Republic, however, there was virtually no link between the confessional church and the state. While the Reformed church was the official church of the Republic, there was little effort on the part of the government to enforce religious conformity in a country with great spiritual diversity that included significant communities of Mennonites, Lutherans, Catholics, Jews, Remonstrants, Socinians, Collegiants, Quakers, and others. Although occupants of public office were required to belong to the Reformed church, no individual was forced to join that church. People were free to belong to one of the other churches, which were permitted to hold their worship services in private, or even to no church at all. The republican government's religious policies reflected the pluralism of interests present in the diverse social and religious situation of the United Provinces. In such circumstances the religious uniformity that was often the goal of absolutist regimes was simply not possible.

The relationship between the state and the official church in the Republic also differed from that in absolutist countries. Although the state owned church buildings and paid the salaries of the Reformed clergy, there was no real state direction of the church, nor was there even much cooperation between the two institutions. Church and state often worked at cross purposes, as was the case in the sabbath controversy. The church repeatedly tried to assert its autonomy, although without much success. The state did not attempt to use the church for its own purposes as much as it tried simply to limit the church's interference in government, society, and economic life. The close relationship between church and state that resulted from the Synod of Dordrecht in 1618-19 was both anomalous and short-lived in a country where diversity rather than uniformity was the rule.

As we have seen, however, confessionalization did take place to a significant extent within the Dutch Reformed church itself. Refugees from the southern Netherlands and Puritan influence from England formed a powerful confessional party that triumphed at the Synod of Dordrecht in 1619. It then fought for the rest of the century to maintain its position against an opposition that would not die.

---

[5]Hsia, 2; Heinz Schilling (ed.), *Die reformierte Konfessionalisierung in Deutschland—das Problem der "2. Reformation"* (Gutersloh, 1986); "The Second Reformation—Problems and Issues," in Heinz Schilling (ed.), *Religion, Political Culture, and the Emergence of Early Modern Society: Essays in German and Dutch History* (Leiden, 1982); *Civic Calvinism* (Kirksville, Mo., 1991); Richard Gawthrop, *Pietism and the Making of Eighteenth-Century Prussia* (Cambridge, 1993).

[6]Hsia, 89-90.

After Calvin's death in 1564, systematic theology came to play a larger role in the training of Reformed clergy throughout Europe as a result of the need to fight polemical battles against Catholics and other confessions. The influence of this Calvinist scholasticism reached into other areas of Reformed thought. In the Dutch Republic, Gomarus and his followers made Calvinism into an increasingly intellectualized system in which emphasis fell on right belief, on "religious truth set forth in carefully reasoned propositions," as F. Ernest Stoeffler has put it. Conformity to confession and catechism was of paramount importance. Preaching focussed on the setting forth of correct doctrine, and thorough knowledge of the catechism was a prerequisite of church membership, although this ideal was not always in practice achieved.

In the years after the triumph of the Gomarists at Dordrecht the Reformed church demanded two things of its members: 1) strict moral conduct, and 2) a thorough knowledge of, and consent to, the church's primary confessional writings—the Formulas of Unity: the Dutch Confession of Faith, the Heidelberg Catechism, and the decrees of the Synod of Dordrecht, including especially the five articles against the Remonstrants. The intellectual structure of Dutch Reformed confessionalism consisted of an alliance between the biblical literalism and scholastic theology of the confessional party on the one hand, and the legalism introduced by English Puritanism and epitomized in Voetius's doctrine of precision on the other hand.[7] The drive within the *Nadere Reformatie* for a reformation of Christian life based on obedience to divine law followed naturally from the strict doctrinal orthodoxy of Gomarus and his successors. While the Gomarists saw themselves as precisely defining divine truth and requiring belief in this truth, Teellinck, Udemans, and other men of the *Nadere Reformatie* accepted this precision of belief as a foundation for precision of conduct.

A number of primary assumptions underpinned the intellectual structure of Dutch Reformed confessionalism, the foremost of which was biblical literalism. The idea that the literal meaning of the Bible was its single, evident sense rested on the interconnected assumptions that Scripture was clear through itself and that the only source of scriptural authority was the text. Literalism necessitated the rejection of allegorical, parabolic, or figurative interpretation as well as the subordination of all external sources of authority to the authority of the text. Literalists saw scriptural interpretation as relatively un-problematic, as an act of rational perception that really involved little need for interpretation at all.[8]   Bible passages stood for themselves without need of context, and this was in fact how they were used as proof texts to supply scriptural authority for the doctrinal propositions of Dutch Reformed confessions and catechisms.

A second basic assumption underlying Dutch Reformed confessionalism was that faith was an explicit and rational process. Confessionalists believed that reason could extract from Scripture the essential truths of faith and cast them in rational, propositional

---

[7]The term "scholasticism" is used here and in what follows to refer to the increasingly intellectualized, systematized, and often highly complex theology focussing on precise definition of doctrine and lengthy explication of dogmatic points that was developed within the Dutch Reformed church by Gomarus and his followers, and later especially by Gisbertus Voetius and other Voetians. This Reformed scholasticism often showed the influence of medieval and early modern Catholic Scholastic philosophy and theology. The terms "Precision" and "Precisionism" are used to refer to the strict application of religious doctrine and biblical precepts to the moral life of the individual believer, a tendency inherited by the Dutch Reformed church from English Puritanism and applied especially by the party of Gomarus and later by Voetius and his followers.

[8]Thomas McGahagan, *Cartesianism in the Netherlands 1639-1676; The New Science and the Calvinist Counter-Reformation* (dissertation, Univ. of Pennsylvania, 1976), 64.

form to create the doctrines of theology without any real interpretation taking place. Believers would then establish their faith and gain entrance into the church by rationally assenting to these doctrines. It was in this way that the Reformed confessions and catechisms were constructed, as were the systematic theological expositions of the confessional documents such as those produced by Voetius. Confessional documents were the heart of confessionalism because of the conception of faith as an act of intellectual assent. Only biblical truth re-cast in such rational, propositional form could be the object of an act of intellectual assent, and such assent was seen as critical evidence of true belief.[9]

In the process of constructing confessions, catechisms, and theological expositions key statements and doctrines were given biblical authority by the use of proof texts. Scriptural texts from which the doctrines or statements were believed to have been derived, or which were seen as confirming the divine truth of the doctrines or statements, were cited (but not quoted or explained) after each doctrine or even, in some cases, within the text of the doctrine itself after each critical point. No further explanation was needed because it was assumed that the scripural texts' literal meaning was their only true meaning and that it was evident through itself. The use of proof texts had been present in medieval Catholic theology as well, but in Reformed confessional documents and theological works these texts were made to stand by themselves without any intellectual support as the sole source of authority for theological doctrine. Confessional theology was thus constructed as "a logical system into which Scripture passages were fitted as proof texts."[10]

The first of the Dutch Reformed Formulas of Unity, the *Nederlandse Geloofsbelijdenis* (Dutch Confession of Faith) was constructed in this way in 1562 and slightly modified later by the Synod of Dordrecht. Subtitled "The Christian Confession Containing the Eternal Salvation of Souls," it consisted of 37 articles containing the essentials of Reformed belief, each article supported by an army of Scripture citations.

Article one, concerning the one true God stated: "We believe from the heart and confess with the mouth that there is one single and simple spiritual being, which we call God, eternal, inscrutable, invisible, infinite, wholly wise, righteous, and good."[11] The scriptural proof texts cited in the margin were II Corinthians 3:17, John 4:24, and Isaiah 40 and 44. II Corinthians 3:17 reads: "Now the Lord is that Spirit: and where the Spirit of the Lord is, there is liberty." John 4:24 reads: "God is a Spirit: and they that worship him must worship him in spirit and in truth." Isaiah 40, containing the prophecy of the forerunner, speaks of God thus in verse 28: "Hast thou not known? hast thou not heard, that the everlasting God, the Lord, the Creator of the ends of the earth, fainteth not, neither is weary? there is no searching of his understanding." Isaiah 44 speaks of God in verse 6: "Thus saith the Lord the King of Israel, and his redeemer the Lord of hosts; I am the first, and I am the last; and beside me there is no God," and in verse 24: "Thus saith the Lord, thy redeemer, and he that formed thee from the womb, I am the Lord that maketh all things; that stretcheth forth the heavens alone; that spreadeth abroad the earth by myself."

---

[9]McGahagan, 62-63, 362.

[10]F. Ernest Stoeffler, *The Rise of Evangelical Pietism* (Leiden, 1965), 114.

[11]*De Nederlandse Geloofsbelijdenis*, from the 1562 text, ed. Dr. A. van der Linde (Nijmegen, 1865), 1.

Article three dealt with the divine authority of Scripture and the Decalogue:

We confess that this word of God has not been sent or brought forth from the will of man; but the holy men inspired by the spirit of God have spoken, as St. Peter said; thereafter through the special care that God has for us and our salvation he commanded his servants and prophets and apostles to write down his revealed word. Yes, and he has even with his own finger written the two tablets of the law. This is why we call such writings holy and Godly.[12]

In the margin beside this article were cited as authority II Peter 1:21; Psalm 102:9; Exodus 17:14, 31:16 and 34:27; and Deuteronomy 5:22.[13]

The uproar caused among the orthodox by Bekker's ideas on spirits becomes more understandable in light of article 12 of the confession, which dealt with angels and devils:

We believe that this one God, according to his pleasure has created the heaven, the earth, and all creatures from nothing, through his Word (his Son) and he gives each creature its essence, form, and figure, and each its own different offices to serve its creator: also he maintains and rules them with his eternal providence and through his infinite strength, serving man so that man can serve God. He also created the angels good to be his servants and servants of his chosen people. Some of these angels fell from the height that God created them in, into eternal damnation. The others through the grace of God remained in their original state. The last, whom we call Devils and evil spirits, are so corrupted that they became enemies of God and all good, leering and standing with all their might against the churches, in order to wholly destroy them with their poison and deceit. They even make people pray to them and promise men great things. And that is no wonder since the devil even dared to come before Christ to make him pray to him: and therefore they are by their own evil doomed to eternal damnation and await their punishment and pain. And we reject the error of the Sadducees, who deny that there are spirits and angels: and also the error of the Manichees, who say that devils had their origin out of themselves and are bad from their own nature and never at any time became corrupt.[14]

As proof texts the confession cited the following passages, the meaning and interpretation of all of which were hotly debated during the dispute around *The World Bewitched*: Isaiah 40:26, Daniel 14:4, Matthew 26:19, I John 15, Acts 5:3, I Corinthians 3:16 and 6:11, Romans 8:9, Colossians 1:16, I Timothy 4:3, Hebrews 3:4, Revelations 4:11 and 11:16, Hebrews 1:14, Psalms 103:21 and 34:8, John 8:44, II Peter 2:1, Luke 8:31, Matthew 25:51, and Acts 23:8.

---

[12]Ibid., 2.

[13]II Peter 1:21 reads :"For the prophecy came not in old time by the will of man: but holy men of God spake as they were moved by the Holy Ghost." Exodus 17:14: reads: "And the Lord said unto Moses, Write this for a memorial in a book, and rehearse it in the ears of Joshua: for I will utterly put out the remembrance of Amalek from under heaven;" Exodus 31:16:"Wherefore the children of Israel shall keep the sabbath, to observe the sabbath throughout their generations, for a perpetual covenant;" Exodus 34:27:"And the Lord said unto Moses, Write thou these words: for after the tenor of these words I have made a covenant with thee and with Israel." And Deuteronomy 5:22 reads: "These words the Lord spake unto all your assembly in the mount out of the midst of the fire, of the cloud, and of the thick darkness, with a great voice: and he added no more. And he wrote them in two tables of stone, and delivered them unto me."

[14]*De Nederlandse Geloofsbelijdenis*, 12.

Biblical proof texts were used in much the same way in the *Heidelberg Catechism of the Reformed Christian Religion*, composed in Heidelberg in 1563 by Zacharias Ursinus, Johannes Veluanus, and Caspar Olevianus. It consisted of 129 questions and answers to be taught over the course of 53 Sundays. The questions were divided into three broad categories: "of the misery of man," "of man's deliverance," and "of thankfulness," and included smaller sections on the sacraments and on prayer. Questions 23-58 consisted of a detailed exposition of the Apostles' Creed, while each of the Ten Commandments was treated individually in questions 92-113. The Lord's Prayer was examined in questions 119-129.

Question one was typical of how citations of biblical passages were used within the text to lend authority to the main points of belief:

Question: What is the only comfort in life or death?

Answer: That both in soul and body (I Corinthians 6:19-20), whether I live or die (Romans 14:7-9), I am not mine own, but belong (I Corinthians 3:23) wholly unto my most faithful Lord and Savior Jesus Christ, who by his precious blood (I Peter 1:18-19) most fully (I John 1:7) satisfying for all of my sins, hath delivered (I John 3:8) me from all the power of the Devil, and so preserveth me (John 6:39, 10:28-29) that without the will of my heavenly father, not so much as a hair (Luke 21:18, Matthew 10:30) may fall from my head: But rather on the contrary all things must be (Romans 8:28) subservient to my salvation. Wherefore by his Spirit also he assureth me (II Corinthians 1:22, 5:7) of everlasting life, and maketh (Romans 8:14, 7:22) me ready, and prepared, that henceforth I may live to him.[15]

Questions 21 and 22 put forward the Reformed confessionalist view of belief and faith:

Question: What is true faith?

Answer: It is not only a true knowledge (John 6:69,17:3; Hebrews 11:3-6) whereby I firmly assent to all things which God (Romans 18:20) hath revealed unto us in his word, but also an assured (Romans 4:16, 20-21; James 1:8; Ephesians 3:12) Trust or Confidence kindled in my heart by the Holy (Romans 1:16, I Corinthians 1:21, Acts 16:14, Matthew 16:17, John 3:5) Ghost, through the Gospel (Romans 10:14-17), whereby I acquiesce in God, being assuredly persuaded that remission (Matthew 9:2) of sin, eternal righteousness (Romans 5:1) and life is given not to others only, but to me (Galatians 2:20) also, and that freely through (Romans 3:24-26) the merits of Christ alone.

Question: What are those things which are necessary for a Christian to believe?

Answer: All things which are promised (John 20:31, Matthew 28: 19-20) us in the Gospel: the sum where of is briefly contained in the Creed of the Apostles, or in the Articles of the catholic and undoubted Faith of all Christians.[16]

Following came a detailed exposition of the Apostles' Creed, point for point, with biblical citations interspersed. The catechism also treated the Ten Commandments at

---

[15]*Heidelberg Catechism of the Reformed Christian Religion* (Amsterdam, 1744), 3-4.
[16]Ibid., 13-14.

length. In its discussion of the First Commandment to "have no other Gods before me" the catechism said that Christians should "shun and fly all Idolatry (I Corinthians 6:9-10, 10:7-14), sorcery (Leviticus 19:41; Deuteronomy 18: 10-12), enchantment, superstition (Matthew 4:10; Revelations 19:10), and invocation of saints or any other creatures," thus lending ecclesiastical and biblical authority to the existence of sorcery and enchantment and categorizing them along with other common practices such as the invocation of saints.[17] Bekker's critics repeatedly charged that his ideas about spirits violated this section of the catechism.

Education was an important tool of confessional conformity, and the catechism lay at the heart of a program of confessional education that was based on control, discipline, and authority. The memorized questions and answers of the catechism were a primary preparation for church membership, and because this preparation was so intensely intellectual some came to believe that rational consent to doctrine was all that belief entailed, if accompanied by a moral life.[18]

Jodocus Lodensteyn was an active proponent of the value of catechizing and he placed great emphasis on purity of doctrine. Under his influence the preachers of Utrecht stressed the teaching of religion through catechism so much that in 1654 sixteen separate catechism sessions were held in the city each week. The catechism regulated admission to the church and guided the spiritual life of members. The Confession Catechism was done by everyone who confessed personal belief in order to be admitted to communion as a member of the church, while the Competence Catechism was demanded of members who displayed good moral conduct but ignorance of doctrine before they could be re-admitted to communion. There were separate catechisms for school children, for girls and boys aged 12-18, and for adults. Bekker's troubles with the confessional party began when he wrote an adult catechism after having successfully completed two others for children. Lodensteyn usually directed no fewer than five separate catechism sessions each week, usually on Sundays, Wednesdays, and Fridays, including a general catechism, one for people preparing for communion, and a practical catechism in the orphanage church.

In the same way that the process of catechizing made belief intellectual and closely tied to education, the systematic reasoning of Voetius and other theologians produced elaborate treatments of church doctrine that grew into a Reformed theology. As doctrine became more complex and confessional orthodoxy more precise, university professors of theology gained great authority as definers of true belief for the church. This new scholastic theology was based on the same assumption that underlay the construction of Reformed confessions and catechisms: that reason could extract the essential points of religious truth from Scripture and formulate them in logical form. Theological works used proof texts in much the same way as did the confessions and catechisms, to lend biblical authority to their doctrines, and thus these works too rested ultimately on the foundation of biblical literalism. While confessions and catechisms were designed primarily to educate the general church membership as a means to enforce intellectual conformity and religious discipline, theological works were intended to do much the same thing among the educated.[19]

The greatest theologian of Dutch Reformed confessionalism was Gisbertus Voetius, professor and preacher in Utrecht. As a successful teacher at the university Voetius

---

[17]Ibid., 63-64, 69.
[18]Hsia, 117; J. C. Trimp, *Jodocus Lodensteyn: Predikant en Dichter* (Kampen, 1987), 181.
[19]Trimp, 44-94.

focussed on dogmatics and ethics, stressing the study of the church fathers and medieval Scholastics as well as church law and practical piety. Voetius also emphasized the doctrinal importance of Reformed religious controversies with the Remonstrants, Catholics, and Socinians. He wrote no textbooks of dogma but instead used regular Saturday public disputations, later collected and published, as the vehicle for his doctrinal teaching. In such disputations Voetius believed that he spoke from the letter and spirit of Scripture and with its authority. He saw theology as the queen of the sciences because it spoke with the full authority of Scripture, and he held the Bible to be the source of all science and art. Voetius was also much concerned with practical theology because, as a member of the *Nadere Refomatie*, he believed that true doctrine had to result in a pious life.[20]

Voetius's method of theology as well as his concern for practical piety were illustrated in his disputation "Concerning Practical Theology" published in Utrecht in 1648 in his collection *Selectae Disputationes Theologicae*. In the broadest sense practical theology was "all theology that follows Scripture or is based upon it, whether expressed in commentaries, the *loci communi*, or catechisms, because all theology among pilgrims here on earth is in its nature practical," Voetius argued. More specifically, Voetius defined practical or casuistic theology as "a practical and specific exposition or application of the context of the polemic or didactic exposition of theological topics."[21] In the narrowest sense, Voetius continued, practical theology was simply the exposition of the Decalogue or particular parts of the Decalogue.[22]

After discussing the opinions of other theologians on the definition of practical theology, Voetius divided its subject matter into three parts. The first part was moral or casuistic theology, and its material was based on questions 86-115 in the catechism, questions discussing good works and explaining the Ten Commandments. The second part was ascetic theology; it taught the practice of devotion based on the catechism section on prayer, questions 116-129. The third part was ecclesiastical polity, and its material was based on the Dutch liturgy, church constitutions, and the catechism section on church discipline, questions 83-85.

Voetius next turned to a discussion of two primary problems of practical theology. First he dealt with the question of whether or not Reformed theologians were really concerned with this kind of theology, answering in the affirmative despite claims made by the Remonstrants that Reformed theology was "purely speculative." The second problem centered on the question of whether practical theology was useful and necessary in the schools and churches. Indeed so, Voetius declared, despite the fact that the enemies of this kind of theology called it "biblical literalism, quarrelsomeness, precisionism, puritanism, anabaptism, legalistic, and anti-evangelical." Perhaps words like "casuistic, scholastic, ascetic, (and) ecclesiastical polity" scared people away from the study of demanding theology, Voetius suggested. He then offered several kinds of proof for the necessity and usefulness of practical theology, including first of all testimony from Scripture in the form of a number of proof texts, among them I Timothy 6:3 and 4:7, Titus 1:1, and Acts 24:16.[23]

---

[20]Ibid., 24.

[21]Gisbertus Voetius, "Concerning Practical Theology," taken from *Selectae Disputationes Theologicae* (Utrecht 1648-49), in John W. Beardslee (ed. and trans.), *Reformed Dogmatics* (New York, 1965), 265.

[22]Ibid., 267.

[23]Ibid., 267-275.

Voetius next dealt with several objections to practical theology. Some said that it introduced into the church a piety more pure than was ordinary and accepted, an objection often made against the English Puritans, Voetius added. But blessed were those Puritans who had a real concern for practice and for purity of heart and conscience, Voetius declared, and he cited as proof texts Matthew 5:8, I Corinthians 5:7, II Corinthians 7:1, I James 3:3, and Jude 23. The "precision of faith and conduct which all the pious are required to seek and desire has now been assigned by some to a hated 'Puritanism,'" Voetius continued, but he added that Puritans were simply "zealous for purity and the orthodox doctrine of the total grace of God."[24]

Still another objection was that practical theology focussed on minutiae while rejecting the true heart of theology. Voetius replied to this criticism by citing Matthew 23:23 and by arguing that no matter how small a sin was, ignoring it did not improve piety. Finally, some objected that practical theologians, by raising so many cases of conscience, disturbed the peace of church and state and subverted ecclesiastical and civil discipline. In his reply to this objection Voetius blamed it on Descartes, whom he called "a man skilled in mathematics but clearly no theologian," and he then referred to the condemnation of Descartes' works by the Utrecht University senate.[25] To end his work Voetius discussed the sources and method of practical theology, answered some frequently asked questions concerning this kind of theology, and dealt with some common errors and fallacies that often crept into moral judgments.

As Voetius's interest in practical theology shows, another important foundation of Dutch Reformed confessionalism was the strict legalism in obedience to divine law that grew out of the Puritan and pietist movements. Once doctrine had been clearly established, the will of God made known, and divine law clearly laid out, complete and total obedience was required as a central mark of piety. The Puritans were profoundly biblical in their attempt to apply the insights of Scripture to the daily life of believers, and they were legalistic in their insistence on strict obedience to what they perceived to be biblical standards of thought and conduct. Religious idealists motivated by the idea that a more perfect Christianity could be achieved on earth, they opposed formalism and externals in favor of devotional literature and exercises to keep believers responsive to God's will. Puritans demanded intense Bible reading, prayer, and strict church attendance, and their sermons were practical, moving, and legalistic.[26]

Under Puritan influence, the proponents of the Dutch *Nadere Reformatie* believed that faith was made explicit through obedience to rules.[27] Within the *Nadere Reformatie,* two distinct tendencies became apparent, the one ascetic and legalistic and often referred to by the name of "precisionism," the other displaying an inclination toward mysticism.

This latter position was represented by Jean de Taffin (1529-1602), who was born in Tournai, an early center of Calvinism in the southern Netherlands, but who fled to the north during the revolt against Spain. In his main work, *Van de Merck-Teeckenen der Kinderen Gods* (The Marks of the Children of God), Taffin argued that the true Christian had both inward and outward marks. The outward marks included willingness

---

[24]Ibid., 282.

[25]Ibid., 280-281, 286-287.

[26]Stoeffler, 10-23.

[27]McGahagan, 87; T. Brienen, *et. al., De Nadere Reformatie: Beschrijving van haar voornaamste vertegenwoordigers* (The Hague, 1986), 5-10, 349-366.

to hear the gospel purely preached and the sacraments purely administered, while the inward marks included the testimony of the Holy Spirit in the heart of the believer, peace of conscience, love of neighbor, and love for and obedience to God. For Taffin, the main source of certainty of personal election was not, as Stoeffler put it, "a series of reasoned convictions gathered from the Bible," but rather an inner feeling of desire brought by the Holy Spirit. He felt that confessional formulas as evidences of faith were secondary to piety in daily experience.[28]

Willem Teellinck, an early participant in the sabbath controversy, deplored what he saw as the spiritual laxity of the church. A true confessionalist, he maintained that the Bible had to be interpreted in the light of the confessional formulas.[29] A similar method of interpreting Scripture was adopted by William Ames (1576-1633), the first important systematic theologian of the *Nadere Reformatie*. Like Taffin, he saw theology not as a collection of assertions about God but as a knowledge of how to live in accordance with God's will. Faith, for Ames, was a trust in the person of Christ and in his revelation. He believed that complete obedience to God's will as revealed in Scripture was man's primary religious duty, and that every detail of man's life had to conform to God's law.[30] In this belief Ames was part of that tendency within the *Nadere Refomatie* known as "precisionism."

The doctrine of precision was the heart of *Nadere Reformatie* legalism. Intimately linked to the drive within confessionalism for religious discipline, it became one of the central issues behind the sabbath debate. Precisionism thus emerged as a chief point of contention between the confessional party and its opponents in the Republic.

Precisionism was based on the belief that a list of precepts could be drawn from the Bible and made into a rule of life for the elect, who would obey this rule out of thankfulness for their election. Pride of place among these biblical precepts was taken by the Ten Commandments, which is why the attack on the Fourth Commandment in the sabbath debate was seen as such a serious threat to the structure of Reformed confessionalism.[31]

The founder of precisionism in the Dutch Republic was Gottfried Udemans, an early participant in the sabbath debate. Udemans saw true piety as centered on the Ten Commandments, the Apostles' Creed, and the Lord's Prayer.[32] But the greatest Dutch theologian of precisionism was without doubt Gisbertus Voetius. For Voetius, piety was "geloofsgehoorzamheid," obedience to the law as expressed in the Decalogue made possible through faith. Man's gratitude for faith was expressed through good works. Voetius held that divine law was expressed in the confessional formulas of the church, and he saw obedience to these formulas as crucial for the purity of the ecclesiastical body. Voetius's piety was both ascetic and militant, intolerant of all that he saw as offensive to pious life. His disputation "On Precision: in Interpretation of Questions 94, 113, and 115 of the Heidelberg Catechism" could perhaps be regarded as the manifesto of the precisionist party.[33] It illustrated particularly well the Reformed confessional alliance between legalism and scholasticism.

[28]Stoeffler, 121-124; Brienen, 56, 65, 366.
[29]Stoeffler, 127-133; Brienen 17-47.
[30]Stoeffler, 134-136.
[31]Stoeffler, 59; Trimp, 195.
[32]Stoeffler, 125.
[33]Trimp, 25.

In the first part of the disputation Voetius defined precision and then discussed its subject, object, causes, adjuncts, effects, and contradictories. In the second part of the disputation he replied to objections made against precision. Voetius defined precision as "the exact or perfect human action conforming to the law of God" as taught by Scripture.[34] The subject of precision was the truly converted believer who pleased God and was accepted by him for salvation, Voetius continued, and he cited as proof texts Hebrews 11:6, Romans 14:23, and Acts 15:9. The object of precision was "the practice of piety or obedience according to God's Word." The primary cause of precision was God, who wanted his children to be pure, holy, and perfect. The most important secondary cause was the Word of God, which was the sole standard for precision, while minor causes included love, fear, and honor for God; hope for salvation; tranquility of conscience; freedom; blessedness; and the glory of believers. As proof texts for these statements Voetius cited Matthew 7:13, 11:12; I John 3:31; I Peter 1:3 collated with 1:12-15; Acts 24:15-16; and II Corinthians 11:27-29 collated with 6:4-11.[35]

Obstacles to precision included the belief that it was burdensome, useless, or adiaphoristic; the bad example of the majority of Christians; imitation of the crowd; and lack of steadfastness due to fear of hatred and scorn from others. Adjuncts to precision, or things that went with it, Voetius divided into necessary, concomitant, and signatory. Necessary adjuncts, things that precision could not do without, included regard for the whole divine law and an effort to conform to it as exactly as possible (proof texts: Psalm 119:104 collated with Matthew 5:19-20); doing good and avoiding evil with the intention of obeying and glorifying God (Psalms 71:8, 34:2, 119:14; Philippians 2:12; Romans 12:11; Matthew 5:16 collated with 22:37; Psalm 119:10); and having faith, courage, fortitude, prudence, knowledge, and the "spiritual eye" (commentaries on James 2:10 and II Peter 1:5-8).

Under concomitant adjuncts (things that would naturally go with precision) Voetius listed spiritual power in the work of the Lord (Matthew 11:29-30, Isaiah 40:31); a multitude of good works (Philippians 1:9, I Corinthians 15:58, II Peter 1:8); spiritual peace (Philippians 4:7); as well as mockery, insults, lukewarm brethren, and alienation from the mass of mankind. Adjuncts that were signatory, or signs of precision, included compassion, humility, dependence on God, and being always and everywhere bound to God's laws. Special effects of precision were that one would not uncritically accept every new, eloquent, or subtle teaching (I Thessalonians 5:21, I John 4:1-2); reformation and purging of public worship (II Kings 18:3-6, 22, collated with 23:13); reformation of life and manners, public and private, down to the very slightest appearance of evil or corruption (Jude 23 collated with I Thessalonians 5:22-23; I Corinthians 9:15, 19, 27, 10:32-33); avoidance of things that lax Christians did not consider wrong, such as drama, gambling, dancing, and luxury in hair or dress; and, finally, the use of private admonishment as well as ecclesiastical censure and discipline.[36]

Among objections to precision Voetius considered the claim that it was impossible. It is our duty, he responded, and that is enough to require preachers to teach it and members of the congregation to work at it. As proof text he cited Ephesians 3:15 ("see that you walk circumspectly, not as fools but as wise"). To the objection that precision

---

[34]Gisbertus Voetius, "On Precision: In Interpretation of Questions 94, 113, and 115 of the Heidelberg Catechism," taken from *Selectae Disputationes Theologicae* (Utrecht, 1648-49), in Beardslee, 317.

[35]Ibid., 318-320

[36]Ibid., 320-323.

destroyed Christian freedom, a claim often heard in the sabbath controversy, Voetius simply replied that such could not be done by the precision required by the word of God. Another objection was that to elevate oneself above one's brethren was a form of pride and disdain for others, to which Voetius replied that the desire to perfectly obey all of the commands of God was supreme humility, and he cited as proof texts Philippians 3:15-16 and Galatians 6:1-7.[37]

While Voetius's disputation discussed precision on a theoretical level, the application of precision to individual conduct was illustrated in Jacobus Koelman's work on observation of the sabbath entitled *De Practijk of dadelijke heyliging der Christelijken Sabbaths, kortelijk voorgestelt* (The Practice or Actual Sanctification of the Christian Sabbath Briefly Presented, Amsterdam, 1682). Koelman held that Christians were obligated by the divine authority of the Fourth Commandment to observe the Lord's Day with religious service and rest from daily work. In the *Practijk* he went to great lengths to define how Christians should observe Sunday and which works were permitted, which forbidden.

According to Koelman, the believer should spend the Lord's Day praying, both in public and private, reading Scripture, meditating on God and his works, examining him/herself, singing Psalms, hearing God's word and discussing it with others, and giving alms. Proper preparation for the day was necessary. The night before the sabbath the Christian should divert his heart from all worldly cares and from the work of his calling in order to prepare to honor God the next day. He should examine his deeds of the past week and repent of all sins of commission and omission. He should pray with special seriousness for peace from what was past in order to be in the proper disposition for Sunday, and he should prepare his heart to serve the Lord by being filled with a feeling of the majesty and holiness of God.

After awaking on the sabbath day the believer should seek the Lord early with his spirit and give himself over completely to the service of God, Koelman continued. He should dress morally and modestly and without taking too much time, keeping his soul free from all thoughts and intentions that were worldly and profane. He should fill his soul with spiritual and useful thoughts so that sinful, vain, and useless ones would be kept out. The believer should inspect his heart in order to truly know how things stood between himself and God.

If he had a family he should do his best to see that God was served in his household, calling his family together for prayer, Psalm singing, and Scripture reading as much as time permitted. He should take his family regularly to public religious service, and while there behave with dignity, morality, and honor, offending no one with word or gesture. He should pay close attention as long as the service lasted, listening closely to what was said in the sermon and putting his full heart into prayer and song. The service over, he should depart honorably and rejoicing in God, and he should remember what was said there.

The rest from work that the believer had to observe on Sunday lasted the whole day, Koelman argued. Even though every minute of the day could not be spent in religious duties, not one minute could be spent in other occupations. The rest of the whole man was demanded, both internal and external, in deeds, words and thoughts, Koelman proclaimed, citing Isaiah 58:13 as proof text. Works that were forbidden on Sunday included all works that led to one's own profit, pleasure, or contentment. All works of

---

[37]Ibid., 329-331.

one's calling were prohibited, and works ordinarily done on the other six days of the week were also forbidden. Works leading to the outward gain or profit of others were forbidden, as were all works that were not necessary. Works of fleshly pleasure such as playing and excessive laughing were forbidden, as were works serving civic ends such as buying and selling. Works that did not go well with praying, reading, and conversation, such as travel or excessive walking in streets or fields, were not permitted. In short, all that was not a religious or spiritual exercise was banned, Koelman declared.

Special sins against the Fourth Commandment included not adequately preparing for the sabbath; having fleshly thoughts and desiring one's own good on the sabbath; carrying on common or un-educational discourse about the weather, one's health, or other such things on that day; going out walking or visiting in order to save time on other days of the week; sitting so far away from the preacher in church that one could hardly hear in order more easily to carry on idle conversation or to sleep; letting one's children run around playing and making noise on the sabbath; spending Sunday doing nothing or sleeping; and not observing the sabbath when one was away from home.[38]

II

The creation of Reformed confessionalism in the Dutch Republic was an ongoing process in which the intellectual structure became steadily more defined. The creation of a Reformed confessional identity marked members of the church as belonging to a religious group clearly distinct from its competitors. The creation of confessional identity was in part a process of exclusion by which the "true" confession was set apart from the many "false" ones through strict adherence to an established set of beliefs and practices. In this process anything that created or highlighted distinctions among confessions was important.

The many religious controversies fought between confessions and between confessional and anti-confessional parties within churches in the Dutch Republic during the post-Reformation period played an important role in both the creation and the defense of confessional identities. In an atmosphere of religious pluralism where Calvinists, Lutherans, Catholics, Mennonites, Socinians, Collegiants, and others met and worshipped more or less openly and spread their ideas to a broadly literate public through a generally free printing industry, most of the religious controversies of the confessional era flourished. Disputes over baptism, preaching, communion, the role of reason in religion, methods and points of exegesis, and many specifics of doctrine, as well as the controversies surrounding the sabbath and the activities of spirits, helped to establish important lines of distinction among the competing religious groups and thus played an important role in the evolution of confessional identities.

These controversies also played an important role in the defense of confessional identities. Competing parties saw in each other's religious polemics attacks on their own confessional and they defended themselves vigorously against these threats, rarely leaving criticism unanswered. In the case of the spirit controversy, the confessional party within the Reformed church saw in the Cartesian and Coccejan attack on biblical literalism an attack on the very structure of confessional identity

[38]Ibid., 104-106.

itself. The threat of a loss of confessional identity caused the confessional party to wage long and sustained warfare against Cartesianism and Coccejanism. This helps to explain the persistence and vehemence of the opposition that followed Bekker's ideas from the appearance of the *Vaste Spyse* in 1670 through the debate around *The World Bewitched* in the 1690s. The confessional party charged its opponents with promoting skepticism and atheism, but what it really feared was a loss of the confessional identity upon which its entire vision of the church was founded.

Voetius spoke for many other confessionalists when he discussed the importance of religious controversies in his disputation on practical theology. For Voetius, it was an obligation and a duty of the Reformed theologian to "dispute with Papists, Anabaptists, and Socinians," and he listed some of the prime issues in dispute between the Reformed and other confessions. Practical questions in dispute with the Catholics included swearing by the saints, divorce for adultery, and marriage without the consent of parents. With the Remonstrants, the Reformed argued about the power of magistrates with regard to the church, religious freedom, coercion of sectaries, and how to deal with speculative or harmless heresy. With the Mennonites, disputed questions included issues of oath taking, magistracy, war, self-defense, and divorce. Voetius categorized all of these disputed issues as "controversial moral questions," as opposed to "non-controversial moral questions" upon which all confessions agreed, such as questions concerning the morality of lying or of charging excessive interest. By making such disputes part of his treatment of the structure of moral theology rather than dismissing them as adiaphoristic, as many humanistic and anti-confessional writers did (for example, Erasmus and many Collegiant authors), Voetius highlighted the importance of religious controversies for the construction and defense of confessional identity.[39]

The function of religious controversies in the construction and defense of confessional identities suggests two further observations about these disputes: 1) they can be understood best not as intellectual debates but as **religious identity games** with their own special rules, and 2) the process of confessional identity formation was linked to that of **personal identity** formation for many of the participants.

Despite the widely varying subject matter of the various religious controversies, they had a great deal in common in terms of the dynamics with which they were carried out. These similarities suggest a common function within the process of confessional identity formation. One could perhaps speak of a set of general rules that governed the conduct of religious disputes as confessional identity games, and also of separate sets of rules specific to each controversy established by the participants themselves.

In general, religious disputes did not take the form of intellectual exchanges of views in which information was transferred and views modified accordingly. Neither did they take the form of the ordinary university disputation in which competing points of view were considered in all their aspects and dealt with as part of the defense of a thesis. Religious disputes took on a highly polemical character in which competing points of view were presented not as arguments subject to modification but as confessional statements or confessions of faith upon which no compromise was possible. Rather than being forums for the development of logical arguments, religious disputes acted as stages for the presentation of confessional declarations and attacks on other confessions.

The goal of writers who engaged in these controversies was not to convince their opponents or the public of their point of view as much as it was to create an image or

---

[39]Voetius, "Practical Theology," 290-291, 298.

definition of their confession and thus of themselves. Polemical writings functioned as personal confessions of faith and helped to establish a link between confessional identity and the personal identity of the authors. Part of personal identity thus came to be defined confessionally in terms of doctrine and practice for the religious thinkers who took part in these debates. The implications of this intellectualization and confessionalization of personal identity for many seventeenth-century religious thinkers needs further exploration.

In the religious controversies that Bekker was involved in from the sabbath dispute down to the spirit controversy, his own Reformed religious identity came to incorporate a clear anti-confessional bias in the form of his exegetical assumptions. This anti-confessionalism not only placed Bekker on one side of a fundamental theological divide within the Dutch Reformed church, it also threatened the very structure of Reformed confessional identity. Perhaps it was the tension that this situation created within Bekker's own confessional and personal identity that led to his sometimes erratic behavior in the confrontations with church councils, classes, and synods that followed publication of *The World Bewitched*. As van Sluis has pointed out, Bekker was sometimes compromising and other times stubborn in defense of his ideas; he often made concessions and promises that he ultimately could not or would not carry through with.[40] Perhaps a confused sense of personal identity created by Bekker's anti-confessional ideas gradually eroding his Reformed confessional identity was at the root of such behavior. At any rate, the tension that Bekker's anti-confessionalism created within the established structure of Reformed confessional identity was certainly responsible for the church process against him that led to his exclusion from the Reformed communion.

Hsia has pointed out some of the relationships that existed between confessional culture and personality structure, suggesting that the psychological structures of confessional society could be investigated through the study of attitudes toward demonic possession, witchcraft, exorcism, melancholy, and suicide.[41] The present study of attitudes toward spirit activity has provided one such entrance into the complex intellectual structure of Dutch Reformed confessionalism. It may also serve to illuminate some of the larger psychological structures at work in the creation and defense of confessional as well as personal identities in the seventeenth century.

The link of personal identity to confessional identity can help to explain the extremely heated and highly personal tone of many of the religious controversies of the time. When opponents' polemics were viewed not only as attacks on confessional identity but also as a threat to an important part of one's personal identity, the stakes in the battle were doubled. Bitterness, personal attacks, and often vicious name calling became a general rule determining the conduct of many religious controversies. Again Voetius is an excellent witness to this phenomenon. In his disputations on precision and on practical theology he catalogued the names that opponents had called his followers. Some were mild enough and actually indicated ecclesiastical or doctrinal stands: precisionists, sabbatarians, double reformers, and Puritans. Other names, however, were more pointed: zealots, hypocrites, long-noses, killjoys, misanthropes, roundheads, foolish-wise, shorthairs (Voetius did in fact preach against overly long hair), joyless, sad-humored, clothed in melancholy, uncouth barbarians, Batavian oracles, stilt-walkers, and salty-sour Zeelanders.[42]

---

[40]See Jacob van Sluis, *Bekkeriana: Balthasar Bekker biografisch en bibliografisch* (Leeuwarden, 1994), 13-44.

[41]Hsia, 162-164.

[42]Voetius, "On Precision," 324; "Practical Theology," 279.

Another general characteristic of religious disputes was that they were governed by a ritual of reply. Writers almost without fail defended their positions by replying to their opponents' charges, often responding in great detail and length, point by point, in the same order as the criticisms were made. This practice led to the publication in each dispute of long series of works containing charges and counter-charges, with the result that the controversies often dragged out for years with very little new being said after the first several works were published. A great deal of repetition was unavoidable, and perhaps functioned to reinforce confessional and personal identities. The sabbath dispute probably held the record for length, stretching out over the greater part of a century. Some disputes were shorter but more intense: the spirit debate took place between the years 1691-1696 but produced a large number of often lengthy publications.

Finally, many of the works published in these disputes were written in the vernacular or translated for wider popular consumption. Many were highly redundant, poorly organized, and poorly edited, indicating that they were written and published in haste as parts of a running controversy. Often these were not works representing a great deal of reflection or original thought. The intellectual standard of such debates generally fell far short of a scholarly exchange of views and much more resembled a heated argument in which statements were made but minds were not changed. But changing minds was not, after all, the point. Measured by these standards, the level of discourse in the spirit controversy was probably higher than that of many other seventeenth-century debates, perhaps because of the serious exegetical issues at stake.

In addition to these general characteristics or rules of religious dispute, upon which there was a surprising degree of tacit agreement among participants, each controversy also had its own particular rules of engagement. These rules were followed by most of the participants even though they were rarely openly formulated. An exception was the sabbath dispute. In his 1682 work *Methode en Bestieringen om klaar te overtuigen de gene, die des Sabbaths en s'Heeren Dags Godlijke verbintenis nu bestrijden...* (Method and Direction to Clearly Convince Those who Dispute the Divine Authority of the Sabbath and the Lord's Day), Jacobus Koelman formulated what amounted to a set of twenty rules of disputation for his side in the controversy. In an opening chapter entitled "Educational and Guiding Address to All Christians who want to Dispute for the Sabbath and the Lord's Day," he instructed his followers: "Before you dispute, make very clear the state of the difference between you and your opponent. Find out what he admits and what he rejects."[43] Does he deny that the Fourth Commandment is binding on Christians? Does he believe that the Fourth Commandment obligates people to rest and engage in religious exercises one day a week? Does he consider the Fourth Commandment ceremonial when it speaks of rest? Does he see the Lord's Day as a human or a divine institution? Does he favor rest on the whole sabbath day, on half of that day, or only for a few hours? Does he consider it a sin against God's commandment to continue daily work on the sabbath, or does he believe that people have freedom on that day for all work and pleasure?

Koelman advised his followers not to argue with those who maintained that there was a ceremonial element in the Fourth Commandment if this ceremonial element was the Saturday sabbath of the Jews or the strictness particular to the Jews. These were

---

[43]Jacobus Koelman, *Methode en Bestieringen om Klaar te Overtuigen de gene/die des Sabbaths en s'Heeren Dags Godlijke Verbintenis nu Bestrijden. Met Aanwijzing van de Voornaamste argumenten, voor de sabbath, en 's Heeren dagh, En oplossing van de principaalste Tegenwerpingen* (Amsterdam, 1682), 4.

not the real enemies of the sabbath because they agreed that people's consciences were bound by the Fourth Commandment to observe the seventh day in rest and holy exercise. But he advised his followers always to carry in their hearts the truth of the Fourth Commandment and to fight, suffer, and speak for what they believed in. They should prefer to have one of their ten fingers hacked off rather than see one of God's Ten Commandments taken away.

Koelman urged his followers not to be satisfied if their opponent admitted that there had to be a time for public religious service called the Lord's Day if he did not also concede that the Fourth Commandment ordered that every seventh day be devoted to religion and that the whole day had to be observed and other work omitted. It was not enough to say that the Lord's Day was observed on human authority, he reminded his partisans. He also advised them to be well supplied with arguments to prove four crucial points: 1) the sabbath law was still binding on all Christians, 2) the Lord's Day was divinely instituted, 3) its observation was not simply a church custom, and 4) the Lord's Day had to be spent entirely in religion with rest from all unnecessary work. Be convinced of the strength of your arguments, Koelman wrote, and use only those most suited to the capacities of your opponent.

Koelman noted five texts from the Old Testament (Exodus 31:13-17, Ezekiel 20:10-12, Deuteronomy 5:15, Nehemiah 9:13-14, and Isaiah 66:23) and five from the New Testament (Colossians 2:16-17, Galatians 4:10-11, Romans 14:5-6, Matthew 12:17, and Mark 2:27-28) from which opponents took most of their arguments. He advised his followers to be prepared to interpret these texts correctly. He also warned them to be prepared to respond to two of their opponents' chief arguments: that the patriarchs before Moses had no sabbath, and that the heathens were not punished for keeping no sabbath as they were for other sins. These objections were easily answered, Koelman said.

In addition, Koelman urged his followers to show opponents that their ideas were "new and novel" and resembled those of the "heretical Socinians and Anabaptists." They should also show them that their ideas contradicted Reformed church synods and catechisms, government decrees, and especially the Fourth Commandment. They should prove to opponents that what they said about the spiritual sabbath of the New Testament did not absolve Christians from the obligation of the Fourth Commandment to observe the sabbath of the seventh day. Do not argue over exactly which works are permitted on the sabbath and which ones forbidden, Koelman added, because opponents love to argue about this. Just insist that by the authority of God's commandment people must rest from all unnecessary daily work. Leave the particulars to the opponents' consciences.

Finally, Koelman advised avoiding all battles over words as vain and useless. But when one saw that someone was an enemy of the sabbath and refused to call the Lord's Day the sabbath in order to give the impression that Christians need not make that day holy with rest, then one should stand up and fight for the name of the sabbath.[44]

III

The development of Reformed confessionalism in the Dutch Republic was marked by opposition from a strong anti-confessional party that presented more serious resistance to confessionalization of religious life than was encountered in absolutist states.

---

[44]Ibid., 3-6.

Resistance to confessional uniformity and the imposition of religious discipline took place both in society at large and within the Reformed church itself. This resistance suffered a temporary setback at the Synod of Dordrecht in 1619 when the Remonstrants were ejected from the Reformed church, but they soon returned from exile to the Republic and formed an independent church. Meanwhile, the battle against confessionalism within the Reformed church was carried on by Cartesians and Coccejans. Their resistance, along with the tacit and sometimes even open assistance of civil authorities, assured that confessionalism would not triumph completely within Dutch church or society. Bekker's role as a leader of this resistance was one of his most important religious contributions and significantly influenced the outcome of the spirit debate.

Resistance to confessionalism within society at large resulted both from the religious pluralism that was a fact of life in the Republic and from the often adversarial relationship that existed between the Dutch state and the Reformed church. Since the Reformation, The Netherlands had become a haven for religious dissidents of all stripes, a situation that the revolt against Spain only encouraged. Confessionalist theologian Hermanus Witsius lamented the situation in which so many religious sects were tolerated in the Republic, saying that "the most horrible kinds come here as to a free inn."[45] Such pluralism made toleration a necessity if society itself were to be held together, if the economy were to function, and if the authority of the government were to be maintained.

Governmental authorities from the national down to the municipal level looked with suspicion upon the efforts of the confessional party within the Reformed church to impose religious discipline and uniformity on public life and institutions in the Republic. Repeated calls for censorship of the press, for banning of dissident religious groups, for actions against individuals who held heterodox views, for ideological uniformity in the selection of Reformed clergy, and for strict enforcement of sabbath observation met with little sympathy and less action on the part of civil authorities. While in absolutist states confessional churches were used by central governments to enforce cultural uniformity and social discipline among subjects, in the Dutch Republic the government, by its lack of cooperation with the official church, often tacitly blocked the advance of a Reformed confessionalism that it felt was unsuited to the pluralistic social and religious situation.[46]

Within the Dutch Reformed church there was a strong tradition of anti-confessionalism that often aligned itself with the civil authorities. The defeat of the Arminians at Dordrecht did not destroy the anti-confessional party within the Reformed church and result in a permanent victory of confessionalism in the Republic in part because state support for the confessional party did not survive the death of Prince Maurice in 1625. In addition, there was a significant intellectual foundation for anti-confessionalism within the Dutch church, and this basis did not disappear after Dordrecht. It was carried on in the thought of men like Bekker and Coccejus.

The intellectual foundations of anti-confessionalism within the Dutch church were built upon the strong influence of biblical humanism in Dutch religious circles, beginning with the work of Erasmus and continuing with humanist religious figures such as

---

[45]Hermanus Witsius, *Twist des Heeren met zijnen Wijngaart..* (Utrecht, 1748), 313-14.

[46]See H.A. Enno van Gelder, *Getemperde Vrijheid: Een Verhandeling over de verhouding van Kerk en Staat in de Republiek der Verenigde Nederlanden en de vrijheid van meningsuiting in zake godsdienst, drukpers en onderwijs, gedurende de 17e eeuw* (Groningen, 1972); S.B.J. Zilverberg, *Dissidenten in de Gouden Eeuw: Geloof en Geweten in de Republiek* (Weesp, 1985).

Dirk Coornhert, Arminius, Hugo Grotius, Simon Episcopius, and later Philip van Limborch. The Erasmian stress on ethical Christian life over dogmatic conformity, and the tendency to see much theological doctrine as adiaphorous, was an important legacy of religious humanism to early Dutch reformers and later Protestant thinkers. The philological tradition of humanism produced a sensitivity to the history and evolution of language and to the meaning of words that resulted in sophisticated textual criticism of the Bible. This textual criticism and sensitivity to the original meaning of biblical language can be seen in Bekker's treatment of the biblical words later translated as "angel," "devil," and "Satan," as well as in his criticism of the States Translation. Humanistic biblical study uncovered the rich texture of meanings present in scriptural language. It produced uneasiness with the idea that the essential truth of the scriptural text could be encapsulated by reason and transferred to propositional form in confessional documents or theology without the intervention of human interpretation to corrupt the divine authority of the doctrines so expressed. Arminius and his followers regarded confessional documents as human products without divine authority and as such they were inferior to the biblical text, a view later adopted by Cartesian theologians.

The Dutch Cartesian separation of religion from philosophy was premised on the assumption that much of biblical truth was beyond the grasp of human reason. This view was incompatible with the instrumental role assigned to reason in the construction of Reformed confessional documents. Cartesians maintained that reason's role in understanding sacred text was not merely instrumental but substantial and thus necessarily involved human interpretation of the text that carried no divine authority. Skepticism about the epistemological foundation underlying Reformed confessional documents, especially doubt about the ability of reason to perfectly grasp biblical truth and then recast it without altering its meaning and corrupting its authority, was the central intellectual foundation for opposition to Dutch Reformed confessionalism.[47]

The tradition of anti-confessionalism in which Bekker carried on produced serious intellectual objections to literalism and confessionalism, objections that contributed to tumultuous controversies over such issues as spirits and the sabbath. Bekker himself was well aware of his own position in the struggle against confessionalism. In 1685 he offered a pointed criticism of Reformed confessionalism and placed himself, his teacher Alting, and Coccejus firmly on the anti-confessional side of the church. In his *Kort Begryp der Algemeine Kerkelyke Historien, zedert het Jaar 1666 daar Hornius endigt, tot den Jaar 1684,* Bekker described Coccejus as "a man of great gifts" who had risen to fame despite the efforts of many to deny him such recognition. Coccejus's enemies were "particularly...those with whom he differs not a little in the common style of teaching, which has up to now been scholastic."[48]

In the *Kort Begryp* Bekker attacked biblical literalism and the use of proof texts, as well as scholastic theology, the cornerstones of Reformed confessionalism. Referring to the many theological disputes that followed in the wake of the Reformation, Bekker argued that those controversies were marked by a distinctive and unfortunate use of the Bible. Writers "have applied the content of Scripture to certain points in dispute and sought to gather proofs here and there in Scripture that appeared to pertain to each point." But Coccejus had seen the error of this method of mining Scripture for proof

[47]McGahagan, 62-139, 347-360.

[48]Balthasar Bekker, *Kort Begryp der Algemeine Kerkelyke Historien, Zedert het Jaar 1666, daar Hornius endigt, tot den jaar 1684* (Amsterdam, 1739), 25.

texts to support theological and controversial points, Bekker continued. "Coccejus thought that it was time to go farther and to trace the thread of Scripture from the beginning on, from which necessarily a new sense would be found for various passages than the ones up to now favored by most interpreters."[49]

Having indicated the important departure that Coccejus made with a more contextual approach to exegesis, Bekker argued that Coccejus opposed the use of human reason to construct the doctrinal formulas used in confessional documents and scholastic theology. Coccejus "believed that most phrases and artificial words (konstworden) used by church teachers were created by human imagination and were not in Scripture. He wanted, therefore, to speak of scriptural things using only the words of Scripture, since the Holy Spirit is the best interpreter of its own words." Coccejus believed that when human words were used to explain scriptural truth, the result was "infinite disputes and word battles," Bekker added.[50]

He went on to discuss the primary points of difference between the theology of Coccejus and that of the confessional party. He discussed Coccejus's interpretation of biblical prophecy, his view of the Old Testament as primarily a foreshadowing of the New Testament, and his view of history as a series of covenants that God made with man. Coccejus believed that there were seven distinct periods of Christian history, and he saw these periods foretold not only in the *Book of Revelations* but in various other places in the Old Testament. Thus "he interprets various prophecies in a new way and not in the way that the printed letter indicates," Bekker added.[51]

Coccejus was "seriously against the errors of bastard Christendom" and an enemy of Socinians and Catholics, Bekker continued. He fought with new wisdom from the "old and Godly military science." Indeed, Coccejus "held much the same position as Descartes, except that he traveled in different waters, wanting to lay aside all prejudice and seek supernatural knowledge only from Scripture, like (Descartes) built natural science on nothing but nature and sound reason."[52]

Bekker put forward his own profoundly anti-confessional view of religion when he claimed that the spread of Coccejan ideas outside the Dutch Republic gave reason to hope "that this theology, along with the philosophy of Descartes, might be the means to re-unite the Protestant churches, a goal long sought in vain by praiseworthy men, most recently by Dury." Because divisions among the churches were "fed by scholastic theology and the mix of philosophies," those who joined with Coccejus to forsake scholasticism and with Descartes to renew philosophy could "escape servitude" and use their new freedom to create the religious unity for which so many hoped, Bekker declared.[53]

Bekker saw himself and his teacher Alting as following in the spirit of Coccejus even though they were not actual Coccejans. Discussing thinkers sympathetic to Coccejus, Bekker commented: "At Groningen the learned Alting held the same style. In the short time that he was professor of theology and thereafter, his teachings supported Coccejus, whose friend he also was." Bekker added that Coccejus and Alting did not have as much in common in doctrine or teaching as they did in the suffering

---

[49]Ibid., 25.

[50]Ibid., 25-26, 36.

[51]Ibid., 28.

[52]Ibid., 29.

[53]Ibid., 36-37. Van Sluis de-emphasizes this ecumenical side of Bekker's thought, saying that Bekker sought a unity of the Protestant churches only if such took place loosely within the Reformed confession.

that they were caused by their opponents. But the fact that the same opponents attacked both men showed the unity of spirit of their work.[54]

Bekker went on to discuss his own role in the Cartesian and Coccejan controversies, including the sabbath debate. In the agitation against Descartes that arose in Friesland in 1668 a central role was played by "a small Latin book by an impartial writer who encountered opposition," Bekker wrote, referring to his own *Philosophia Cartesiana admonitio candida et sincera*.[55] He continued:

> Therefore this writer, because he was held for a Cartesian, could not escape serious troubles brought upon him by the accusations of several scholars to the classes and synods of two provinces regarding another book that he published in 1670 about the catechism in Dutch: so much that it was without investigation first forbidden, and thereafter condemned, and again forbidden. And although this writer agreed little with Alting and less with Coccejus, some took this opportunity to urge the classes and synods to oppose the novelties of Descartes and Coccejus.[56]

Thus Bekker himself saw the controversy surrounding the *Vaste Spyse* as a result of his association with the positions of Coccejus, Descartes, and Alting. Little did he know in 1685 how much these associations would influence the controversy around his later work on spirits.

Attempts to prevent the spread of Coccejanism actually had the opposite effect of helping to spread the ideas, Bekker argued. The many books published on both sides of the dispute only served to make Coccejus's ideas better known, and when people saw that Coccejan ideas did not actually contain the terrible things that opponents said they contained, more people began to follow them. Thus efforts to keep Coccejan ideas out of churches and schools only helped them to penetrate all the more deeply. "Coccejus was most attacked where he differed from other teachers in explaining points of doctrine, and it was here that he was least defeated," Bekker proclaimed.[57]

IV

Bekker's account of his own ideas and those of Alting and Coccejus showed that he was conscious of being a part of a distinct anti-confessional party within the Dutch Reformed church. With its insistence on the acceptability of non-literal biblical exegesis the anti-confessional party helped to open the way for the acceptance within the Dutch Republic of many new ideas, from Cartesianism to Copernicanism.[58] Once the obstacle of biblical literalism was removed, many ideas previously blocked by a rigid and conservative interpretation of Scripture could flourish. Heliocentricism, philosophical rationalism, and a wide complex of related ideas gained broader acceptance in the Republic by the end of the seventeenth century in part as a result of the struggle against literalism and confessionalism.

[54]Bekker, 29.
[55]Ibid., 30.
[56]Ibid., 30.
[57]Ibid., 31-38.
[58]See Rienk Vermij, *Secularisering en naturwetenschap in de zeventiende en actiende eeuw: Bernard Nieuwentijt* (Amsterdam, 1991)

In Germany, as Hsia has pointed out, the confessional competition among the churches aided in the desacralization of society as elites vied with each other for the allegiance of the people and attacked popular religion. Especially Protestant confessions tried, somewhat unsuccessfully, to wipe out popular religion, popular magic, and belief in witchcraft, and they raised serious doubts about the power of the devil as well. Thus confessional competition in Germany ultimately led to an increase of toleration and helped to pave the way for the secularization of society.[59]

In the Dutch Republic in the seventeenth century it was the battle against confessionalism that secularized society by opening the way for the growing influence of Cartesianism and subsequently for other elements of the new science and philosophy. The anti-confessional party led by Coccejus and Bekker promoted secularization of society with its battles against spirit belief, diabolic power, and rigorous observation of the sabbath. It did so, however, not in the name of modern science and philosophy, but as part of a long struggle within the Dutch church against the strictures of literalism, legalism, and confessionalism. The confessional party in the Dutch Republic was in turn placed in the somewhat unusual position of defending the very spirit belief and spirit magic that Protestant confessionalism in other countries attacked.

As the eighteenth century dawned, the traditional religious worldview began to lose its grip on educated European minds in favor of a new secular worldview dominated by empirical science and rationalist philosophy. It can perhaps be suggested that this great intellectual transformation was brought about, in the Dutch Republic at least, not by the triumph of science over religion but by the gradual internal decay of the religious worldview itself. Racked by internal disputes, and in particular by the reaction against the wave of confessionalism that followed in the wake of the Protestant Reformation, the old worldview found itself with powerful critics and an eroding intellectual foundation.

If Bekker's ideas had the effect of encouraging a secularized worldview by changing the way that educated people conceived of the spirit world, interpreted the Bible, and spent their time on Sundays, it was only because he felt deeply that the confessional model of religion and biblical literalism undermined religious belief and distorted the Reformed religious community that he himself never ceased to love. Bekker and those who excluded him from the Reformed church quarreled over distinctly different models of religious and ecclesiastical life, a quarrel that ultimately helped to open the door to a much broader and more profound intellectual transformation in the Dutch Republic. In this process of intellectual change Bekker was less a revolutionary than a reformer disenchanted with the old regime but determined to improve it, not to overthrow it. That his steps were followed by those more radical than he was not of his own doing, and the resultant erosion of the religious worldview during the course of the following century was a development he neither foresaw nor desired. Perhaps this above all else made Bekker a quintessential example of, and a key figure in, this momentous intellectual transition. The ultimate consequences of his ideas were born of intentions and purposes as remote as he himself was from the new intellectual world he helped to create.

---

[59]Hsia, 153, 183-184.

The Death of an Atheist

I

Just over three months after Balthasar Bekker was excluded from the communion of the Dutch Reformed church an event, took place in Westminster, England, that bore ironic resemblance to Bekker's experience in the spirit debate. The unhappy nobleman who died in Westminster on December 8th, 1692, had had the benefit, in his younger years, of an excellent education in religion and morality. He learned much faster than most boys of his age, becoming highly skilled in Latin and Greek by the age of 16, and he was zealous in the exercise of religion as well. He went on to university, where he stayed five years and again did very well. His friends considered him a blessing and the jewel of his family.

At the age of 21 the young man came to the city of London to study law, which he wanted to know well enough to protect his possessions. It would have been better had he died at this point in his life without indoctrination into the evils of the city, the narrator of his story tells us, but such was not to be the case. His fellow students and companions mocked him because of his virtue and upright behavior, and so in order to avoid such embarrassment he pretended to the same profanity and godlessness that was their way of life. But while he showed himself terrible and slovenly, his heart was not in it. His judgment was too great and well founded for his personality to really be changed by a little mockery. When his fellows laughed at his ideas he said: "people who use reason cannot be transported and bewitched by the temptation of pleasure...nor can a little laughing make them reject all that they believe."[1]

Then one day one of his older companions replied to the young man's profession of religious faith by pointing out that Mohammed had more followers than Christ, that Islam also had its confessors and martyrs, that the Indians would surely die for their religion, and that every nation had its own wonderful examples of deeds and sufferings. It was not from religion that people got ideas of heaven and hell, the immortality of the soul, the future state of souls, and the demands of conscience, he continued. Rather, these ideas were promoted by wicked priests and governments in order to enrich themselves and intimidate the common people, who were by their nature superstitious and fearful. These arguments so poisoned the grounds of belief of the poor nobleman

---

[1]Hermanus Witsius, *Een Tweede Fra. Spira, Zijnde een Vreesselijck Exempel van een Atheist, welcke Verloochent hadde de Christelijcke Religie, en Sterfte in Waanhoop in Westminster, de 8 December 1692. Als ook een brief van een atheist aan hem, en een Antwoordt dar op, door J.S., Leeraar van de Kerck van Engeland, die hem geduerigh bezocht heeft, duerende de geheele Sieckte* (Goes, 1714), 6.

that he was instantly molded in the same vile fashion as those who made the arguments. He converted not only to the same wretched ideas but also to the same godless, unrighteous, and idle life.

Seven years later the young nobleman was part of a cabal of lawyers who met to discuss how best to put their godlessness into practice through abuse of the law. They sought loopholes in the law, looked for places where it had no provisions covering this or that knavery, and considered what looseness could be used in interpreting the law in order to allow various kinds of misconduct. These were useful lessons for the young man, still a relative newcomer to godlessness. But he was too educated and cautious to reveal all of his base ideas to everyone. He kept up a regular correspondence with old friends who suspected nothing, and he behaved moderately in unfamiliar places. Thus he lived for some years being secretly as Godless as he prudently could.

But his sensual and immoderate life led him to become hopelessly ill on November 30, 1692. As soon as he realized the seriousness of his condition, he was surprised and frightened by the idea of death. No matter how hard he tried, he could not escape the thought of the payment awaiting him in the next life, a prospect he could not reject or laugh at any longer. Highly disturbed he took to his bed, where he said to himself:

> What does this war inside me mean? What grounds do I now have to defend myself against what I have done? I hold that there is no hell, but do I feel it in my bosom? Am I so certain...that there is no punishment in the hereafter when I already see a judgment in myself? Can I say that my soul is just as mortal as my body when I see my body weaken but my soul is as strong as ever? Oh! if somebody could just restore me to my old holy and unpunishable state. But it is too late. Miserable as I am, where will I flee from myself, what shall become of me?[2]

Having heard of his condition one of his old colleagues came to visit him, and finding him thus disturbed, asked why. He answered:

> The reason is that you and the rest of your friends have given me grounds which, now that I need them most, leave me in an anxiety of hopelessness and confusion. What advice or comfort can you give me now to strengthen me against the fear that I have for the expectation of the next life? Are you certain that my soul is bodily and mortal? And that I will pass away with my body?[3]

This conversation broke off when a pastor entered the room. Saying that he had heard of the nobleman's condition, the pastor considered it his Christian duty to visit and offer him advice and comfort. "I thank you," said the sick man, "and would to that end request of you that you prove to the nobleman who sits there that the soul is not bodily or mortal." To this request the pastor replied: "That the soul is not material or bodily Descartes has proved in his *Discourse on Method*. He showed that the soul is independent of the body."[4] The pastor continued by saying that Locke had proved in *On Human Understanding* that a body could not move itself. But the best proof of the point was this, he added: all philosophers hold that a body in itself is indifferent to motion and rest, and thus it is certain that something at rest will remain thus unless

---

[2]Ibid., 8.
[3]Ibid., 9.
[4]Ibid.

something else moves it. And if something else moves it, it will move unless the interference of another body hinders the motion.

Now there are those who say that the soul is made of a very fine, pure material, the pastor continued. They also believe that this soul moves the body by moving the animal spirits, which move the loins, which move the legs, and in this way the one part moves the other and the body is set in motion. But we have seen that it is impossible for a material body to move itself, the pastor argued. So the soul could not be part of the body, because then the soul moving the body would be the same as the body moving itself, which could not happen, he concluded.

It was certain, however, that the soul moved the body without the aid of any intervening body. "From this it follows that the soul is no material body," the pastor declared.[5] To this argument the sick man "gave a sad sigh, as if his heart had broken," and his friend suddenly left the room. Then the man said:

> Alas, my lord, you have helped me out of my deceit now that it is too late. I was afraid of nothing so much as that my soul is immortal, and now that you have assured me of that you have at the same time assured me that there is a hell, a terrible expectation of judgment for those who have fallen away from religion, a laid-away fate for the God deniers and forsakers of Christ. You have sealed my damnation by waking up my conscience, which makes me aware of my sins and makes a big register of them, for which I must now give account. Oh disastrous fallen one, from how great a hope have I fallen. Oh had I never known what religion was, I would never have denied my savior and inherited such destruction.[6]

II

This account of the creation and conversion of an atheist was translated from the English and published by Hermanus Witsius in 1693 under the title *Een Tweede Fra. Spira, Zijnde een Vreesselijck Exempel van een Atheist, welcke Verloochent hadde de Christelijcke Religie, en Sterfte in Waanhoop in Westminster, de 8 December 1692...door J.S., Leeraar van de Kerck van Engeland, die hem geduerigh bezocht heeft, duerende de geheele Sieckte* (A Second Father Spira, Being a Fearful Example of an Atheist who had denied the Christian Religion and Died Hopelessly in Westminster on 8 December 1692...by J.S., Pastor of the Church of England, Who Constantly Visited Him during his entire Sickness). In his introduction to the work, Witsius wrote that among "sicknesses of the soul" the two most common were superstition and atheism. Although these two illnesses were at opposite extremes of spiritual life, they were equally fatal to man's hopes for eternal life.

For a long time superstition had the upper hand in Europe, Witsius wrote, and in what followed it became clear that by superstition he meant Catholicism. From pure ignorance of Gods' will men occupied themselves with external things that they believed would bring them salvation but which actually contradicted sound reason as well as God's revealed will. Nevertheless, they insisted with hypocritical boldness that

[5]Ibid.
[6]Ibid., 10

in these things alone was true religion. "But in the course of time the human race became more clever and uncovered the vanity, baselessness, and absurdity of such ideas and practices." Then people went immediately to the other extreme of profanity and atheism, "Godless unbelief and wanton neglect of all, and especially of revealed religion."[7]

This unbelief now was the master of the age, Witsius lamented. It had won over the hearts of all kinds of people, but most of all those who were "taken in by the delusion of elevated wisdom and who want to excel others in cleverness of reason." These people pointed their reason against holy Scripture, formed societies, and encouraged each other to storm heaven. "Under the pretext of rejecting all prejudice they have corrupted their reason with the most horrible of all prejudices, having become a slave to their hellish lusts, and are busy rubbing away from their hearts the engraved seal of divinity."[8]

As professor E.G.E. van der Wall has pointed out, fear of atheism filled religious literature of the early Enlightenment. While many believed with Voetius that no one rejected the existence of God in principle because all people had an inborn natural idea of God, practical atheism was considered a real and deadly threat. Practical atheists were those who out of bad faith or malice acted as if there were no God despite the inborn idea that they had of him. They thus lived contrary to his will and commandments. Just as skepticism was seen by conservative religious thinkers as an act of bad will in doubting certain truth, so atheism was seen as an act of bad will in living a godless life and professing irreligious views. Thus skepticism was closely linked to atheism: both were acts of bad faith, obstinate and willful rejections of clearly evident reality rather than legitimate intellectual positions, and the lesser act could easily introduce people to the greater sin.[9]

The role of doubt in Cartesian philosophy was one of the central reasons that the confessional party condemned Cartesianism as leading to atheism. Descartes' philosophical doubt was seen as leading to outright skepticism rather than to the certainty that it was designed to produce, and from there atheism was an easy next step. Witsius himself had condemned Cartesian doubt about God's existence for these reasons, and one of the most common attacks made by confessionalists against Cartesianism was that it promoted atheism. In this context, the atheist that Witsius actually discovered deserves a second look.

When Witsius wrote in his introduction that the people most attracted to atheism were those who believed that they had great wisdom, who wanted to excel others in the cleverness of their reason, and who pretended to reject all prejudice, he was no doubt referring to Cartesians. His nobleman was indeed led into atheism by the seeds of doubt sowed by his companions regarding the uniqueness of Christianity and the motivations of those who taught belief in hell and the immortality of the soul. It was not, however, Cartesian doubt or materialistic ideas of the new science or philosophy that drew the noble away from God, but rather traditional, if radical, skeptical arguments. The materialist conception of the soul that the atheist adopted, as well as his position that the materiality and mortality of the soul reduced fear of death, seemed closer to ancient Epicureanism than to any ideas of Gassendi or Hobbes. Indeed, the atheist was

[7] Ibid., 3.

[8] Ibid., 3-4.

[9] Theo Verbeek, "From 'Learned Ignorance' to Scepticism: Descartes and Calvinist Orthodoxy," in *Scepticism and Irreligion in the Seventeenth and Eighteenth Centuries*, ed. by Richard Popkin and Arjo Vanderjagt (Leiden, 1993), 32-33; E.G.E. van der Wall, "Orthodoxy and Scepticism in the early Dutch Enlightenment," in Popkin and Vanderjagt, 122-123, 131.

converted **back** to God by arguments taken from the new science and philosophy: Cartesian dualism, ideas from Locke, and a confused version of Galileo's principle of inertia. This episode would have confirmed Descartes and some Coccejans in their conviction that Cartesian ideas could be a useful support for religious faith rather than the great danger to belief feared by the conservatives.

Witsius argued in his introduction that the great flood of atheism in Europe began immediately after Catholic "superstition" was rejected by a human race that had become "more clever," possibly a reference to the Protestant Reformation. What was the relationship between the Reformation and the growth of atheism hidden between these lines? Did Witsius recognize the great harm done to religion by the theological quarrels among the churches born of the Reformation movement? Did he realize the damage done to belief by the rise of confessionalism? In the last decades of his life Witsius developed somewhat more sympathy for Coccejanism. Thus even for him, the relationship between the decline of religious belief and the coming of modern science and philosophy was not so clear as others tried to portray it.

In the seventeenth century, propagandists for religious orthodoxy and confessionalism repeatedly made a direct connection between the growing influence of the new science and philosophy and the feared triumph of materialism and atheism, the victory of a secular worldview. Beginning in the eighteenth century, propagandists for the Enlightenment continued to draw this connection from a different point of view, seeing the coming of modern science as leading to the victory of the modern secular worldview over the old worldview of religious superstition, opening the door for the eternal progress of mankind. The episode Witsius reported seemed to contradict his own stated position on the relationship between Cartesianism and atheism, while his other comments seemed to suggest a link between religious doubt and the Reformation.

As Witsius's atheist and our own investigation into the decline of spirit belief shows, both versions of the direct and adversarial, or dialectic, relationship between science and religion were naive and simplistic. Just as modern science did not suddenly appear on the scene to defeat belief in spirits, neither did it overwhelm and replace the traditional religious worldview by the force of its superior truth. The actual relationship between the new science and philosophy and traditional religious belief in the seventeenth century was far more complex. In the case of the Dutch Republic at least, the growing influence of Cartesianism was to some extent a result of developments within the religious worldview brought on by the Reformation. The struggle between confessionalism and anti-confessionalism would almost certainly never have occurred without the revolution in religious life begun by Martin Luther, and the ideas of Descartes would likely not have attracted the interest that they did among Dutch religious thinkers like Balthasar Bekker had the threat of literalism and confessionalism not been present.

The case of the atheist converted back to religious belief by arguments taken from the new science and philosophy was paradoxically similar to the case of the Reformed pastor Bekker. Both used new ideas as instruments within an older intellectual context. The converted atheist died just over three months after the Reformed church had excommunicated Balthasar Bekker. Just as the former atheist on his death bed was sure that he was destined to hell for his sins, Bekker's exclusion from the communion of his church was for him a deeply felt and tragic end for his life. A world had not yet dawned in which these two men could meet happier ends.[10]

[10]Parts of this chapter appeared in "Atheism in the Early Dutch Enlightenment," *Publications of the American Association of Netherlandic Studies* XII.

Bibliography

There are several extensive published bibliographies covering the works of Bekker and his opponents. The most venerable is Antonius van der Linde, *Balthasar Bekker. Bibliografie,* published in 1869 by Martinus Nijhoff in The Hague. Van der Linde continued his work with "Bijvoegsels tot de Bekkeriana" in *Bibliographische adversaria* 2 (1874-1875), 13-16. More recently there is the comprehensive *Bekkeriana: Balthasar Bekker biografisch en bibliografisch* by Jacob van Sluis, published by the Friesian Academy in Leeuwarden in 1994. Below is a list of contemporary sources on the Bekker controversy compiled during work on *Fallen Angels.*

WORKS BY ANONYMUS AUTHORS

Aanmerkinge op de Handelingen der twee laatste Noordhollandsche Synoden, in de sake van B. Bekker. Enkhuizen. 1692.

Aanmerkingen op de Lasteringen en Smaatreeden door Haggebher Philalethes en Bloemardus Thusius, Uitgebraakt Tegens het onwederleggelik Boek De Betoverde Weerelt. 1691

Aanmerkingen van eeniges rechtzinnige Broederen over de Articulen van Satisfactie, waarop men met D. B. Bekker een Verdrag gemaakt heeft. Leiden. Haring. 1692.

Acten ofte Handelingen van de Noord-Hollandsche Synodus, gehouden binnen Edam en Alcmaar, 1691-1692. Rakende Dr. Balthazar Bekker, en sijn Boek de Betoverde Wereld, met alle de Documenten daar toe behoorende.Y Amsterdam. G. Borstius. 1692.

Antwoord op een Brief geschreven van een Vriend tot Uytrecht, Den 2/12 July 1691. Zynde een Korten Inhoud van het Tweede Boek genaamd de Betoverde Wereld. Amsterdam? 1691?

Artikelen voor te Stellen aen Dr. B. Bekker. 1691.

Autentyke Copye van de Articulen Die van het Eerwaarde Consistorie van 23 Aug. 1691 opgestelt zyn om voor te houden an D. B. Bekker. En de anbieding die Dr. B. Bekker daar op gedaen heeft den 30 Augusti 1691. Amsterdam. G. Borstius. 1691.

B.L.B. *De Betooverde Weereld. Onderzoekende wie haar betooverd heeft, De Duivel, of 't Zo= Genaamde Boek? En de moogelyke werking der Geesten op de Lighaamen uit de Reeden Toonende.* 1691.

Balthazar Bekkers En insonderheyd sijner Voedsterlingen onkunde, Onbescheidentheyd, en Dwalingen Kort en Klaar ontdekt door een discipel van.. J. vander Waeyen. Franeker. Hans Gyzelaar. 1696.

Bekker door Bekker Overtuygt. Uytgewerckt in een Brief hem schriftelijk toegesonden. The Hague. Barent Beek. 1692.

Beschryvinge van een Vremd Nagt-Gezigte, Vertoont aan een toehoorder der predikatie die door Ds. Johannes Molinaeus tegen den Aucteur van 't boek de Betooverde Weereld... "Logoochoorion." Krisis. 1691.

Brief, Geschreven van Uitregt, Aan een Vriend tot Amsterdam over het Boek genaamd de Betoverde Wereld. Als mede wat daar omtrent is voorgevallen. Utrecht. 1691.

Brief van L. P. aan Herman Bouman; eerst in 't bysonder aan hem geschreven, en nu door hem, met verlof van den Autheur, gemeen gemaakt: Behelsende sommige redenen waarom hij de soo genaamde Sleutel der Geesten van M. van Diepen en J. Hubener, niet, ofte niet zoodanig alsse daar ligt, behoorde te beantwoorden. Amsterdam. R. Blokland. 1699.

Brief van L. R. Tot Antwoord Aan Dr. Everard van der Hoocht. Amsterdam. D. van den Dalen. 1692.

Brief van N.N. aan Balthasar Bekker. "Uyt Rotterdam, den 1 Februarij, 1692."

Brief van N.N. aan den Predikant Balthasar Bekker, en Sijne Aenhangers. Veer. Cornelis Pietersz. 1691

Brief van N. N. aan Dr. Balthasar Bekker. Rotterdam. 1692

Brieven Van eenige Kerkenrade buyten de Provintie van Holland, Namentlyk van 't .. classis van Walcheren, van de.. Kerkenraaden van Middelburg, Utrecht, Leeuwarden, Groningen, Aan de.. Kerkenraad van Rotterdam, Tot Antwoord op haren Circulaire Brief, rakende de sake van Dr. B. Bekker. Rotterdam. R. van Doesburg. 1692.

Copye van een Brief aen N. N. Behelsende Eenige Consideratien (over het Boek van Dr. Bekker genaamt de Betoverde Werelt) Aangaande de Geesten. Waar in duydelyk aangewesen wort, dat D. Bekker, in die stoffe verwart is, en sich selve tegenspreekt. Dienende, met ook tot bewijs, dat de Philosophie niet moet zijn de Uytlegster der Schriftuur...Door een Liefhebber van de Vrede enz... 1691?

Copye van een Brief Geschreeve aan een Heer, woonende tusschen Rotterdam en Dort. Rakende het gepasseerde Saak van Dr. B. Bekker; Door een liefhebber van Vreede en Waarheid. Dordrecht. G. Abramsz. 1692.

De Betoverde Predikant Dr. Balthasar Bekker... Door de Boose-Geest des vooroordeels misleydt, In sijn Boeck de Betoverde Werelt, handelende van den Aert, en 't vermogen der Geesten. "Vrystadt." L. Waermont. 1691.

De gebannen Duyvel Weder-Ingeroepen. Ofte Het Vonnis van Dr. Bekker over den Duyvel geveldt, in Revisie gebragt. Hoorn. Kortingh and Beels. 1692.

De Geest van David Joris, Sprekende zijn eygen taal, in dese Laatste Eeuwe. Waar men als in een Spiegel sien kan, dat veel der stellingen die den Heer Bekker in sijn Tweede Deel van de Betoverde Weerelt stelt, uyt dit Monster sln voortgeteelt. Middleburg. P. Jansz. 1691.

De Herstelde Duyvel, ofte Waerachtige Historie van het bedrijf van den Boosen Geest tot Nieukerken... Om te dienen te oovertuyginge van den Heere B. Bekker ende wederlegginge van desselfs vreemde stellingen in zyn B. W... "Gedrukt onder de Degel." 1695.

De redenen voor de onmagt der Geesten, In het oordeel der Wysgeren gewogen, en te licht bevonden door E. S. S. The Hague. 1694.

Den Predikant D. Balthasar Becker, seediglyk Ondersogt so in zijn Persoon als Schriften... met zijn Andtwoord provisioneel daar op gevolgt... Utrecht. W. Jansz. 1692.

Der Verkeerden Duyvel van den Throon geschopt, En den rechten weder hervoort gebragt, verhandelende van Engelen en Duyvelen, hare macht ende werkinge. Door K. A. H. Amsterdam. N. Holbeex. 1692.

d'Onttoverde Werelt, Handelende Van de Duyvelen, en Tovenaers, haer macht en onmacht, etc. Tegens die gene die niet geloven datter Duyvelen of quade Geesten zijn, uyt de H. Schrift en met verscheyde Historien bevestigt. Amsterdam. J. Boekholt. 1691.

Een Brief van N. N. Behelsende nader Deductie en bekrachtiging over L. Joosten's Verdediging.. van 't Gebruik der Reden, En van de Engelen Gods buyten de Zielen der Menschen. Leiden. 1697.

Een Keunings-Kaarsje voor den Siender van een Vremt Nagtgesigte... "Ezelenburg." 1692.

Eenige Extracten uyt Dr. Bekker's Betooverden Weerelt, Tweede Deel. Dar beneffens een Extract uyt de synoden den 10 Augusti, 1691 tot Edam, raakende Dr. Beckers Betooverde Weerelt, Beneffens desselfs Veroordeling. 1691.

Eenvovdige Aanmerking over 't geene in de boek van Dr. B. Bekker is gepasseert, vergeleken met de handelingen der Roomsche Geestelijkheyd hier in overeenkommend.... Amsterdam. 1692.

Extract van 't gepasseerde in de Synodus tot Edam 10 Aug 1691 raakende B. Bekker. 1691.

Gestroojde Zeegen-Palmen, Op het doorwrogte Werk van Balthasar Bekker Genaamd De Betooverde Wereld. 1691.

Het Sterfbed van Dr. Balthasar Bekker Verdeedigt, Tegen de liefdeloose Misduydingen van den Autheur der soo genaamde Noodige Aanmerkingen, etc. Vervat in Twee Brieven. Amsterdam. A. van Damme. 1699.

J:P.L:R., *De Volmaakte kragt Godts Verheerlykt. Nevens eenige Aanmerckingen over de drie Predikatien van Dr. Petrus Schaak. Gedaan over Psalm 72:18, Gen. 18:1-2 en Gen. 32:24-25Y* Amsterdam. D. vanden Dalen. 1691.

Klinkende Bel; of Uytroep om den verlorenen Duyvel, Door last van sijn Liefhebbers. Rotterdam. P. van Veen. 1691.

Kort Begrip van de twee boeken der Betooverde Weereld opgesteld door een Redenlievenden hater van bygeloof.. Rotterdam. Iz. van Ruynen. 1691.

Kort Beschouwinge van de Naekte zoo genaemde uyt-beelding die Dr. Bekker onlangs heeft uitgegeven van de vier boeken van sijn Betooverde Weereld door een liefhebber van Waerheit en Gods Vreeze. Amsterdam. Borstius. 1693.

Kort en waaractig Verhaal Van 't gebeurde tsedert den 31 Mey 1691. tot den 21 Aug. 1692. In de Kerkenraad en Classis van Amsterdam, en de Synode van Noord-Holland. In de sake van Balthasar Bekker... Amsterdam. D. vanden Dalen. 1692.

Liefdelooze Acterhoudinge van Dr. Everardus van der Hooght Gebleken in syn Schriftelyke onderhandelingen met Arent Haak. Amsterdam. D. vanden Dalen. 1693.

Missive van M. D. E. P. Aan een Vrind over de zaak van Dr. B. Bekker. Rotterdam. J. Gysen. 1692.

Nodige Bedenkingen op de Niewe Beweegingen, Onlangs verwerkt door den Circulairen Brief en andere Middelen, Tegen den Auteur van 't Boek de Betoverde Weereld. Amsterdam. D. vanden Dalen. 1692.

Omstandig Bewijs, Dat de Daemones overgeset Duyvelen, Geen quade Geesten, maar Zielen van menschen geweest zijn als ook datter maar ene Duyvel of Satan is, Welk gevoelen met dat van.. Bekker.. over een stemt. Getrokken uyt de Schriften van d'Heer Daillon Frans Predikant. The Hague. M. Uytwerf, 1692.

Oogmerck Van Everardus van der Hooght, In sijn Brabbelen Tegen het Boek De Betoverde Wereld Genoemd. Amsterdam. D. vanden Dalen. 1691.

Op de Betoverde Wereld door Dr. B. Bekker. Amsterdam. D. Van Dalen. 1691.

Reedelyk Bewys, Dat het On-reedelikheid is, uit de Reeden D'onmogelyke werking der Geesten op Ligchaamen aan te dringen: Een steevige Storm-ram, om de Grondpilaar van een onlangs half-op getimmerd gevaarte te vellen, en 't zelve in te doen storten. Amsterdam. J. Boeckholt. 1692.

Remonstrantie in de Eerw. Synoden van Noord Holland, jegenwoordig vergederd tot Alkmaar, ingedediend often van wegen Balthasar Bekker op den 5 Aug. 1692. Amsterdam? s.n. 1692.

Request Aan de Eerwaarden Kerkenraad van Amsterdam, overgelevert den 20 Maart 1692, ten eynde de suspensie van Dr. Balthasar Bekker mochte werden gecontinueert. Amsterdam. G. Borstius. 1692.

Request van eenige Ledematen der Gemeente, Aan de Kerkenraad van Amsterdam. Overgelevert den 20 Maart 1692. Amsterdam. J. Boekholt. 1692.

Rescripsie op seker Missive, Aan seker Vriend, om sijn Advijs of goed bedunken eens te mogen sien, wegens de omswevende Brieven van eenige Kerken-raden: en wel bysonder die van RotterdamY wegens de saken van Dr. Balthasar Bekker Amsterdam. D. vanden Dalen. 1692.

S.W.S.F.. *Aanmerkinge Over de Predicatie van.. Dr. Adrianus van Wesel den 25 November over Matt. 4:5-7. Discourswyse Voorgestelt Hier neevens, Eenige opening, hoe men Dr. B. Bekker in sijn XIX Hooftstuk, des II Boeks, rakende, t' gene sijn Eerw. seght, van de verleydinge der Eerste Menschen, verstaan moet.* Amsterdam. D. van den Dalen. 1691.

Seedige Aanmerkinge Over de Voorreden, Genaamt: De Godtslasteringe van den Amsterdamsche Predikant Dr. Bekker Wederleyt, in de Voorreden voor de Toetsteen der Waarheyt, ende der meyninge, door Henrikus Brink, etc Door N. N. Amsterdam. D. vanden Dalen. 1691.

't Onkragtig en Nietig Bewys van J. V. K. SY Amsterdam. 1693.

J.V.K.S. *Bewys dat de Zedige Aanmerkinge van J. W. geen doel treft. Waar in met een getoont word, het gewigte.. gevoelen van Dr. B. Bekker.* Amsterdam. G. Borstius. 1693.

Triumph-Digt op de Medailje, of penning, Gemaakt ter Eeren en eeuwegier gedagtenisse van Balthasar Bekker. Rotterdam. P.van Veen. 1692.

Twee Predicatien Gedaan door Dr. Henricus Vos en Dr. Johannes Colerus Predicanten van de onveranderde Augsburgse Confessie binnen deeze Stad Amsterdam, Handelende van de magt en het gewelt des Satans ontrent Mensch. Amsterdam. Jadocus Olchers. 1692.

Twee Requesten opgestelt door verscheidene Ledematen der Gereformeerde Kerke in Amsterdam. Ter saak van Dr. Balthasar Bekker Amsterdam. D. vanden Dalen. 1692.

Tweeden Brief aan Jacobus Shuts: En deeze tot beantwoordinge van zijn zoo genaamde Nader Verklaaringe over de nodige aanmerkingen op het Sterf-bedde van B. Bekker. Door M. G. Amsterdam. 1699.

Verscheyde Gedichten, so voor, als tegen het Boek, Genaamt: de Betoverde Weereld. 1691.

Wederlegging van de gewaande macht des duivels, door Dr. B. Bekker in sijn onweederleggelik boek De Betooverde Wereld. 1691.

WORKS OF KNOWN AUTHORSHIP

Aalstius, Johannes, and Steenwinkel, Paulus. *Zedige Aanmerkingen Waar in de Gronden en de daar op gebouwde redeneringen van Dr. Balth. Bekker Nopender den aard en Werkingen der Geesten aan Gods woort en de Reden getoetst worden.* Dordrecht. Dirk Goris. 1693.

Amsterdam, Classis of. *Drie Resolutien Des Classis van Amsterdam, By deselve genomen op den 22 Jan, 8 April en 21 July deses jaars, in de sake van Balthasar Bekker.... Betreffende sijn Boek De Betoverde Weereld...* Amsterdam. D. vanden Dalen. 1692.

Analda, Ruardus. *Uiterste Verleegentheid van Balt. Bekker Duidelyk aangewesen door wederlegginge van alle syne Aanmerkingen door een disciple van J. van der Waeyen...* Franeker. Gyzelaar. 1696.

Bekker, Balthasar. *Aamerkinge op de handelingen der twee laatste Noordhollandsche Synoden.* Amsterdam? 1692.

——————— *Articulen tot satisfactie van de Eerw. Classis van Amsterdam. Van Dr. Balthasar Bekker, overgeleverd den 22 Jan. 1692. Wegens syn Boek genaand de Betoverde Wereld.* Leuwarden. Hero Nauta. 1692.

——————— *B. Bekker's Naakt Verhaal van alle de kerkelijke Handelingen, voorgevallen in den Kerkenraad en de Classis van Amsterdam alsmede in de Synoden van Noordholland, 31 May 1691-21 Aug 1692. Na vervolg des tijds uit de eigene Acten en bygevoegde stukken der voornoemde Kerkelike Vergaderingen tsaamgesteld, en met Aantekeningen van den Auteur.* Amsterdam, D. van Dalen, 1692.

——————— *Beright van den kinderdoop.* Amsterdam, 1690.

——————— *Brief van Balthasar Bekker Aan Dr. Joannes Aalstius... ende Dr. Paulus Steenwinkel.* Amsterdam. D. vanden Dalen. 1693.

——————— *Brief van Balthasar Bekker.... Aan.. Joannes van der Waeyen... In Antwoord op desselven Brief waarmede hy hem sijn Boek tegen de Betoverde Wereld heft toegesonden....*Amsterdam. 1693.

——————— . *Brief van Balthasar Bekker Aan de Heeren Joost de Smeth, Willem Weyer, en Nicolaas van der Hagen tot antwoord op den Brief van den Professor van der Waeyen aan desselven.* Amsterdam. D. vanden Dalen. 1693.

——————— *Brief van den Schrijver des Boeks de Betoverde Weereld genaamd, Aan Everhard van der Hooght, Yverigen Leeraar van's Heeren Gemeente tot Niewendam.* Amsterdam. G. Borstius. 1691.

——————— *Brief van Dr. Balthasar Bekker, aan zijn Huisvrouw, Frouk Fullenia. Benevens een Antwoord van de Christellke gemeente t' Amsterdam, op de selve: Mitsgaders den Fameusen Antwoorden Rustigh afgeslagen: waar by gevoeghd, een Antwoord op de naam van deselve Frouk Fullenia.* Utrecht. J. Michielsz. 1691.

———————————— *De Betoverde Weereld.* Amsterdam. D. van Dalen. Four Volumes. 1691-1693.

————————————*De leeraar van de Hoge School door voedsterlingen van de Kerk ondersocht en Wederleid, zynde aanmerkingen van ongestudeerde personen op het boek van der Wayen tegen de Betoverde Weereld van B. Bekker.* Amsterdam, D. vanden Dalen. 1694.

———————————— *Kort Beright van Balthasar Bekker Aangaande alle de Schriften, Welke over sijn Boek de Betoverde Wereld Enen tyd lang heen en weer verwisseld sijn.* Franker. L. Strik. 1692.

———————————— *Kort en Waarachtig Verhaal van >t gebeurde tsederd den 31 Mey 1691 tot 21 Aug. 1692 in den Kerkenraad en Classis van Amsterdam, en de Synod van Noord-Holland, In de sake van Balthasar Bekker.* Amsterdam. D. van den Dalen. 1692.

————————————*Naakte Uitbeeldinge van Alle de vier Boeken Der Betoverde Weereld, uitgegeven door Balthasar Bekker vertonende Het Oogmerk van den Schrijver, de Schikkinge van 't werk, en sijn eigentlyk gevoelen daar in vorergesteld tot wechneemingen van vooroordeelen, en een Kort begryp des ganschen Werx* Amsterdam. D. vanden Dalen. 1693.

———————————— *Omstandig Bericht, van Balthasar Bekker van sijne particuliere Onderhandelinge met Dr. Laurentius Homma... Beneffens Ontdekte Lagen van Everhardus van der Hooght en Jakob Lansman tegen denselven.* Amsterdam. D. Van Dalen. 1693.

———————————— *Ondersoek en Antwoord van Balthasar Bekker op 't Request Door de Gedeputeerden der Noordhollandsche synod tot Edam, in den Herfst 1691 ingegeven aan de Staten van Holland tegen sijn Boek de Betoverde Weereld.* Amsterdam. D. vanden Dalen. 1693.

———————————— *Ondersoek van de betekeninge der kometen, by gelegentheid van de genen die in de Jaren 1680, 1681, 1682 geschenen hebben.* Leuwarden. Hero Nauta. 1683.

———————————— *Protest van Balthasar Bekker ter Synode van Noordholland binnen Alkmaar ingeleverd, den 7 Aug 1692* Alkmaar? 1692.

———————————— *Twee Brieven aan E. V. d. Hooght 25 Sept. 1691 + 13 Jan 1692.. Met een Kort bericht over de voorrede van seker Opstel van Aanmerkingen door J. J. F. B.* Franecker. L.Strik. 1692.

————————————*Twee Brieven van Balthasar Bekker aan Everhardus van der Hooght.* Franecker. L. Strik. 1692.

———————————— *Uytlegging van den Propheet Daniel.* Amsterdam. 1688.

———————————— *Viervoudige Beantwoordinge van Beswaarnissen, voorgesteld aan Balthasar Bekker.. over syn Boek, genaamd De Betoverde Weereld. Zynde I Extracten, door Gecommitteerden des Kerkenraads, met de Korte Aantekeningen van den Auteur, die tot mondelinge conferentie hadden mogen dienen. II de XIII Artykelen, hem eerst van den Kerkenraad, en daarna van de Classis, vorergesteld: met syn Antwoord op de selve, en ene Acte van satisfactie daar by van hem aangeboden III. De VI Onderhandelingen der Gecommitteerden van de Classis, met den Auteur gehowden. IV D'Artykelen van Satisfactie, hem laatst van de Synodus tot Alkmaar voorgehowden, met sijn Antwoord naderhard daar opgesteld.* Amsterdam. D. van Dalen. 1692.

Bekker, Johannes. *Sterf-bedde, van.. Dr. Balthazar Bekker.. ofte een oprecht bericht hoe hij sich gedurende syne Siekte gedragen heeft.. En sulks na een voor-of-gaande kort ontwerp van sijn leeven, volgens sijn eigen hand-schrift, gevonden onden sijn nagelatene papieren.* Amsterdam. D van Dalen. 1698.

Bouman, Hermann. *Aanleydinge Om klaar te konnen uytvinden wanneer men in de H. Schriftuur van Duyvel, Satan, Boose Geest In ons Nederduyts leest, het selve te Verstaan.* Amsterdam. R. Blokland, 1700.

———————— *Aanmerkinge Over de woorden van den Evangelist Lucas, Beschreven in sln H. Evangelium Cap. 4: 1-14. Daar verhaalt word hoe den Saligmaker Jesus Christi is versogt van den Duyvel, en aangetoond wat voor een Duyvel deselve kan geweest zln.* Amsterdam. R. Blokland. 1699.

———————— *Brief van Lambert Joosten, met een Antwoord op de selve van H. Bouman.* Amsterdam. A. van Damme. 1696.

———————— *Disputatie over den Duyvel, of deselve is een geschaapen Geest, dewelke afgevallen is, ofte niet? Voorgevallen tusschen J. van Kuyk en H. Bouman, ten Huyse van Cornelis Slock, schoolmeester, 26. Dec. 1694.* Amsterdam. E. Webber. 1695.

———————— *Disputatio van verscheyde saaken...* Amsterdam. J. Smets and P. Dibbits. 1695.

———————— *Eenige Nodige Aanmerkingen op Lambert Joostens Verdediging...* Amsterdam. R. Blokland. 1696.

Brink, Henricus. *Ongenoegsame satisfactie, Gedaan Door den Auteur van het Boek, de Betoverde Wereld.* Utrecht. Widow of W. Klerck. 1692.

———————— *De Godslasteringen van de Amsterdamsche Predikant Dr. Bekker, Ter Waarschouwinge van alle Vroome in den Lande, Wederleyd In de Voorreden voor de Toet-steen der Waarheid en der Meyningen, door Henricus Brinck, Dienaar de Gemeente Christi tot Utrecht.* Utrecht. Widow of W. Clerck. 1691.

———————— *Ontdekkingen van de Gevoelens van Willem Deurhof, waar in gesien word, hoe deselve gantsch tegenstrijdig zijn met de Christelyke Gereformeerde leere.* Utrecht. Th. Appels. 1701.

Costerus, Florentius. *De gebannen Duyvel weder in geroepen, Ofte Het Vonnis van Doctor Bekker over den Duyvel gevelt, in Revisie gebraght. Gedrukt voor de Vreedlievende w.z.* Hoorn. S. Kortingh and J. Beets. 1691.

van Dalen, Anthony. *Lasteringen van Jacob Koelman, In sijn zoo genaamde Wederlegging van B. Bekkers Betooverde Wereld, Zediglyk aangewesen in een brief aan een vriend in Rotterdam.* Rotterdam. Iz. Van Ruynen. 1692.

Deurhoff, Willem, en Blyenbergh, Willem. *Klaare en beknopte Verhandeling van de Natuur en Werking der Menschelyke Zielen, Engelen en Duivelen, Vervat In gewisselde brieven tusschen de heer Willem van Blyenbergh en Willem Deurhoff.* Amsterdam. Jan ten Hoorn. 1692.

Deurhoff, Willem. *Brief van Willem Deurhoff aan Jacobus Schuts Vervattende een Verdeediging van de Natuur en Werking der Geesten, Teegen het Geschrifte genaamd W. Deurhoffs Geestelooze Geesten* Amsterdam. Jan ten Hoorn. 1693.

——————————— *Willem Deurhoff aan Henricus Brink, Vervolg van de klare en Beknopte Verhandeling van de Natuur en Werkinge der Menschellke Zielen, Engelen en Dvivelen.* Amsterdam. Jan ten Hoorn. 1693.

Groenewegen, Henricus. *Pneumatica, ofte Leere van de Geesten, zynde Denkende en Redelike Wesens uytgegeven by gelegentheyd van 't Boek De Betooverde Wereld door Henricus Groenewegen, pastor te Enchuysen.* Enkhuysen. Hendrik van Straalen. 1692.

——————————.*Verhandeling van de Mirakelen of Wonderen, Die van de Visitatoris: Door ordere des E. Classis van Enchuysen, uyt het Boek genaamd Pneumatica, van Dr. H. Groenewegen, verwonen zln.* 1692.

van Gunst, Lucas, *Den Gevallen Engel; Weereloos, En desselfs Onmacht, en Krachteloosheyd, klaarllck vertoont uyt de H. Schriftuur, het Geestellck en Wereldllck Recht, als mede uyt de Historien. Door Mr. Lucas van Gunst, Rechtsgeleerde.* Amsterdam. J. and G. Janssonius van Waesberge. 1692.

Hammer, Petrus. *Den Swadder, Die Eric Walten op Cartesianen en Coccejanen Geworpen heeft in syn twee Deelen van Aardige Duivelarye Zuiver af-gevaagt, met een het geschil dat Dr. Bekker Ongegrond opwerpt, als of Daimoon, etc. niet wel Duivel overgezet weird, Kortelyk voldongen, en in Staat van wyzen gebracht, door Iiratiel Leetsosoneus.* Amsterdam. G. Borstius. 1692.

——————————— *Volstreckte wederlegging van deen Herren Orchard, de Daillon en Bekker over de werkinge der geesten uitwarts, en met name der Duivelen. By occasie en tegen Dr. Bekker's Betoverde Wereld....* Dordrecht. Cornelis Willegaarts. 1693.

——————————— *Voorlooper tot de Volstrekte Wederlegginge van het gene de Heeren Orchard, Daillon en Bekker Hebben aen het licht gebragt. Aengaende de werken en macht der Geesten en met name der Duivelen.* Dordrecht. Cornelis Willegaarts. 1692.

van der Hoogt, Everardus. *Aanmerkingen van Haggebher Philaleethes, op de Invorgselen van Dr. Balthasar Bekker Zynde een Aanhangsel van de Vyfden Brief.* Amsterdam. G. Borstius. 1691.

——————————— *Antwoord van Everardus van der Hooght, Aan Dr. Balthasar Bekker (29 Sept. 1691).* Amsterdam. G. Borstius. 1691.

——————————— *Derde Briev Over Het Vervolg van de Kerkelyke Proceduuren tegen den Persoon van Dr. Balthasar Bekker.* Amsterdam. G. Borstius. 1691.

——————————— *Een Brief. Haggebher Philaleethees, Geschreeven Aen Zynen Vriend NN Over Den Persoon en het Boek van Dr. Balthasar Bekker.* Amsterdam. G. Borstius. 1691.

——————————— *Een en Deugd van De Duivel; verdeedigd door de Kloeke Man, Haggebher Phoolaleethees. Tegen die On-eerbiedige Schendnaam van Bandreekel, so ongemanierd op de Duivel uitgeschooten, door de Schrijver des Boeks De Betooverde Wereld.* 1691.

——————————— *Korte Aanmerkingen van Everardus van der Hooght over de laatste Schriften van Balthasar Bekker.* Amsterdam. D. vanden Dalen. 1693.

——————————— *Sesde Briev vervattende I. Een Afwysing van vyfdeley gewaande Voorspraaken van. D. Bekker. II Een Verhandeling van de De Daimonia.* Amsterdam. G. Borstius. 1691.

——————————— *Tweede Brief... Over De ordentelyke Kerkelyke Proceduuren, gehouden tegen den Persoon ende het Boek van Dr. Balthasar Bekker.* Amsterdam. G. Borstius. 1691.

——————————— *Vierde Briev... Over Het Weesen, Denken, Willen, Vermoogen ende de Plaats der Engelen, in het gemeen, ende der quade Geesten, in het byzonder.* Amsterdam. G. Borstius. 1691.

——————————— *Vijfde Briev... Over de Versoekinge Christi in de Woestyne.* Amsterdam. G. Borstius. 1691.

——————————— *Zeedige Ondersoek van het Boek Genaamt de Betoverde Weereld Door Evarardus van der Hooght Met des Auteurs Antwoort op de Brieven van B. Bekker.* Amsterdam. D. Boekman. 1692.

Jacobs(e), K. *Een klaer Bewijs van de Onmacht des Duyvels, voorgestelt in Antwoort op de vierde Brief van... Haggebher Philaleethees.* Amsterdam. 1691.

——————————— *Een klaare Uytlegginge, over de Versoekinge Des Heere Jesu Christi In de Woestyne. An antwoord Op de vijfde Brief van Philaleethees.* Amsterdam. 1691.

——————————— *Verhandelinge Van de Eerste Predicatie, Door Dr. P. Schaak. Gedaen in de Oude Kerk, op den 30 Sept. 1691. Tot een Grondslagh op de Wederlegginge van het Boek, genaamt de Betoverde Wereld Over de woorden Psalm 72:18.* Amsterdam. Pieter Rotterdam. 1691.

——————————— *Verhandelingh van de Tweede Predicatie, Door Dr. P. Schaak. Gedaen in de Nieuwe Kerk, op den 7 October 1691. Tot Wederlegginge van het*

Boek, genaamt de Betoverde Wereld Over den woorden Genesis 18:1-2, en eenige volgende des Capittels, en uyt Genesis 19, eenige Versen. Amsterdam. 1691.

de Jonge, D.T.S. Een Brief van Utrecht, van D. T. S. de Jonge, Geschreven aan sijn Vriend H. V. G. tot Amsterdam. The Hague. Eldert van der Stoce. 1692.

Joosten, Lambert. Verdediging van de wezentheyt en werking van Engelen Gods. Amsterdam. 1696.

Koelman, Jacobus. Eenige Originele Brieven Geschreven aan Dr. Balthasar Bekker over syn Boek de Betoverde Werelt. Amsterdam. D. vanden Dalen. 1692.

——————————— Wederlegging van Dr. B. Bekkers Betooverde Werelt. Amsterdam. 1692.

Leydekker, Melchior. De Godlikheid en Waarheid der H. Schriften, te gelyk van den Christeliken Godsdienst, verdedigd tegen de Betoverde Weereld van B. Bekker... 1692.

——————————— Melchior Leydekkers Historische en Theologische Redenering, Over het onlangs uitgegeve Boek van Balthasar Bekker, Strekken tot bevestinge der Waarheit en Authoriteit van de H. Schriftuur Waarachter gevoegt is Een Brief van de Hr. D'Aillon, wegens sijn gevoelen van de Eenheit des Duyvels. Utrecht. Widow of W. Clerck. 1692.

Molinaeus, Johannes. De Betoverde Werelt van D. Balthazar Bekker Onderzogt en Wederleydt. In twee Predikaetien. Rotterdam. B. Bos. 1692.

——————————— Paraenesis, ofte Ernstige Aenspraek aen den Siender van een Vremt Nagtgesigt. Rotterdam. B. Bos. 1692

Muys van Holy, Nicholas. Overwegging van het Hooft punct in Dr. Bekkers Boek genaamt de Betoverde Werelt, Te weten, of de Duyvel op een Mensch werken kan. Amsterdam. P. Rotterdam. 1692.

Noomtijns, Zalomon. Briev aan Dr. Everardus van der Hooght waar in uit zlijne schriften tegen Dr. B. Bekker, de kragteloosheid zijner bewyzen voor de magt en werking des Duivels, duidelyk vertoont... en het Boeksken genaamd Spiegel voor den Verwaarden en Warzoekende Haggebher Philaleethees Verdedigd word... door Zalomon Noomtijns. Amsterdam. Nathaniel Holbeecx. 1693.

——————————— Spiegel voor Den Verwarden, en Warzoekende Haggebher Philaleethees. Waarin, ult zln 6 Brieven getoond ward, zijne onkunde en verwarring, zoo in Taal als in Zaken. Ofte, een briev van Zalomon Noomtijns tot Amsterdam. Inhoudende voornaamelyk, eenige Aanmerkingen over den Perzoon en de 6 Brieven van Haggebher Philaleethees. Als mede over de Briev, en Perzoon van Everhardus van der Hooght. Mitsgaders d'Ontdekking, der lasteringen van Brink..... Amsterdam. D. vanden Dalen. 1692.

Orchard, Nicholas (Pred. In Nieuw Engeland). De Leeringe Der Duyvelen, Beweezen te zyn de Groote afval deerer Laatste tyden. Of een Proeve, strekkende om die *onbehoorlyke kundigheden en bevattingen, welke de menschen van de Demons en Quaade Geesten hebben, te verbeteren. In 't Engelsch geschreeven, vertaeld door Wm. Geivel.* Amsterdam. J. Broers. 1691.

Pel, J. *De Leeringe der Duyvelen Verwoest, door J. Pel.* Amsterdam. D. vanden Dalen. 1694.

142——————— *De Wonderdaden des Alderhoogsten waar in anngewesen word wat mogellker en waarschlnellker is, de verleidinge van den Mensch door sig selfs, of door dat ding dat een afgevallen Geest word genoemd.* Amsterdam. D. vanden Dalen. 1693.

Rotterdam, Church Council of. *Circulaire Brief van de Eerwaarde Kerken-raad van Rotterdam, geschreven aan de Respective Kerken-raden van zuyd ende Noord Holland; misgaders aan de voornaamste Steden van de verdere geunieerde Provincien, wegens de saake van Dr. Balthasar Bekker.* Amsterdam. J. Dale. 1692.

——————— *Circulaire Brief van de Eerwaarde Kercken-raad van Rotterdam, aan de 10 Kerken-raden van de Steden in Zuyd-Holland en de andere nederlandsche provintien aan de Kerken-raad van een Stad der selver.* Utrecht. Widow of W. Clerck. 1692.

——————— *Nader en particuliere Missive van de Kerkenraad van Rotterdam, Aan de Kerkenraad van Amsterdam, speciael dienende tot een aenmaningh om doch ernstigh te zijn ontrent de Saek wegens Dr. Balthasar Bekker.* Amsterdam. J. Dale. 1692.

Sergeant, Anthony. *Brief van Anthony Sergeant aan Henricus Brink.. over de ontdekking van de gevoelens van Willem Deurhoff...* Amsterdam. J. ten Hoorn. 1701.

Shuts, Jacobus. *Bekker's Sterf-bed ongelukkig verdedigt. Vertont in een brief van M. G. tot Amsterdam. Door Jacobus Shuts.* Amsterdam, 1699.

——————— *Brief van Jacobus Schuts aan Willem Deurhoff. Vervattende een nader bewls van W. Deurhoffs Geesteloose Geesten.* The Hague. Uytwerf. 1693.

——————— Consideratien over het boek van de Heer Doctor Balthasar Bekker, genaamt De betoverde weerelt. Amsterdam. G. Borstius. 1691?

——————— *De Betoverde Bekker, ofte een Overtuygent Bewijs Dat het Boek van de Heer Bekker, genaamt de Betoverde Weerelt, door saeyt is met onredelijkste Redenering, notoirste Onwaarheden en anden schadelijcke gevolgen.* The Hague. B. Beek. 1691.

——————— *Missive Aen D. Balthasar Bekker In 't Korte Ontdekkende de gronden van sijn Mis-grepen,..... in sijn drie Tractaten: De Betoverde Werelt, over den Prophet Daniel, en van de Cometen.* The Hague. Barent Beek. 1692.

——————— *Nodige Aanmerking over het Sterf-Bedde van Balthasar Bekker. Vertonende De openbare valsheyt van dat syn gevoelen, dat hij op sijn dood-bedde segt hem voor Paart en Wagen verstrekt te hebben om hem te voeren na den Hemel.* The Hague. Pieter van Tol. 1698.

——————————— *Tweede Missive aen Balthasar Bekker over syn Betooverde Wereld, Daniel, en Cometen.* The Hague. Barent Beek and Meinard Uitwerf. 1692.

——————————— *W. Deurhofs Geesteloose Geesten, ofte Gevaarlyke Grondregels.* Rotterdam. 1692.

Silvius, J. *Consideratien Over het Boek van Bathasar Bekker, genaamt De Betoverde Wereld, Voorgestelt door J. Silvius.* Amsterdam. G. Borstius. 1691.

Utrecht, Church Council of. *Briev van de Kerkenraad van Utrecht aan de Kerkenraad van Amsterdam, Daar toe tendereende dat de Auteur van het Boek, de Betoverde Wereld genaamt, niet Wederom tot de bedieninge van het Predik-ampt in de Gereformeerde Kerke mach werden toegelaten.* Amsterdam. J. Boekholt. 1692.

Verryn, Johannes. *Aenmerckingen op de Betoverde Werelt van Dr. Balthazar Bekker, Nopende de Geesten, en hun vermogen, en byzonderlick den Staet en magt des Duyvels.* Amsterdam. G. Slaats. 1692.

de Vries, Simon. *Overdenkinge op het Boek den Satan. In zijn Weesen, Aard, Bedryf.....* Amsterdam. D.vanden Dalen. 1691.

vander Wayenm Johannes. *De betooverde wereld van D. Balthasar Bekker ondersogt en wederlegt...* Franeker. Strik and Horreus. 1693

Walten, Eric. *Aardige Duyvelary, Voorvallende in dese dagen. Begrepen in een Brief van een Heer te Amsterdam, geschreven aan een van sijn vrienden te Leeuwarden, in Vriesland.* Rotterdam. P. van Veen. 1691.

——————————— *Brief aan de Heer Graaf van Portland, Rakende de Person en het gevoelen van Dr. B. Bekker.* The Hague. Uytwerf. 1692.

——————————— *Brief Aan een Regent der Stad Amsterdam. Behelsende een Regtsinnige uytlegginge en redenmatige verklaringe, van de Articulen die D. Balthasar Bekker op den 22 Jan. 1692 heeft overgeleverd aan de Classis van Amsterdam...* The Hague. Uytwerf. 1692.

——————————— *Den Triumpheerenden Duyvel Spookende omtrent den Berg van Parnassus.* Middleburg. Gillis Horthemels. 1692.

——————————— *Vervolg van de Aardige Duyvelary, Voorvallende in deser dagen. Begrepen in een twede Brief.* Rotterdam. P. van Veen. 1691.

Note: Original spellings and capitalizations have been retained.

Index

ARCHIVES INTERNATIONALES D'HISTOIRE DES IDÉES

*

INTERNATIONAL ARCHIVES OF THE HISTORY OF IDEAS

1. E. Labrousse: *Pierre Bayle*. Tome I: *Du pays de foix ã la citÇ d'Erasme*. 1963; 2nd printing 1984   ISBN 90-247-3136-4
   For Tome II *see below under Volume 6.*

2. P. Merlan: *Monopsychism, Mysticism, Metaconsciousness*. Problems of the Soul in the Neoaristotelian and Neoplatonic Tradition. 1963; 2nd printing 1969   ISBN 90-247-0178-3

3. H.G. van Leeuwen: *The Problem of Certainty in English Thought, 1630–1690*. With a Preface by R.H. Popkin. 1963; 2nd printing 1970   ISBN 90-247-0179-1

4. P.W. Janssen: *Les origines de la rÇforme des Carmes en France au 17ᵉ SiÐcle*. 1963; 2nd printing 1969   ISBN 90-247-0180-5

5. G. Sebba: *Bibliographia Cartesiana*. A Critical Guide to the Descartes Literature (1800–1960). 1964   ISBN 90-247-0181-3

6. E. Labrousse: *Pierre Bayle*. Tome II: *Heterodoxie et rigorisme*. 1964   ISBN 90-247-0182-1

7. K.W. Swart: *The Sense of Decadence in 19th-Century France*. 1964   ISBN 90-247-0183-X

8. W. Rex: *Essays on Pierre Bayle and Religious Controversy*. 1965   ISBN 90-247-0184-8

9. E. Heier: *L.H. Nicolay (1737–1820) and His Contemporaries*. Diderot, Rousseau, Voltaire, Gluck, Metastasio, Galiani, D'Eschemy, Gessner, Bodmer, Lavater, Wieland, Frederick II, Falconet, W. Robertson, Paul I, Cagliostro, Gellert, Winckelmann, Poinsinet, Lloyd, Sanchez, Masson, and Others. 1965   ISBN 90-247-0185-6

10. H.M. Bracken: *The Early Reception of Berkeley's Immaterialism, 1710–1733*. [1958] Rev. ed. 1965   ISBN 90-247-0186-4

11. R.A. Watson: *The Downfall of Cartesianism, 1673–1712*. A Study of Epistemological Issues in Late 17th-Century Cartesianism. 1966   ISBN 90-247-0187-2

12. R. Descartes: *Regul ad Directionem Ingenii*. Texte critique Çtabli par Giovanni Crapulli avec la version hollandaise du 17ᵉ siÐcle. 1966   ISBN 90-247-0188-0

13. J. Chapelain: *Soixante-dix-sept Lettres inÇdites ã Nicolas Heinsius (1649–1658)*. PubliÇes d'aprÐs le manuscrit de Leyde avec une introduction et des notes par B. Bray. 1966
                                                                            ISBN 90-247-0189-9

14. C. B. Brush: *Montaigne and Bayle*. Variations on the Theme of Skepticism. 1966
                                                                            ISBN 90-247-0190-2

15. B. Neveu: *Un historien ã l'Ecole de Port-Royal*. SÇbastien le Nain de Tillemont (1637–1698). 1966   ISBN 90-247-0191-0

16. A. Faivre: *Kirchberger et l'Illuminisme du 18ᵉ siÐcle*. 1966   ISBN 90-247-0192-9

17. J.A. Clarke: *Huguenot Warrior*. The Life and Times of Henri de Rohan (1579–1638). 1966
                                                                            ISBN 90-247-0193-7

18. S. Kinser: *The Works of Jacques-Auguste de Thou*. 1966   ISBN 90-247-0194-5

19. E.F. Hirsch: *Damião de Gois*. The Life and Thought of a Portuguese Humanist (1502–1574). 1967   ISBN 90-247-0195-3

20. P.J.S. Whitemore: *The Order of Minims in 17th-Century France*. 1967   ISBN 90-247-0196-1

21. H. Hillenaar: *FÇnelon et les JÇsuites*. 1967   ISBN 90-247-0197-X

22. W.N. Hargreaves-Mawdsley: *The English Della Cruscans and Their Time, 1783–1828*. 1967
                                                                            ISBN 90-247-0198-8

23. C.B. Schmitt: *Gianfrancesco Pico della Mirandola (1469–1533) and his Critique of Aristotle*. 1967   ISBN 90-247-0199-6

24. H.B. White: *Peace among the Willows*. The Political Philosophy of Francis Bacon. 1968
                                                                            ISBN 90-247-0200-3

ARCHIVES INTERNATIONALES D'HISTOIRE DES IDÉES
*
INTERNATIONAL ARCHIVES OF THE HISTORY OF IDEAS

ARCHIVES INTERNATIONALES D'HISTOIRE DES IDÉES
*
INTERNATIONAL ARCHIVES OF THE HISTORY OF IDEAS

ARCHIVES INTERNATIONALES D'HISTOIRE DES IDÉES

*

INTERNATIONAL ARCHIVES OF THE HISTORY OF IDEAS

70. R. Simon (Çd.): *Henry de Boulainviller. Œuvres Philosophiques, Tome II.* 1975
ISBN 90-247-1633-0
For Œuvres Philosophiques, Tome I see under Volume 58.

71. J.A.G. Tans et H. Schmitz du Moulin: *Pasquier Quesnel devant la CongrÇgation de l'Index.* Correspondance avec Francesco Barberini et mÇmoires sur la mise à l'Index de son Çdition des Œuvres de Saint LÇon, publiÇs avec introduction et annotations. 1974   ISBN 90-247-1661-6

72. J.W. Carven: *Nàpoleon and the Lazarists (1804–1809).* 1974   ISBN 90-247-1667-5

73. G. Symcox: *The Crisis of French Sea Power (1688–1697).* From the *Guerre d'Escadre* to the *Guerre de Course.* 1974   ISBN 90-247-1645-4

74. R. MacGillivray: *Restoration Historians and the English Civil War.* 1974
ISBN 90-247-1678-0

75. A. Soman (ed.): *The Massacre of St. Bartholomew.* Reappraisals and Documents. 1974
ISBN 90-247-1652-7

76. R.E. Wanner: *Claude Fleury (1640–1723) as an Educational Historiographer and Thinker.* With an Introduction by W.W. Brickman. 1975   ISBN 90-247-1684-5

77. R.T. Carroll: *The Common-Sense Philosophy of Religion of Bishop Edward Stillingfleet (1635–1699).* 1975   ISBN 90-247-1647-0

78. J. Macary: *Masque et lumiÐres au 18ᵉ [siÐcle].* AndrÇ-Franèois Deslandes, Citoyen et philosophe (1689–1757). 1975   ISBN 90-247-1698-5

79. S.M. Mason: *Montesquieu's Idea of Justice.* 1975   ISBN 90-247-1670-5

80. D.J.H. van Elden: *Esprits fins et esprits gÇomÇtriques dans les portraits de Saint-Simon.* Contributions à l'Çtude du vocabulaire et du style. 1975   ISBN 90-247-1726-4

81. I. Primer (ed.): *Mandeville Studies.* New Explorations in the Art and Thought of Dr Bernard Mandeville (1670–1733). 1975   ISBN 90-247-1686-1

82. C.G. Nore/a: *Studies in Spanish Renaissance Thought.* 1975   ISBN 90-247-1727-2

83. G. Wilson: *A Medievalist in the 18th Century.* Le Grand d'Aussy and the Fabliaux ou Contes. 1975   ISBN 90-247-1782-5

84. J.-R. Armogathe: *Theologia Cartesiana.* L'explication physique de l'Eucharistie chez Descartes et Dom Robert Desgabets. 1977   ISBN 90-247-1869-4

85. BÇrault Stuart, Seigneur d'Aubigny: *TraitÇ sur l'art de la guerre.* Introduction et Çdition par lie de Comminges. 1976   ISBN 90-247-1871-6

86. S.L. Kaplan: *Bread, Politics and Political Economy in the Reign of Louis XV.* 2 vols., 1976
Set ISBN 90-247-1873-2

87. M. Lienhard (ed.): *The Origins and Characteristics of Anabaptism / Les dÇbuts et les caractÇristiques de l'Anabaptisme.* With an Extensive Bibliography / Avec une bibliographie dÇtaillÇe. 1977   ISBN 90-247-1896-1

88. R. Descartes: *RÐgles utiles et claires pour la direction de l'esprit en la recherche de la vÇritÇ.* Traduction selon le lexique cartÇsien, et annotation conceptuelle par J.-L. Marion. Avec des notes mathÇmatiques de P. Costabel. 1977   ISBN 90-247-1907-0

89. K. Hardesty: *The 'SupplÇment' to the 'EncyclopÇdie'.* [Diderot et d'Alembert]. 1977
ISBN 90-247-1965-8

90. H.B. White: *Antiquity Forgot.* Essays on Shakespeare, [Francis] Bacon, and Rembrandt. 1978
ISBN 90-247-1971-2

91. P.B.M. Blaas: *Continuity and Anachronism.* Parliamentary and Constitutional Development in Whig Historiography and in the Anti-Whig Reaction between 1890 and 1930. 1978
ISBN 90-247-2063-X

ARCHIVES INTERNATIONALES D'HISTOIRE DES IDÉES

*

INTERNATIONAL ARCHIVES OF THE HISTORY OF IDEAS

ARCHIVES INTERNATIONALES D'HISTOIRE DES IDÉES
*
INTERNATIONAL ARCHIVES OF THE HISTORY OF IDEAS

114. S. Pines and Y. Yovel (eds.): *Maimonides* [1135-1204] *and Philosophy*. Papers Presented at the 6th Jerusalem Philosophical Encounter (May 1985). 1986   ISBN 90-247-3439-8
115. T.J. Saxby: *The Quest for the New Jerusalem, Jean de Labadie* [1610–1674] *and the Labadists (1610–1744)*. 1987   ISBN 90-247-3485-1
116. C.E. Harline: *Pamphlets, Printing, and Political Culture in the Early Dutch Republic*. 1987   ISBN 90-247-3511-4
117. R.A. Watson and J.E. Force (eds.): *The Sceptical Mode in Modern Philosophy*. Essays in Honor of Richard H. Popkin. 1988   ISBN 90-247-3584-X
118. R.T. Bienvenu and M. Feingold (eds.): *In the Presence of the Past*. Essays in Honor of Frank Manuel. 1991   ISBN 0-7923-1008-X
119. J. van den Berg and E.G.E. van der Wall (eds.): *Jewish-Christian Relations in the 17th Century*. Studies and Documents. 1988   ISBN 90-247-3617-X
120. N. Waszek: *The Scottish Enlightenment and Hegel's Account of 'Civil Society'*. 1988   ISBN 90-247-3596-3
121. J. Walker (ed.): *Thought and Faith in the Philosophy of Hegel*. 1991   ISBN 0-7923-1234-1
122. Henry More [1614–1687]: *The Immortality of the Soul*. Edited with Introduction and Notes by A. Jacob. 1987   ISBN 90-247-3512-2
123. P.B. Scheurer and G. Debrock (eds.): *Newton's Scientific and Philosophical Legacy*. 1988   ISBN 90-247-3723-0
124. D.R. Kelley and R.H. Popkin (eds.): *The Shapes of Knowledge from the Renaissance to the Enlightenment*. 1991   ISBN 0-7923-1259-7
125. R.M. Golden (ed.): *The Huguenot Connection*. The Edict of Nantes, Its Revocation, and Early French Migration to South Carolina. 1988   ISBN 90-247-3645-5
126. S. Lindroth: *Les chemins du savoir en SuÐde*. De la fondation de l'UniversitÇ d'Upsal ā Jacob Berzelius. tudes et Portraits. Traduit du suÇdois, prÇsentÇ et annotÇ par J.-F. Battail. Avec une introduction sur Sten Lindroth par G. Eriksson. 1988   ISBN 90-247-3579-3
127. S. Hutton (ed.): *Henry More (1614–1687). Tercentenary Studies*. With a Biography and Bibliography by R. Crocker. 1989   ISBN 0-7923-0095-5
128. Y. Yovel (ed.): *Kant's Practical Philosophy Reconsidered*. Papers Presented at the 7th Jerusalem Philosophical Encounter (December 1986). 1989   ISBN 0-7923-0405-5
129. J.E. Force and R.H. Popkin: *Essays on the Context, Nature, and Influence of Isaac Newton's Theology*. 1990   ISBN 0-7923-0583-3
130. N. Capaldi and D.W. Livingston (eds.): *Liberty in Hume's 'History of England'*. 1990   ISBN 0-7923-0650-3
131. W. Brand: *Hume's Theory of Moral Judgment*. A Study in the Unity of *A Treatise of Human Nature*. 1992   ISBN 0-7923-1415-8
132. C.E. Harline (ed.): *The Rhyme and Reason of Politics in Early Modern Europe*. Collected Essays of Herbert H. Rowen. 1992   ISBN 0-7923-1527-8
133. N. Malebranche: *Treatise on Ethics* (1684). Translated and edited by C. Walton. 1993   ISBN 0-7923-1763-7
134. B.C. Southgate: *'Covetous of Truth'*. The Life and Work of Thomas White (1593–1676). 1993   ISBN 0-7923-1926-5
135. G. Santinello, C.W.T. Blackwell and Ph. Weller (eds.): *Models of the History of Philosophy*. Vol. 1: From its Origins in the Renaissance to the 'Historia Philosophica'. 1993   ISBN 0-7923-2200-2
136. M.J. Petry (ed.): *Hegel and Newtonianism*. 1993   ISBN 0-7923-2202-9

ARCHIVES INTERNATIONALES D'HISTOIRE DES IDÉES
*
INTERNATIONAL ARCHIVES OF THE HISTORY OF IDEAS

137. Otto von Guericke: *The New (so-called Magdeburg) Experiments* [Experimenta Nova, Amsterdam 1672]. Translated and edited by M.G. Foley Ames. 1994   ISBN 0-7923-2399-8
138. R.H. Popkin and G.M. Weiner (eds.): *Jewish Christians and Cristian Jews. From the Renaissance to the Enlightenment.* 1994   ISBN 0-7923-2452-8
139. J.E. Force and R.H. Popkin (eds.): *The Books of Nature and Scripture.* Recent Essays on Natural Philosophy, Theology, and Biblical Criticism in the Netherlands of Spinoza's Time and the British Isles of Newton's Time. 1994   ISBN 0-7923-2467-6
140. P. Rattansi and A. Clericuzio (eds.): *Alchemy and Chemistry in the 16th and 17th Centuries.* 1994   ISBN 0-7923-2573-7
141. S. Jayne: *Plato in Renaissance England.* 1995   ISBN 0-7923-3060-9
142. A.P. Coudert: *Leibniz and the Kabbalah.* 1995   ISBN 0-7923-3114-1
143. M.H. Hoffheimer: *Eduard Gans and the Hegelian Philosophy of Law.* 1995   ISBN 0-7923-3114-1
144. J.R.M. Neto: *The Christianization of Pyrrhonism.* Scepticism and Faith in Pascal, Kierkegaard, and Shestov. 1995   ISBN 0-7923-3381-0
145. R.H. Popkin (ed.): *Scepticism in the History of Philosophy.* A Pan-American Dialogue. 1996 ISBN 0-7923-3769-7
146. M. de Baar, M. Lwensteyn, M. Monteiro and A.A. Sneller (eds.): *Choosing the Better Part.* Anna Maria van Schurman (1607–1678). 1995   ISBN 0-7923-3799-9
147. M. Degenaar: *Molyneux's Problem.* Three Centuries of Discussion on the Perception of Forms. 1996   ISBN 0-7923-3934-7
148. S. Berti, F. Charles-Daubert and R.H. Popkin (eds.): *Heterodoxy, Spinozism, and Free Thought in Early-Eighteenth-Century Europe.* Studies on the *TraitÇ des trois imposteurs.* 1996   ISBN 0-7923-4192-9
149. G.K. Browning (ed.): *Hegel's* Phenomenology of Spirit: *A Reappraisal.* 1997   ISBN 0-7923-4480-4
150. G.A.J. Rogers, J.M. Vienne and Y.C. Zarka (eds.): *The Cambridge Platonists in Philosophical Context.* Politics, Metaphysics and Religion. 1997   ISBN 0-7923-4530-4
151. R.L. Williams: *The Letters of Dominique Chaix, Botanist-CurÇ.* 1997   ISBN 0-7923-4615-7
152. R.H. Popkin, E. de Olaso and G. Tonelli (eds.): *Scepticism in the Enlightenment.* 1997   ISBN 0-7923-4643-2
153. L. de la Forge. Translated and edited by D.M. Clarke: *Treatise on the Human Mind (1664).* 1997   ISBN 0-7923-4778-1
154. S.P. Foster: *Melancholy Duty.* The Hume-Gibbon Attack on Christianity. 1997   ISBN 0-7923-4785-4
155. J. van der Zande and R.H. Popkin (eds.): *The Skeptical Tradition Around 1800.* Skepticism in Philosophy, Science, and Society. 1997   ISBN 0-7923-4846-X
156. P. Ferretti: *A Russian Advocate of Peace: Vasilii Malinovskii (1765–1814).* 1997   ISBN 0-7923-4846-6
157. M. Goldish: *Judaism in the Theology of Sir Isaac Newton.* 1998   ISBN 0-7923-4996-2
158. A.P. Coudert, R.H. Popkin and G.M. Weiner (eds.): *Leibniz, Mysticism and Religion.* 1998   ISBN 0-7923-5223-8
159. B. Fridén: *Rousseau's Economic Philosophy.* Beyond the Market of Innocents. 1998   ISBN 0-7923-5270-X
160. C.F. Fowler O.P.: *Descartes on the Human Soul.* Philosophy and the Demands of Christian Doctrine. 1999   ISBN 0-7923-5473-7

ARCHIVES INTERNATIONÁLES D'HISTOIRE DES IDÉES
*
INTERNATIONAL ARCHIVES OF THE HISTORY OF IDEAS

161. J.E. Force and R.H. Popkin (eds.): *Newton and Religion*. Context, Nature and Influence. 1999
ISBN 0-7923-5744-2
162. J.V. Andreae: *Christianapolis*. 1999 ISBN 0-7923-5745-0
163. Reserved
164. T. Verbeek (ed.): *Johannes Clauberg (1622-1665)*. And Cartesian Philosophy in the Seventeenth Century. 1999 ISBN 0-7923-5831-7
165. A. Fix: *Fallen Angels*. Balthasar Bekker, Spirit Belief, and Confessionalism in the Seventeenth Century Dutch Republic. 1999 ISBN 0-7923-5876-7

KLUWER ACADEMIC PUBLISHERS – DORDRECHT / BOSTON / LONDON